THROUGH PERIL TO THE STARS

Other books by Dilip Sarkar: -

SPITFIRE SQUADRON: *19 Squadron at War 1939-41*
THE INVISIBLE THREAD: *A Spitfire's Tale*
ANGRIFF WESTLAND: *Three Battle of Britain Air Raids*
A FEW OF THE MANY: *Air War 1939-45, A Kaleidoscope of Memories*
BADER'S TANGMERE SPITFIRES: *1941, The Untold Story*
BADER'S DUXFORD FIGHTERS: *The Big Wing Controversy*
MISSING IN ACTION: *Resting in Peace?*
GUARDS VC: *Blitzkrieg 1940*
BATTLE OF BRITAIN: *The Photographic Kaleidoscopes Vols I - IV*
FIGHTER PILOT: *The Photographic Kaleidoscope*
SIR DOUGLAS BADER: *An Inspiration in Photographs*
JOHNNIE JOHNSON: *Spitfire Top Gun, Parts 1 & 2*
BATTLE OF BRITAIN: *Last Look Back*
SPITFIRE!: *Courage & Sacrifice*
Dilip also contributed a chapter on historical accuracy to the late Robert Rudhall's best-selling BATTLE OF BRITAIN: *The Movie* (being re-printed 2006).

Most of Dilip's books have been out of print since shortly after their release dates. **Victory Books** will be re-printing the majority of these works so that, for the first time, all will be concurrently available from May 2006 onwards. To receive early notification of our publications and signed limited editions, join the Victory Books privileged customer mailing list.

Through Peril to the Stars
© Dilip Sarkar MBE, 1993
ISBN: 0-9550431-9-0

Second Edition: Victory Books International, 2006.

For further information regarding further books by Dilip sarkar MBE, and or other titles, please contact: Victory Books International, PO Box 573, Worcester WR5 3WU, UK. Tel: 07921 503105. Fax: 01905 767735. www.victorybooks.co.uk

Design & layout by Victory Books, printed and bound in the UK.

THROUGH PERIL TO THE STARS

RAF FIGHTER PILOTS
WHO FAILED TO RETURN
1939-45

by

Dilip Sarkar

RAMROD PUBLICATIONS

For my son, James,
whom I hope will fly,
but not to the stars.

Through Peril To the Stars

Contents

Through Peril to the Stars

Foreword

Group Captain Peter Townsend (right) with the late Squadron Leader James "Ginger" Lacey during the making of the "Battle of Britain" film, 1968.
Group Captain P. Townsend.

Dear Dilip,

Although we have been corresponding for many years, we have never met. So here comes another letter, this time in praise of your latest book *"Through Peril to the Stars"*, Per Ardua ad Astra, a theme which has been engraved in my mind since I joined the RAF sixty years ago.

Your efforts of research have been prodigious and, I know, taken you several years - years of patience and distant journeys, of sympathy and understanding for the relatives and friends of deceased British and German airmen who have helped you with your task of research.

I know you became mad about flying and aeroplanes at the tender age of seven - you beat me by a year or two! But without actually joining the happy band of aviators, you have perfectly understood their spirit - their slang, their particular expressions, their peculiar sense of humour and their simple way of relating even their most horrific experiences. This, indeed, was essential to their morale and their survival.

Another remarkable thing, you have understood so well the mysteries of air strategy and tactics, and this has enabled you to write an accurate, lively and deeply touching story, or rather the stories, of friend and foe, all of whom died in battle. There, I imagine, you have a unique theme, and a noble one.

Once, when describing an air combat with my 8 year-old son, he asked *"But why did you have to kill them?"* Truthfully, I have never wanted to kill anybody and least of all a young man of my age who shared with me a passion for flying, young men in their late teens or early twenties. That is the tragedy of war.

Dilip, you have already written two successful books, *"Spitfire Squadron"* and *"The Invisible Thread"* and you have created the Malvern Spitfire Team and founded the Surma Memorial Trust for Youth, the entire proceeds generated from the latter being donated to that charity with your customary generosity. I admire you all the more for this, because Britain is your adopted, not your native country, for you were born in Calcutta, son of an Indian father and a British mother. What a happy get-together which, in a way, brings our association closer; In 1935 I spent my 22nd birthday at Dum-Dum airport, Calcutta, having landed there, with my squadron, in my dear old Vickers Vildebeeste, cruising speed 100mph.

Another thing which pleases me is that you are a police officer, which no doubt explains the quality of your research, which is largely detective work. And with your colleagues you protect Britain from crime and tyranny which is what, in our youth, we were doing against Nazism. I go along with you all the way in your heartfelt ambition to inform the youth of today that we, when their age, were doing our best to make a better Britain for them.

Warmest congratulations to you for your great efforts both in the literary and humanitarian field.

Group Captain Peter Townsend CVO, DSO, DFC RAF Rtd,
France, June 1993

Introduction

Dilip Sarkar (centre) with Malvern Spitfire Team members at the launch of "The Invisible Thread" in 1992. Left to right: Brian Owen, Tony Bramhall, Bob Morris, Andrew Long (secretary and co-founder), Dennis Williams and Mark Postlethwaite.

The atmosphere was electric; as the car approached Little Rissington airfield, aircraft began appearing overhead. Within the gate was utopia. I was nine years old and at my first air show. By that time I had already watched, fascinated, many of the films made in the wake of the Second World War, such as *"The Dambusters"*, *"Reach for the Sky"*, and later *"The Battle of Britain"*, and unfailingly watched from the armchair Raymond Baxter's annual Farnborough commentaries. My bedroom ceiling closely resembled the Battle of Britain, with here and there a 1/72nd scale Airfix fighter going down trailing cotton wool *"smoke"*. I was, according to my mother, *"aircraft mad"*. That particular day, however, I saw a real Spitfire for the first time, P7350 of the Battle of Britain Memorial Flight. I was spellbound and, once discovered, I strayed not far from it. Not for me the fast jets and suchlike, but there was something remarkably special about this, almost serene, piston-engined fighter that was possessed of an indefinable quality that even today I am unable to adequately describe. Around the same time, on a family outing, my parents stopped at the station plot of a former wartime airfield to show me the graves of the aircrew within. I read their names, their ages, and their positions in the aircraft. But that was not enough. I wanted to know what they were like, and how they died. I remember as we got in the car to drive away, thinking how sad it was that those brave men, whose names were obviously not well known like my heroes, Douglas Bader and Guy Gibson, had neither today or tomorrow. Thus the scene was set for a fascination that will endure a lifetime.

Strangely enough this book was not actually researched as such. Following publication of my last title, *"The Invisible Thread: A Spitfire's Tale"*, I thought that another interesting book could be made by putting together a selection of fighter pilots' biographies that I had researched over the years, the common denominator being that all had failed to return. As I wrote the book, however, I realised that the dates of death, and the various aircraft and periods of flying that each pilot was involved with, actually covered the greater part of the Second World War, i.e. from May 31st, 1940, when Pilot Officer Jack Pugh was the first to fall even before Dunkirk, to Pilot Officer John Thould, on October 13th, 1944, during the opening stage of the Battle for Germany itself. By using original background research material, I resolved to cover this period in detail, thus offering the reader a fair idea of the fighter pilot's war over north-western Europe. I do not believe *"Through Peril to the Stars"* to be either in the mould or wake of books that have dealt specifically with the aerial battles and campaigns fought between 1939-45, but, following on from my previous two books, is an original idea in retaining an essentially human element throughout. Between them, although all are hitherto *"unknowns"*, these pilots flew on some of the most complex of operations and participated in bitter fighting from the days when Britain stood alone, until the liberation of Nazi dominated Europe and the new jet age. Enough, I believe, has been written about the Baders, Stanford-Tucks et al, but not so of the ilk of men such as those who represent the anonymous mass of courage that went about its duties unrelentlessly, and often without recognition, until Hitler and his evils had been defeated. Without the like of Robin Rafter, George Lock, Tommy Drinkwater and the rest, that ultimate victory would never have been made possible. To me there are no warriors in the history of arms more worthy than wartime aircrew. They were, I believe, a special breed, although the survivors, modest men all, would probably not agree with me.

Regarding the subjects of this book, my biographical studies have been so intense, often having read the subject's diaries and other most personal of papers, that it is almost as if I actually knew each of the young airmen concerned. Together we have travelled, therefore, on the adventure that the compilation of this book has been. I grieved when each one fell, grieved for mankind because of the terrific potential snuffed out in an instant. I too have stood deeply moved at several of their gravesides; the average age of the pilots in this book was just twenty-one. Perhaps I now even walk with ghosts.

I am privileged to have received the co-operation of their relatives and friends during my research, many families having allowed me to enter a very painful and private area of their lives. All, however, gave immediate and unfailing support, for which I am extremely grateful. Out from many attic boxes came long forgotten documents, photographs and other mementos of the fallen. Similarly privileged do I feel, as a result of these researches, to have met and interviewed numerous survivors, many of whom I now count amongst my close friends, despite the years between us.

A small selection of memorabilia collected by Dilip Sarkar during the research for this book; items of interest are, clockwise: Squadron Leader T.H.D. Drinkwater's DFC, a message of sympathy from the King and Queen sent to Mr and Mrs Lock upon the death of their son, Sergeant G.C. Lock, the second Pilot's Flying Log Book of Pilot Officer John Thould, the silver cigarette case of Squadron Leader Brian Lane DFC (see "Spitfire Squadron", also by Dilip Sarkar), the medals of Pilot Officer W.P.H. Rafter, the RAF peaked-cap of Pilot Officer H.L. Whitbread, the NCO cap-badge of Sergeant K.C. Pattison, the silver American Army Air Corps "wings" of Sergeant G.C. Lock, the Pilot's Flying Log Book of Sergeant K.C. Pattison, and a letter written to his mother by Pilot Officer H.L. Whitbread from the Officers' Mess, RAF Hornchurch, September 14th, 1940, just six days before his death in action.

Mark Postlethwaite.

I would also like to ask you all to spare a thought for the other unsung heroes, the groundcrews, who laboured long and arduous hours, often in difficult and primitive conditions, to keep the aircraft flying. Without them there would have been no victories.

The reader will note much detail regarding the creation, organisation and undertaking of the Operational Training Unit in some chapters, and for which I make no apology. I have never read such detail elsewhere, so hope that the publication of this information will fill a gap in the historical material currently available to students of the air war. Also, and perhaps more importantly, I am delighted to have the opportunity to set the record straight with regard to the true sequence of events preceding the capture of Oberleutnant Franz von Werra, *"The One That Got Away"*, and Oberleutnant Arnim Faber who delivered an intact Focke Wulf 190 to the RAF. Perhaps even more important than the foregoing, the truth is only now told regarding a little-known action fought over Gloucestershire during the summer of 1940, and the victor, a hitherto unheard of Hurricane pilot, finally credited accordingly.

As an historian of relatively recent times I am fortunate, at the moment, in being able to reach out to the people who were there, and look at their faded Velox images of a time now past. The research process is continuous, so if anyone has any extra information regarding the personalities studied in this volume I would be pleased to hear from them via the publisher. I am particularly anxious to obtain further information regarding Sergeant *"Chuck"* Dales of the Telecommunications Flying Unit, Sergeant 1346507 H. Clarke of 52 OTU in early 1943 and who is known to have later been seriously injured whilst flying with another training unit, Squadron Leader William Radclyffe Assheton who flew with 222 Squadron as a Pilot Officer during the Battle of Britain, and Flight Lieutenant John Purkis DFC, formerly of 263 Squadron.

Still on the subject of research, I was amused following the publication of my second book to receive a letter from a reader who mentioned that authors had *"access to information denied the general public."* Absolute nonsense. The only way authors succeed is through sheer hard work and dedication alone. The official documents consulted during the research for this book are available to anybody and are held at the Public Record Office. Other sources include the Ministry of Defence's Air Historical Branch, again whose material is available for inspection, and previously published sources. First hand material is collected through correspondence and personal interviews. To appreciate the volume of work involved, my postage records indicate that since I started research during 1986, I have written over one thousand letters per annum. Visits to the Public Record Office are also an effort, two or three times a month rising at 5 am for a long car journey ending in the London traffic, all day then spent studying documents and extracting information before eventually heading for home and the end of a fourteen hour day. Then of course we have our full-time jobs!

Finally, I would like to repeat part of a speech made on November 12th, 1940, by Britain's wartime Prime Minister, Winston Spencer Churchill, which aptly describes how I feel about my work: *"History with its flickering lamp, stumbles along the trail of the past, trying to reconstruct its scenes, to revive its echoes, and kindle with pale gleams the passion of former days."*

Dilip Sarkar, Malvern, April 1993

Chapter One

BROTHERS IN ARMS

Pilot Officers Jack and Bob Pugh.
Squadron Leader R.M. Pugh.

A t the outbreak of the Second World War, Fighter Command was the only Command to oppose Air Ministry plans for establishing special units to train newly qualified pilots from Flying Training School to operational standard prior to them being posted to the squadrons. The Commander-in-Chief of Fighter Command, Hugh Dowding, considered it to be a waste of operational aircraft for this purpose when such instruction could be given by the squadrons themselves. Ironically, at the time, Fighter Command were the only Command to possess such a unit. No 11 Group Pool had been formed at Andover on January 16th, 1939, and equipped with four Demon biplane fighters to train eight pilots at a time on two month courses. The Air Ministry considered that three pools would actually be required to back the thirty-six squadrons. However, shortages of aircraft, personnel and aerodromes delayed the expansion process. In March 1939, 11 Group Pool had moved to

St Athan in South Wales, and re-established with more modern aircraft, namely eleven Fairey Battles and twenty-two Hurricanes. In September 1939, however, the unit was seriously below establishment and its energies were therefore largely devoted to the advanced training of volunteer reservists. Shortly after the outbreak of war, the Battles were replaced with Harvard trainers and 11 Group Pool was soon only five Hurricanes short of its authorised establishment. The course length was halved to four weeks, and syllabus hours reduced from forty-five to thirty hours per pupil. Producing twenty-four pilots every four weeks, it was hoped that the Pool would provide three hundred pilots trained to operational standard per year.

Fighter Command remained sceptical regarding the value of Pools for training at the expense of front line strength. Dowding vigorously contested the need, making it clear at conferences on September 15th and 21st, 1939, that new pilots from FTS should be trained in squadrons, 11 Group Pool at St Athan being used only for reinforcements to France. The Commander-in-Chief went further by saying that the need for a 12 Group Pool based at Aston Down in Gloucestershire was unnecessary. The Air Ministry parried with the argument that the lack of Group Pools would mean a lack of casualty replacements when the fighting became intense, and if necessary Group Pool aircraft could be taken for operational use. Fighter Command therefore agreed, albeit reluctantly, to open 12 Group Pool on a limited basis, on the understanding that it did not absorb any Spitfires or Hurricanes. Training was still to be ongoing in squadrons, and the constant need for it was impressed upon the Group Commanders.

12 Group Pool became operational at Aston Down on September 25th, 1939, equipped with six Harvards, three Blenheims and eleven Gladiators. The schedule was to train some two hundred and thirty pilots per year. Both pools were handicapped by a shortage of cine-camera guns, reflector gunsights, lack of proper armouries, and having no ground R/T facilities. However, when the general adequacy of Group Pools was compared with FTS output in October, it was found to be satisfactory. The planned Group Pool capacity at full establishment almost equalled that of the FTSs with 1,100 fighter pilots per year. In reality the Group Pools were far below establishment and therefore capable of dealing with less than half of those proposed numbers. Due to lack of aircraft, the Pools were able to do little Blenheim training and no Spitfire training at all. To remedy the former deficiency, a few pupils were given conversion courses at Hendon during December 1939.

In January 1940, Fighter Command eventually agreed in principle that an adequate operational training system for fighter squadrons should be established. Both 11 and 12 Group Pools were renamed Operational Training Units the following March, and became 6 and 5 respectively. The OTUs remained under the command of their respective Fighter Command Group areas, but in June 1940 were placed under the direct control of 10 Group. By April 1st, 1940, the fighter training organisation had expanded and three OTUs were planned with a total strength of forty-eight Hurricanes, thirty-four Spitfires, twenty Blenheims, four Defiants, two Gladiators and twenty-four Harvards or Battles.

These decisions were not altogether welcomed by Fighter Command who disagreed that the recent spate of flying accidents prompting the Air Ministry's action was due to inadequate training, and still saw OTUs as an unaffordable luxury. Dowding particularly objected to a third OTU being formed before all front line squadron requirements were met. His arguments were once again to no avail as the Air Ministry decided to go ahead. At that time the total strength of operational aircraft held by OTUs was twenty, as opposed to the authorised one hundred and thirty-two. Their combined pilot output was barely enough to back the Hurricane squadrons in France serving there with the Advanced Air Striking Force as a component part of the British Expeditionary Force, and also fulfil the requirement to supply ninety Blenheim pilots to Fighter Command. In France the fighter squadrons criticised the standard of training provided by OTUs, the replacement pilots being received by them direct from St Athan and Aston Down having just ten hours flying experience on Hurricanes or Spitfires, and no high altitude, oxygen or fighter attack experience.

In May 1940, the urgent need for fighter pilots suddenly became more than apparent as the Hurricane squadrons in France started suffering heavy losses. 5 and 6 OTUs were at that time achieving a maximum output of eighty pilots per month, against a monthly requirement of two hundred for casualty replacement alone, and three hundred if raising squadron establishments was taken into account.

By May 1940, Germany had already occupied Poland, Denmark and Norway. On the morning of May 10th, Hitler's legions invaded Belgium, Holland, Luxembourg and France. Three days later General Guderian's XIX Panzer Corps emerged from the early morning mist and crashed across the River Meuse at Sedan. By May 21st, both Rotterdam and Antwerp had fallen. The Germans had crossed the Somme, advancing ever westwards. The British Expeditionary Force was soon in full retreat against the onslaught of the German war machine and its relatively new tactic, "Blitzkrieg", or "lightning war". It seemed that nothing could stop, much less defeat Hitler's forces as they recorded one victory after another. By this time any hope of a successful counter-attack was out of the question, and the British Expeditionary Force was soon retreating towards the port of Dunkirk, from where the tattered remnants would later be evacuated in June.

These current events must have been uppermost in the minds of the embryonic fighter pilots posted to 5 OTU at Aston Down during the Battle for France. One such young man was Pilot Officer John "Jack" Connolly Pugh who arrived for his fighter course in mid-May 1940. Having successfully flown the single-engined Harvard trainer, Pilot Officer Pugh progressed to the Spitfire, the ultimate goal. On May 21st, 1940, he took off from Aston Down on a training flight in Supermarine Spitfire Mk Ia, P9517.

High over the town of Leominster in Herefordshire, P9517's Rolls-Royce Merlin III engine, No. A143801, suffered a malfunction. Pilot Officer Pugh was high enough to have taken to his parachute, but instead attempted a wheels down forced landing to therefore try and save his Spitfire, the value of which had no doubt been impressed upon him.

P9517 had been built at the Supermarine Aviation Works near Southampton and flown for the first time by test pilot Jeffrey Quill, from Eastleigh airport, on April 26th, 1940. *"Production test, 30 minutes"* is recorded in the pages of his log book. The Spitfire was then taken on charge by No 24 Maintenance Unit at Ternhill on April 29th, and allocated to 5 OTU on May 11th. The fact that P9517 was such a new machine could also have influenced Jack Pugh's decision to make a forced landing as he lost height and searched for a suitable field in which to do so. The fire in the engine seemed well contained and there appeared no danger of it spreading to the rest of the aircraft.

Present-day Spitfire owner David Pennell, operator of Mk IX MJ730, and who provided a magnificent flying display in that machine over Malvern in 1992 at the launch of my last book, *"The Invisible Thread: A Spitfire's Tale"*, once told me that to land a Spitfire he required a flat strip of open ground some 800 yards long by 50 yards wide. Such a feature Pilot Officer Pugh must have desperately sought, eventually finding a suitable field about four miles southwest of Leominster, at Alton Cross, in the parish of Dilwyn, a small village which lay a mile to the north-west of the chosen field. By now the Spitfire, trailing black smoke, had attracted a great deal of attention from watchers on the ground. Lionel Weaver and Dennis Fletcher, young boys from Dilwyn, clearly saw the crippled fighter circling overhead as Pilot Officer Pugh searched for a landing place.

Thick black smoke and oil was pouring from the Spitfire, seriously reducing the pilot's forward visibility. Jack lined up on the field, reduced his airspeed, pressing down the small lever on the top left-hand side of his instrument panel to lower the flaps, and also lowered the undercarriage using the hand pump on the right-hand side of his cockpit; the green light on his instrument panel indicated that the wheels were safely locked in the *"down"* position. Probably, to reduce the risk of the fire spreading, Jack had already cut off the fuel supply and would have been in a glide, Air Ministry Pilot's Notes recommending the speed for such a *"non-power assisted"* landing as being about 90 mph Indicated Air Speed.

Literally at the last second of Pilot Officer Pugh's approach, fate played an unexpected card. Suddenly through the smoke he saw a man working a horse in the field right in his path. Without hesitation Jack heaved back on his control column, desperately climbing his Spitfire to avoid a collision with both. Immediately the fighter stalled. Out of control, the Spitfire hit two oak trees in the hedgerow of a field across a narrow lane from the meadow in which farmer Leonard Deakin and his horse had suddenly loomed. Straight away Mr Deakin ran to the crash site with his wife and young daughter, Kathleen, to offer what assistance they could to the pilot. Kathleen takes up the story :-

"When the pilot tried to miss Dad the Spitfire was so low that, as it passed above, his shirt was covered in the black oil leaking from the 'plane, which was also trailing thick black smoke. Immediately the pilot swerved to miss Dad the Spitfire crashed in the next field between the trees. Dad, Mum and myself were at the scene and I can remember it to this day, seeing the pilot there with the 'plane burning. The flames were so fierce we just could not get near him. He saved my father's life and in doing so lost his own."

Leonard Deakin, whose life Pilot Officer Jack Pugh saved by sacrificing his own.
Mrs Stanfield.

Pilot Officer Pugh's body was removed by villagers and kept in Dilwyn overnight in a wooden hut near the church. His remains were later laid to rest at St.Mary's Roman Catholic Church, Woodchester, near Stroud, Gloucestershire. The grave is inscribed *"In Loving Memory of My Son JC Pugh Pilot Officer RAF. Killed on Active Service 21.5.40."*

As a result of my research into local crash sites back in the mid-1980s, I had known for some time that Spitfire P9517 had crashed near Leominster and that its pilot was killed in the accident. Information at MoD Air Historical Branch and the Public Record Office, however, gave no other clue as to the exact location of P9517's crash site. Malvern Spitfire Team vice-chairman Bob Morris had made enquiries in Leominster but had drawn a blank. The surrounding area is very rural, but small villages such as Dilwyn and Weobley abound in the Herefordshire countryside. Therefore I was confident that someone, somewhere, must recall the incident. In September 1987 I set out to solve the mystery and record the story behind the accident which befell P9517.

Having obtained a copy of the Spitfire's service record card, or Air Ministry Form 78, I contacted Team patron Jeffrey Quill, former Supermarine Chief Test Pilot, to ascertain whether he test flew P9517. Jeffrey promptly confirmed that he had done so and provided the date of the flight.

A telephone call to the Commonwealth War Graves Commission provided the pilot's full name, service number, grave location and details of his parents. I now knew that Pilot Officer John Connolly Pugh RAF was the son of Thomas Garnet Pugh and Agnes Mary Pugh of Farnborough, in Hampshire.

Whilst awaiting a result from my letter to the Farnborough newspaper, appealing for contact with the Pugh family or friends of the unfortunate pilot, I visited the pilot's grave along with three other members of the Malvern Spitfire Team, Tony Bramhall, Andrew Long and my younger brother, Neil. Despite a two hour search the grave could not be found, so overgrown was the churchyard. With the use of the priest's map of plots, we eventually discovered the grave in which were also buried Pilot Officer Pugh's mother's ashes. The grave did not have the service headstone we were seeking, therefore not assisting our search, but a privately purchased kerb surround which bore an inscription. We cleared away the grass and weeds, returning a few days later with a stone cleaning solution and commenced restoring the grave to its former state. A sack of white Spanish gravel was scattered on top of the grave replacing the existing very discoloured chippings. On the final visit, in November 1987, a wreath of bright red poppies was left on the grave, a vibrant contrast against the brilliant white gravel. Before this work was carried out permission was obtained from the church, who were informed of the problem, and an article relating to our efforts subsequently appeared in the parish magazine.

Mark Waldron, a reporter with the *"Farnborough Mail"*, traced Pilot Officer Pugh's family and I was contacted by the pilot's brother, Squadron Leader RM Pugh AFC RAF Rtd. It transpired that Bob Pugh was the youngest of three brothers, all of whom were wartime pilots, but the only survivor of the conflict. Bob was delighted with our interest and was able to tell me a little more about Jack and the Pugh family.

Jack was born the middle of the three boys on June 19th, 1919, in Hong Kong, where Mrs Pugh, a Queen's Army schoolmistress, had gone to join her husband who was a teacher in the Army Education Corps. The family returned to England in 1920, where Bob was born in 1921. In 1924, Mrs Pugh was posted to India and was accompanied by her three sons, Tom, Jack and Bob, not returning to Farnborough, their home town, until 1927. All three boys were educated at the Salesian College, Farnborough, along with the Woods-Scawen brothers, Patrick and Tony, who were both to become fighter "aces" during the Battle of Britain, that at that time lay some years ahead, only to be killed in combat within twenty-four hours of each other. In 1934, Jack and Bob accompanied their mother on her latest posting to Cairo. Elder brother Tom remained at Salesians, completed his education and joined the RAF as a pilot in 1936, on a Short Service Commission. Jack and Bob returned from Egypt in April 1939, both also applying for Short Service Commissions in the air force and subsequently being accepted for flying training in August 1939.

Jack's service record states that he was granted a Short Service Commission and became an Acting Pilot Officer, on probation, in the General Duties Branch of the RAF on October 13th, 1939, was graded as a Pilot Officer on probation on May 18th, and lost his life in the flying accident at Dilwyn just three days later. He had gained his Private Pilot's Licence at the Civilian Flying School, Yatesbury, and commenced his training to become a service pilot with 3 Initial Training Wing on October 23rd, 1939, moving on to 6 Flying Training School on November 6th. Jack subsequently arrived at 5 OTU, Aston Down, in mid-May 1940. Had he survived his course and been posted to a fighter squadron, he may even have participated in Operation Dynamo, the air operation covering the evacuation of the BEF from Dunkirk in June, and undoubtedly in the Battle of Britain of summer 1940.

Three other young pilots joined the unit on the same day, all of whom did fly in the Battle of Britain. Pilot Officer Ray Aberhardt, just nineteen years old, went on to fly Spitfires with 19 Squadron. He was killed on August 31st, 1940, the day of Fighter Command's heaviest losses, when his Spitfire overturned on landing, due to his flaps having been damaged in combat over the Thames estuary (see "Spitfire Squadron" also by this author). Pilot Officer Robert Dewey, also nineteen years old, flew Spitfires with both 611 and 603 squadrons during the Battle, in which he destroyed an Me 109. Dewey was killed on October 27th, 1940, when shot down by an Me 109 in a surprise attack south of Maidstone. Only one was to survive the summer of 1940, Sergeant Fred Killingback, who flew Hurricanes with 249 Squadron. Though Killingback survived the Battle he did not do so unscathed; he was wounded when his Hurricane was hit by Me 109s over Maidstone and was forced to take to his parachute.

Returning to the tragic accident in which Pilot Officer Jack Pugh lost his life, Bob Pugh was only able to relate to me what he and brother Tom had been told at Jack's funeral. Representatives from Aston Down had told the brothers that Jack was killed in a forced landing incident in which he had swerved to avoid collision with a farm worker. Jack, who was doing very well on his fighter course, was considered to have made an *"excellent effort in setting up a perfect forced landing under difficult conditions."*

Further enquiries in Leominster by Team members to locate P9517's crash site, and appeals in the local newspaper for eye-witnesses had drawn a complete blank. Tony Bramhall and I felt that if the story about Pilot Officer Pugh avoiding a farm worker was true, then surely someone must remember the incident. Subsequently we contacted Nigel Edwards at our local radio station, Radio Wyvern, who had already done the Malvern Spitfire Team excellent service in connection with other projects. Only too pleased to assist, Nigel described the incident and our predicament on the morning news in late October 1987. Within minutes we were contacted by a number of eye-witnesses who identified the site as being at Chadnor Court, near the village of Dilwyn, and not the town of Leominster, as stated in official records.

The eye-witnesses also confirmed the story of Pilot Officer Pugh's selfless sacrifice. When interviewed by Nigel Edwards on Radio Wyvern's lunchtime news, Mr Lionel Weaver, who had lived in Dilwyn all his life, related the events of that tragic day, describing Pilot Officer Pugh's bravery as *"Remarkable."*

In 1987 Dilip Sarkar searches for a fragment of Spitfire P9517. The adjacent oak tree still bears the scars of what was a most tragic accident.   Andrew Long.

Permission was then sought and obtained from Mr Powell, the landowner at Chadnor Court, for a site investigation. On December 13th, 1987, I visited the site for the first time, with Bob Morris and Andy Long, where we were met by eye-witnesses Lionel Weaver and Dennis Fletcher. Both oak trees remained in the hedgerow and still bore the scars of the accident, with several boughs being damaged and others missing from the trees. It was with great sorrow, however, that we learned of Mr Weaver's sudden death only a few days after our meeting.

A recovery licence was issued by the Ministry of Defence, in accordance with the Protection of Military Remains Act 1986, but a subsequent site investigation proved disappointing, only a thumb-nail sized, once molten, ingot of aluminium being found.

I also discovered at this time that the farm worker's name was Leonard Deakin, who after the war had settled in Dudley, West Midlands. Through the "*Express & Star*" newspaper I was able to trace Mrs Kathleen Stanfield, Mr Deakin's daughter, who explained that her father was forty-two at the time of the accident but had died in 1970. Kathleen related her version of events to me and stressed that her father had no doubt that Jack Pugh's action had saved his life. *"Never a day went by that Dad did not say something about the pilot's bravery and that if he had not been working in that particular field at the time the young man would still be alive."*

It seemed extremely sad to me that Jack Pugh should have given his life so nobly and yet, forty-eight years after the event, nothing remained as tribute to his bravery or to mark the spot of the dramatic incident in which he died. It is remarkable to think that such an occurrence now would be front-page news, but, due to wartime censorship, Jack Pugh's heroic act did not even make the local newspaper. Only the villagers of Dilwyn, Mrs Stanfield, and the Pugh family remembered Jack Pugh for his sacrifice.

The team decided that a permanent memorial should be erected, telling the story of Pilot Officer Pugh's bravery. Support was immediately forthcoming from Squadron Leader Pugh, who told the Farnborough Mail, *"It is very heart-warming that these young people of the Malvern Spitfire Team should think of pilots like my brother. They are doing a good job"*. Bob also pointed out *"this is not being done by retired old gents but by young people who feel that they owe something to people like my brother. It is a great honour."*

The next step was to decide where the memorial should be erected. The crash site is remote and was therefore rejected, so the village green at Dilwyn, reputedly the best kept village in Herefordshire, was mooted by the Team as a more suitable location. Permission and support was then granted by Dilwyn Parish Council, with whom the Team had a number of meetings to plan the project, scheduled for Saturday, August 20th, 1988.

Eye-witness Dennis Fletcher, a committee member of the Herefordshire Aero Club, based at Shobdon, near Leominster, offered the club's services in providing a fly-past tribute to Pilot Officer Pugh, a much appreciated offer that was eagerly accepted. Flight Lieutenant Tony Saville RAFVR(T), CO of 151 (Leominster) ATC Squadron offered his unit as guard of honour and to maintain the memorial after the event.

It was decided that the tribute would take the form of a brass plaque, photo-etched with the team logo, a black Spitfire silhouette above the Malvern Hills, in both top corners. The wording of the plaque would tell the story of Pilot Officer Pugh's accident and of its unveiling. The plaque was set in a steel back-plate and stand featuring another Spitfire silhouette. The memorial was then ready for erection at the site the day before the event. On that day, Andy Long, Bob Morris and I visited the village and met representatives from the Parish Council. The memorial was duly erected and an adjacent hole prepared for Squadron Leader Pugh to plant a silver maple tree in honour of his brother. Both the plaque and tree were provided by the Team. One of our honorary members, Brian Owen, Keeper of Collections at Worcester City Museum and with whom we have worked closely regarding several major exhibitions, supplied a set of display boards on which my research notes and photographs were displayed at the village hall along with a 1/72nd scale model of P9517 made by a villager. All those attending the service were to be invited back to a buffet provided by the village at the nearby hall.

On the eve of the big day, Squadron Leader Pugh and his wife, Sheila, arrived in Malvern with their family. A very enjoyable evening was spent by team members with the Pugh family in the lounge of an hotel high on the slopes of the Malvern Hills over which Jack Pugh may even have flown during his Spitfire training at Aston Down.

At 2.30pm on Saturday, August 20th, 1988, the Pugh family joined members of the team and Dilwyn Parish Council at the village hall, where 151 Squadron's cadets formed up to lead the procession the short distance to the village green. Squadron Leader Ashcroft, RAF Hereford's Community Relations Officer, also joined us for the procession. The Pughs were able to meet Kathleen Stanfield and her husband, with whom they had only previously corresponded since I put them in touch early in 1988.

About three hundred people were waiting at the village green and all traffic was brought to a standstill by Leominster police for the duration of the service. Flight Lieutenant Saville formed his squadron into a guard of honour and Mr George Bray, Chairman of Dilwyn Parish Council, opened proceedings by delivering a speech, in which he said *"It is right for Pilot Officer Pugh to be remembered in this way as he was the only person to be killed on active service in the parish during the Second World War."* On behalf of the Team I followed Mr Bray and explained that *"The Malvern Spitfire Team was formed (at that time) less than two years ago to record the histories and preserve the memories of the many young men, like Jack Pugh, who gave their lives for freedom in the air war over western Europe, and to whom we all, without exception, owed a debt we could never repay. The year 1988 may be time to remind modern society of the quality of young men like Pilot Officer Pugh."* I also had the pleasure of introducing Squadron Leader Pugh, who told of how he had *"attended Jack's funeral forty-eight years ago, but then had no idea that his brother would one day be honoured in this way"*. Bob also publicly paid tribute to the work of the Malvern Spitfire Team and thanked Dilwyn Parish Council for giving the project their support and permission for the event to take place.

The Rev. Mike Kavannagh, 151's chaplain, dedicated the memorial, which was draped in an ATC ensign and unveiled by Squadron Leader and Mrs Pugh. Bob then planted the silver maple and, after a short silence, a lone bugler played the *"Last Post"*, the tones of which were carried far across the surrounding countryside by the strong wind. As the final notes faded, four light aircraft of the Herefordshire Aero Club flew low over the green in a missing man formation which provided an extremely moving and fitting finale to the service.

The crowd then made their way to the village hall where many had the opportunity to meet the Pugh family and see the exhibited research material. Later in the afternoon members of the team took the Pugh family to the site where Jack and P9517 had met their end in 1940. Bob Pugh was shown the field in which his brother had attempted to land and the trees which had claimed his young life. *"From a professional point of view my brother chose an excellent location for a forced landing"*, he remarked.

The memorial project aroused interest from the national press and reports appeared in both the Daily Mail and the Telegraph. All local and regional newspapers carried the story and the televised service was shown on Central TV's Sunday lunchtime news.

It is fitting that such a courageous young man as Pilot Officer Jack Pugh should be remembered with the first such memorial to an airman in the county of Herefordshire.

His elder brother Tom had gone to France flying the ill-fated Fairey Battle light bomber with 103 Squadron on September 2nd, 1939, the day before war was declared on Germany. Upon his return to the UK, after the collapse of France, he was posted to 263 *"Fellowship of the Bellows"* Squadron, who were flying Hurricanes at Grangemouth. During the Battle of Britain, in which the squadron took no direct part, it was equipped with Hur-

Squadron Leader R.M. Pugh AFC with Dilip Sarkar at the unveiling of the memorial to Pilot Officer Jack Pugh at Dilwyn, Herefordshire.

Andrew Long.

ricanes but was converting to the new twin-engined, single-seat fighter, the Westland Whirlwind. Tom Pugh rose to command the squadron, the first to be equipped with the Whirlwind, and was awarded the Distinguished Flying Cross (*see Chapter 11*). Tom later formed 182 Squadron, equipped with Hawker Typhoons. At the same time Denis Crowley-Milling, another distinguished young airman, formed 181. In 1988 Air Marshal Sir Denis Crowley-Milling KCB CBE DSO DFC recalled the following of Tom Pugh:-

"I knew Tom Pugh very well and admired him greatly. There was great rivalry between our two squadrons, particularly with regard to the number of operations against German airfields and other targets in Northern France. Tom Pugh was to have taken over 16 Wing, 121 Airfield, as Wing Commander. Sadly, Tom was killed before he could do so when he was lost during a dive bombing attack on Dieppe harbour on August 2nd, 1943. I took over in his place, so although he held the rank he sadly never actually became wing leader."

Squadron Leader Tom Pugh DFC.
Squadron Leader R.M. Pugh.

Wing Commander Tom Pugh DFC RAF was twenty-five years old at the time of his death and has no known grave. He is remembered on the Runnymede Memorial dedicated to all of the Commonwealth airmen who remain *"missing"*.

Photographs of both Jack and Tom Pugh appeared in a post-war Salesian College magazine published in honour of those former pupils who had made the ultimate sacrifice. Below each photograph appears a poem, one by Seamus Haughey of the RCAF, killed in action 28.9.43, and one by PH Pearse. The last line of Pearse's poem could well be the epitaph of both Jack and Tom Pugh:-

"My sons were faithful and they fought".

Squadron Leader Bob Pugh was born on June 26th, 1921, and received a Short Service Commission at the same time as Jack. He flew throughout the war and remained a regular officer in the post-war RAF with a number of important and varied appointments. I make no apology for quoting his extensive service details in full.

Bob trained at Perth and Kinloss before joining 502 Squadron at Aldergrove, Northern Ireland, in April 1940, flying twin-engined Avro Ansons on convoy escort and anti-submarine patrols. It was during this time that he and brother Tom attended Jack's funeral. Selected for a flying instructor course at the Central Flying School (CFS), Upavon, he graduated in October and instructed at 11 Service Flying Training School (SFTS), Shawbury, until November when posted to 14 SFTS, Carberry, Manitoba, Canada.

Back in the UK in August 1942, Bob attended 3 (Coastal) OTU at Cranwell, and in January 1943 flew a new Wellington to Malta, continued to Egypt and completed a night torpedo dropping course at 5 Middle East Training School (METS), Shallufa, before being posted to 38 Squadron, flying 'Wimpeys' from Berka, near Benghazi in Cyrenacia, Libya. The unit was operating convoy escort and anti-submarine patrols in the Mediterranean and offensive night torpedo operations in the Ionian and Aegean seas. At this time he was promoted to Acting Squadron Leader and became commander of 'A' flight.

In August 1943, Bob was posted to the UK, at his mother's request following Tom's death in action, but did not arrive home until October upon the completion of his tour. After a Qualified Flying Instructor's (QFI) refresher course at Upavon in February 1944, Bob was posted as a Flight Commander to 3 (Pilot) Advanced Flying Unit, South Cerney, but in July returned to Upavon and joined 3 Flying Instructor's School (FIS) as a QFI. In March 1945 he went to 7 FIS at Lulsgate Bottom as commander of a new flight and whilst with that unit was awarded the Air Force Cross. 3 and 7 FIS amalgamated in May 1946 at Little Rissington, where he became a Flight Commander at the post war CFS. In June Bob attended the Air Ministry for interview and was consequently posted as the regular adjutant to 616 Squadron of the Auxiliary Air Force, which was reforming as a Mosquito bomber unit at RAF Finningley. Between September and October 1948, he completed the Day Fighter Leaders Course at Central Fighter Establishment (CFE), West Raynham, and assisted in converting 616 back to the fighter role on jet Meteor IIIs.

Following a short spell as Group Chief Flying Instructor (GCFI), at 62 Group, Rudloe Manor, Bob became founder member of the Reserve Command Training Flight at White Waltham. The flight was upgraded and renamed Home Command Examining Unit with responsibility for the flying standards of all units in the Command.

Posted to the 2nd Tactical Air Force in Germany in October 1950, he assumed command of 2 Squadron, flying Griffon engined Spitfire XIVs and XIXs at Buckeburg. Soon after the squadron converted to jet Meteor FR9s and PR10s, though the Meteor PR10s soon went to 541 PR Squadron and 2 retained the FR9s.

Squadron Leader Pugh AFC returned from Germany in June 1953 and thereafter followed a series of varied appointments; Station Admin Officer at RAF Newton, Air Staff 25 Group at RAF Manby, Group Recovery Executive at RAF Boulmer, Command Land Air Warfare Representative, OC Near East Land/Air Warfare Training Team, HQ NEAF at Episkopi, Cyprus, and staff appointments at the Ministry of Defence. Throughout these he continued to fly as much as possible. Squadron Leader Pugh retired from the RAF in 1968 and joined Airwork Ltd on contract to the Royal Saudi Air Force, becoming squadron commander of the first basic jet training course, flying Strikemasters, at the Air Academy, Riyadh. After conversion training in the USA he transferred as senior instructor to the fighter OCU, with T33 and F86 jets, at Dhahran. The T33 and F86 were phased out in his fifth year in Saudi, after which he spent a further two years in the Arab state as Administration Manager at Tabuk with BAC.

After his return to England he became temporarily employed as a course organiser and lecturer at the Centre for International Briefing which led to a full time post as Director of Human Resources in London for an American company with interests in Saudi Arabia and the Middle East, and from which he resigned in 1979.

In 1981, at the age of sixty, Bob qualified as a microlight pilot and still flies with his eldest son, Michael, who holds a private pilot's licence and is also a qualified glider pilot. Michael Pugh is an army Major and formerly a member of the British Olympic bobsleigh team. Bob Pugh's total flying time is an impressive 6,667 hours on 65 types. He has also flown gliders, made a parachute jump, *"had a go at a hovercraft"* and made a flight in a hot air balloon.

I think that Bob Pugh's antecedents clearly indicate the potential of wartime pilots, being largely well educated and intelligent young men. I am personally deeply moved by the sacrifice of those unfortunates like Jack Pugh, all of their potential for the future being lost in an instant. Without Pilot Officer Jack Pugh, and the thousands like him, the world has undoubtedly been a poorer place.

Chapter Two

THE "STRONG MAN"

Pilot Officer Jack Royston Hamar.
Fred Hamar.

Jack Royston Hamar was born on December 21st, 1914, at Knighton, in Radnorshire, the son of Arthur Thomas and Sarah Anne Hamar. The family ran a long established wholesale and retail grocery and provisions business, William Hamar & Son, supplying customers and village shops within a thirty mile radius of Knighton. Transport was generally horse-drawn until the army took all the firm's horses but one for service in the Great War. From then on Model T Ford motor vans were used, although the one remaining horse was still used to reach remote places in rural Radnorshire.

Jack attended Knighton Primary School until he was eleven years old, when he moved on to the John Beddoes Grammar School in Presteigne. By this time he had already developed an interest in speed, perhaps not surprisingly; his grandfather was a great horseman and always had the fastest horses in town, and, before the Great War, his father and three uncles were motorcycle

The Hamar family business in Knighton, 1936. Jack is fifth from right, and his younger brother Fred third from left.   Fred Hamar.

enthusiasts, known collectively as the "*Mad Hamars*". One female pillion passenger of Alfred Hamar's remembers being left sitting on air after he made a sudden take off! The same uncle Alfred ran three cinemas before the 1914-18 war, in Knighton, Presteigne and Rhayader, and travelled between his premises in a Model T Ford.

The seeds of a flying career were perhaps sown for Jack at an early age, as two of his uncles had flown with the Royal Flying Corps. Lieutenant Alfred Hamar became a pilot early on in the Great War, banging away at the enemy with revolvers and rifles. After one leave he even returned to the front with his mother's fur coat, so cold were the open cockpits of biplanes in service at that time. Returning from a successful bombing raid on Sunday, 8th April, 1917, with two other aircraft of 55 Squadron, Lieutenant Alfred Hamar and his observer, Lieutenant Myburgh, were caught by thirty enemy aircraft, perhaps of von Richthofen's "*Flying Circus*". Hamar's was the only machine to escape the German interception, albeit severely damaged and both pilot and observer fatally wounded. However, Lieutenant Hamar managed to get his aircraft home, only losing consciousness when attempting to land and suffering further injuries in the resulting crash. Alfred Hamar died at 3.50 pm that afternoon in the New Zealand Stationary Hospital, his observer having died only after being carried from the wreckage and imparting invaluable information. Lieutenant Hamar was later buried at Amiens, aged twenty-seven years. No 55 Squadron's Commanding Officer, Major Jack Baldwin, later described the manner of his death as *"one of the finest acts of endurance I have heard of in this entire war"*. Possibly as a result of his brother's death in action, Richard Clarence Hamar, who had emigrated to Canada before the war, joined up and commenced ab initio pilot training. After successfully making his first solo flight, on June 4th, 1918, his aircraft was involved in a mid-air collision with a second machine, which was out of control. Cadet Hamar was killed and buried at Beamsville, Canada, aged twenty-three years.

Jack Hamar's uncle, Lieutenant Alfred Hamar of the RFC, who was killed in action during the Great War.

Fred Hamar.

Jack Hamar (left) pictured with two unknown fledgling fighter pilots during their pre-war flying training days and posing with a Hawker Fury.

Fred Hamar.

During the early 1930s, Jack Hamar worked in the family business, and vastly expanded the animal and poultry feed department. In pursuance of his passion for speed, young Jack progressed from an Ariel 250 cc motorcycle to an Ariel Red Hunter, which he rode successfully on a number of hill climbs. After motorcycles came fast sports cars, first a three-wheeler Morgan, then an Aero Minx and finally an MG. Like numerous other intelligent young men during the late 1930s with a love of speed and adventure, Jack joined the Royal Air Force Volunteer Reserve, on May 16th, 1938, learning to fly with the Civilian Flying School at Yatesbury in Wiltshire. On June 17th, Jack received his licence to fly *"private flying machines"*, covering *"all types of landplanes"*. As the clouds of war gathered over western Europe, the men such as Jack

Hamar who had stepped forward to become pilots with the RAFVR would soon be needed to supplement the strength of the regular air force in the battles ahead. Although the volunteers were not wanting in either numbers or enthusiasm, the time left to train these men was short. Jack Hamar was lucky, having joined so early. Having successfully completed his service flying training, he received the full fighter course at 12 Group Pool before reporting for operational duties with 151(Fighter) Squadron, at North Weald, Essex, on March 4th, 1939. At that time he was still an Acting Pilot Officer, later being commissioned as a Pilot Officer on probation in the General Duties Branch of the Royal Air Force on May 16th.

151 Squadron had been formed at North Weald in August 1936 from a flight of 56 Squadron's Gauntlet biplanes. In November 1938 the squadron had re-equipped with the new eight-gun monoplane fighter, the Hawker Hurricane, and operated this type when Pilot Officer Hamar joined the unit. 12 Group Pool, as we have already discussed when considering the quality of training provided to Pilot Officer Jack Pugh in 1940, was equipped with Demon biplanes before the war, so Jack Hamar's conversion to the Hurricane took place in 151 Squadron, the type of experience that Fighter Command's Commander-in-Chief would have

Pilot Officer Jack Hamar with his 151 Squadron Hurricane shortly before the outbreak of the Second World War and at North Weald in Essex. Note the fixed-pitch wooden propeller and the half-white-half-black undersurfaces.

Fred Hamar.

preferred all of his new pilots to have.

The pre-war peacetime flying taking place at North Weald was largely uneventful, and this situation continued beyond September 3rd, 1939, the fateful day on which Britain and France had declared war on Nazi Germany. However, on February 11th, 1940, Pilot Officer Hamar crashed in a Magister aeroplane at Debden airfield. During landing the aircraft stalled, its undercarriage collapsed and the airscrew was smashed; fortunately the pilot was unhurt.

Following the declaration of war, the British Expeditionary Force, supported by the Hurricanes and Fairey Battles of the Advanced Air Striking Force, was sent to France, there to await Hitler's next military move which was rightly anticipated as being an offensive in the west. 151 Squadron's Commanding Officer, Squadron Leader Edward Donaldson, recalled before his death in 1992, that *"the Low Countries refused to allow British troops in before the Germans broke through France. Then the French bolted, including their air force. I have never seen so many people running so fast anywhere, so long as it was west. The poor British soldiers were continuously let down when the Dutch, Belgian and French soldiers surrendered by the division. The British were marvellous and finally fought their way to the flat beaches of Dunkirk."*

A visit to 151 Squadron by Sir Kingsley Wood, Secretary of State for Air. Squadron Leader "Teddy" Donaldson appears in the black flying suit fourth from left, and Pilot Officer Hamar sixth.

Fred Hamar.

The Supermarine Spitfire fighter had flown several months after the Hawker Hurricane's maiden flight, so production of the former more technically advanced design had commenced later, not having lent itself to mass production at this early stage. Recognising the value of the Spitfire, and in view of the military disaster in France, it was decided that only Hurricanes, the mainstay of Fighter Command in 1940, would be committed to battle on the continent, Mitchell's potent Spitfire being retained for the defence of Britain which

Dowding knew lay ahead. To reinforce the battered Advanced Air Striking Force, a number of Hurricane squadrons based in England were sent to France on a daily detachment basis, amongst them 151.

At 8.30 am on May 17th, 1940, Pilot Officer Hamar and his fellow pilots arrived at Abbeville aerodrome, near the Somme Estuary, taking off at 10 am and carrying out an offensive patrol of the Lille to Valenciennes areas. An hour later, at 12,000', the Hurricane pilots sighted the enemy for the first time: two Junkers 87 Stuka dive bombers, some considerable distance away to the south east. Squadron Leader Donaldson ordered Blue and Yellow Sections to remain above whilst he and Red Section went to investigate. Twenty Stukas were found, and after ensuring that there were no enemy aircraft above the squadron, Blue and Yellow Sections also joined in the attack, which took place at a very low altitude. Subsequently the Hurricanes claimed the destruction of six Stukas confirmed, and a number of unconfirmed claims were made, including two by Pilot Officer Hamar. Donaldson later commented *"It was fairly easy as the Germans were grossly over-confident."* However, Jack's first sortie could well have been his last; his machine was later discovered to have ten bullet holes in it. Donaldson also recalled that 151 Squadron had no option but to return to Manston that night *"as we had several damaged Hurricanes and no ground crews to mend them. Next day we were back to France and this continued every day because our airfields in France were heavily bombed. Whilst pilots could get away to sleep off the airfield, the Hurricanes would take a terrific beating on the ground."*

151 Squadron flew to Vitry airfield at 2pm the following day, and by 3.30 pm were again in action. The squadron diary records that *"a colossal dogfight took place above the aerodrome in which about twenty Messerschmitt 109s came out of the sun and attacked a squadron of Hurricanes taking over escort duties."* At 6.45 pm, 151 Squadron was scrambled from Vitry to intercept several Me 109s sighted above the aerodrome, believed to be escorting a force of bombers. Three miles north-west of Vitry, Pilot Officer Hamar caught an Me 110:-

"I climbed to 7,000' and attacked two Me 110s, succeeding in getting onto the tail of one E/A. I opened fire at 300 yards with a burst of 5 seconds. Whilst closing in I noticed tracer passing over my head, from behind, and looking round I discovered the other E/A on my tail. I immediately half rolled away and noticed two Hurricanes chasing another E/A which was diving to ground level. I followed down after the Hurricanes and as they broke away I continued the chase, hedge-hopping, but did not seem to gain on E/A. I got within 500 yards and put in a five second burst. I saw my tracer entering both wings, but did not observe any damage. As my windscreen was by this time covered in oil from my own airscrew, making sighting impossible, I broke away and returned to Vitry."

Pilot Officer Jack Hamar, in black flying suit, Squadron Leader Donaldson (adjacent to Jack's Morgan sports car), and other 151 Squadron pilots snatch a precious few moments' sleep during the Battle for France.

Fred Hamar.

Having again returned to Manston, on May 22nd three sections of 151 Squadron took off to escort three Ensign transport aircraft to Merville aerodrome. On the return journey, twenty-four Stukas were seen dive- bombing St Omer. Donaldson's Hurricanes attacked, the subsequent *"bag"* being four confirmed destroyed and two unconfirmed. Pilot Officer Hamar was again amongst the successful pilots, claiming one confirmed destroyed and a second unconfirmed:-

"The leader ordered Red Section to attack and we dived towards the Junkers 87s. I lost sight of my leader and circled to select a target. I closed on one which·was diving, but failed to attack before the E/A dropped its bombs on a village. As the E/A pulled up I attacked giving a five second burst at 200 yards which killed the rear gunner. I closed to 100 yards and after a 7 second burst the E/A turned on its side with smoke pouring from its engine. It went into a steep dive and crashed in a field. I attacked another E/A at which I fired a short burst from 200 yards, after which I experienced no further fire from the rear. I closed to 100 yards and opened fire, which tore off the side of the fuselage and top of port wing. I was forced to break away without observing what happened to this E/A because I ran into another five Ju 87s. I did not see any

further E/A crash but I saw a parachute descending. Having turned the petrol supply on to the gravity tank, and having just fifteen rounds per gun remaining, I returned to base."

Jack was in action again on May 25th:-

"Whilst flying as Red Two with Yellow and Blue Section carrying out a general sweep in the Calais - Boulogne district, a Junkers 88 suddenly appeared out of the clouds, passing slightly above and across our formation. The leader ordered a No 1 attack. The E/A dived for sea level, and after Red 1 (Squadron Leader Donaldson) broke away, I attacked. My sights were set 80' at 200 yards range. I used full throttle and gradually closed, opening fire at 300 yards. The slip stream effect was noticed and keeping the sights dead on I fired two long bursts, finishing at 50 yards, using all of my ammunition. I then broke away. During the attack I noticed three large pieces drop from the port side of the E/A which may have been bombs. No other damage was noticed."

On May 29th, 151 Squadron flew as escort to a formation of Boulton Paul Defiants patrolling the Dunkirk area, protecting the seemingly endless lines of soldiers below from enemy air attack. At 15,000' a fierce dogfight took place with Me 109s, and a Junkers 88, believed to be a decoy, was destroyed by Squadron Leader Donaldson and Pilot Officer Hamar. The latter's combat report describes the action:-

"Whilst flying as Red Two on a high escort patrol over Dunkirk, a Ju 88 was seen flying approximately due east at 7,000'. The leader ordered Red Section into line astern and delivered a No 1 Fighter Attack. The leader also ordered Yellow One to take over and remain above on guard. As I followed the leader into attack I saw a large formation of Me 109s high above. As the leader broke away, I saw white smoke pouring from the E/A's port engine, and it started flying crab-like. Thinking that this may be a ruse, I decided to attack again, aiming at the port engine. I opened fire at approximately 150 yards and continued the burst until at about 20 yards. Large pieces of the port engine were seen to drop off. I did not experience any fire from the rear of E/A, which neither executed any evasive actions other than a fast dive towards cloud, nearly on its side. I then re-joined Red 1."

As the evacuation of the BEF from Dunkirk by the "Little Ships" continued, 151 Squadron returned to North Weald to re-form, leaving the fighting of Operation Dynamo to fresh squadrons, the majority being Spitfire equipped and meeting the enemy for the first time.Donaldson recalled:-

"151 Squadron flew as many as seven sorties a day against overwhelming odds. At Dunkirk we even stayed on patrol after running out of ammunition to complete a one hour patrol. This hindered the Luftwaffe from attacking the defenceless troops on the ground. When we finally returned to North Weald we were involved in escorting RAF bombers attacking German communications and the thousands of invasion barges massing along the Pas de Calais beaches, rivers and canals. Most, if not all, of the Hurricane squadrons which had operated from French airfields had by this time been rested, except 151. Basil Embry, a man without fear, was commanding a bomber squadron in those days, and always asked for 151 as escort because we always stayed close.

"One of the pilots we lost at Dunkirk was Allen Ives, a friend of Jack Hamar's. He was partially trained to be a doctor, so I gave my permission for him to remain on the beaches to help treat badly wounded soldiers. He put up a marvellous show before getting on a boat. This was sunk and 'Ivy' was swimming in the water when shot through the head by a German soldier who was lying on the bow deck of an 'E'-boat. An eye-witness account of the incident was given to me by another 151 Squadron pilot, a New Zealander, also shot down over Dunkirk.

"After the fall of France and the Dunkirk evacuation, the Luftwaffe switched their attacks to British shipping in the English Channel, and our radar stations and airfields so that they could win aerial supremacy, thus enabling Operation Sealion, the proposed invasion of England to take place. Of course it was our job to stop them. Altogether I flew 303 sorties, missing only one; Victor Beamish, the North Weald station commander, wanted me for something important, although I was able to get back to the airfield and greet the squadron on its return.

"Our Group Commander, Air Vice-Marshal Keith Park, told me at the time that he was sorry to have to work the squadron so hard, thus giving us more than our fair share of harder jobs. However, he explained that as we were battle hardened he could rely on 151 Squadron to fully do its duty."

As France collapsed, Britain's Prime Minister, Winston Churchill, ominously predicted "The Battle of France is over; the Battle of Britain is about to begin." Churchill was quite right. Hitler was already making plans for the occupation of the British Isles by a foreign power for the first time in 874 years. Operation Sealion, his War Directive No 16, stipulated that:-

"As England, in spite of her hopeless military position, has so far shown herself unwilling to come to any compromise, I have decided to begin preparations for, and, if necessary, to carry out the invasion of England.

This operation is dictated by the necessity to eliminate Great Britain as a base from which the war against Germany can be fought. If necessary the island will be occupied. I therefore issue the following orders:-

1. The landing operation must be a surprise crossing on a broad front extending approximately from Ramsgate to a point west of the Isle of Wight. The preparations must be concluded by the middle of August.

2. The following preparations must be undertaken to make a landing in England

possible:

a) The English air force must be eliminated to such an extent that it will be incapable of putting up any substantial opposition to the invading troops..."

Flying from newly acquired bases in France, thus increasing the operational range of its aircraft, the Luftwaffe set about attempting to destroy Fighter Command. The first skirmishes between the opposing air forces took place over Channel convoys which were bringing much needed food and ammunition to Britain, now an island fortress under siege. Although the Battle of Britain is deemed to have begun officially on Wednesday, July 10th, 1940, much fighting over the Channel had taken place for some time previously. On July 9th, 151 Squadron was involved in bitter combat twenty miles north east of Margate, with a formation of German aircraft numbering someone hundred, comprising Heinkel 111 bombers escorted by Me 109s and 110s. Pilot Officer Hamar damaged an Me 110:-

"At 1430 hrs 'A' flight of 151 Squadron was ordered to patrol a large convoy about five miles off the coast, just north of the Thames Estuary. I was flying as Red 2 in the formation. At 1540 hrs a large number of E/A in several waves were sighted flying N.W. at about 10,000'. It was impossible to attack the first wave, which consisted of Heinkel 111 bombers, because of the large number of escorting fighters which were very near us. Red 1 therefore ordered line astern and attacked the nearest formation of fighters, which consisted of 12 Me 110s. No 1 Fighter Attack was used, and after Red 1 had broken away and attacked the rear Me 110. I closed to 150 yards and gave it a 5 second burst. I saw my bullets tearing into the fuselage and wings of the E/A, which staggered badly. I then had to break away quickly as the air seemed full of enemy aircraft.

"I then saw bombs exploding near the convoy which I approached at full throttle. I chased a section of three E/As away from northern end of the convoy but failed to get into a position to open fire. I then continued to patrol the convoy for about 15 minutes as the air had by this time cleared of E/A. No ships in the convoy had been hit, so I then returned to base as my fuel was running low."

Hurricane pilot, circa 1939. Pilot Officer Jack Hamar at North Weald. Note the 'D' type canvas oxygen mask and sidcot flying suit.

Fred Hamar.

A Midshipman Wightman later reported seeing an enemy aircraft dive into the sea, which was possibly that claimed by Jack Hamar, or one damaged by Wing Commander Beamish and Flying Officer Forster.

The Battle of Britain officially began the following day, when a dogfight involving over one hundred aircraft took place over the Channel. Pilot Officer Hamar next reported a combat claim on July 14th, a day which saw further attacks on shipping off Swanage and Dover:-

"At 1500 hrs the squadron was ordered off from Rochford to intercept E/As south of Dover. At approximately 1520 hrs, when the squadron was almost over Dover, a bunch of Me 109s were sighted about 5000' above our formation. I was flying Red 2 in the formation. As it looked as though the E/A were about to attack us, the leader ordered our defensive line astern tactics. As we turned sharply to port, two Me 109s were seen diving to attack the last aircraft in our formation. Milna leader attacked the leading Me 109 and I attacked the second. I turned inside the E/A, which had pulled up into a steep left hand climbing turn. I closed rapidly and opened fire at about 250 yards with a 45 degree deflection shot. The E/A seemed to falter and straightened out into a dive. I placed myself dead astern at about 50 yards. I opened fire, closing to almost no distance. I saw a large explosion just in front of the pilot and a large amount of white smoke poured from the E/A which was by this time climbing steeply. I was then forced to break away quickly due to fire from the rear, and lost sight of the E/A and therefore did not see it crash. This action was also seen by Flying Officer Forster."

On July 23rd, 151 Squadron received a signal to the effect that Pilot Officer Hamar's gallantry had been recognised by the award of a Distinguished Flying Cross. The King himself had approved the Air Ministry's recommendation for the award, which was worded as follows: "Since December this officer has participated in all operations and most of the patrol flights undertaken by his squadron. He has shown coolness and courage of a high order and has personally destroyed six enemy aircraft." Tragically, the muscular young pilot from Radnorshire, known as the "Strong man", was never to receive the medal from his King, or sew onto his tunic the coveted medal's diagonally striped mauve and white ribbon.

On Wednesday, 24th July, 1940, just two weeks into the Battle of Britain, the 151 Squadron diary recorded:-

"Jack Hamar brought down three confirmed enemy aircraft and six others probably destroyed; it is particularly tragic that his death should occur as the result of an accident. Green section were taking off on patrol when Pilot Officer Hamar's aircraft was seen to dive into the ground."

The true facts of the matter were a little different, as Edward Donaldson recalled, paying tribute to his friend:-

"Jack Hamar was my No 2. A leader has to navigate as well as co-ordinate and lead attacks. He can only do this if he has a good No 2 whom he can completely rely on. A CO then knows that no-one can creep up behind him as long as his No 2 is in place. I always knew that Jack would be there. If he were shot down, I knew that the last thing he would do would be to tell me on the radio that he had 'had it'. Looking after me was an extremely hazardous task. Jack did it loyally and even so managed to shoot down six and a half enemy aircraft. The half was for a German bomber which we shared; I had damaged it but it may have returned to its base, so Jack blew it out of the sky in flames. I made nine forced landings in total, but was never shot down with Jack Hamar as my No 2.

"Jack and I were extremely close; I loved the fellow. From mid-July we slept the night in dugouts on the airfield at North Weald. There were eight pilots on camp beds at the beginning. By July 24th only Jack and I were left. On the previous night Jack had sat on my bed and said "Sir, I think you and I will live through this. We have been to hell and back together and are still alive."

"I said "For God's sake don't say that. It's bad luck."

"The next morning the weather was appalling. I got an urgent telephone call from the Air Officer Commanding. He said "The weather is awful, but I have an unidentified aircraft circling Felixstowe at 10,000', I don't like it. As the weather is so bad I must ask you, not order you, if you can go after him."

"I said to Jack, "What about it?"

"He said, as I knew he would, "Let's get the bastard." Air Vice-Marshal Park said "Thanks a lot", so off we went. Visibility was down to about a quarter of a mile. The danger at North Weald was the international radio masts. These went up several hundred feet, and whilst the controllers could get pilots back to the field, to avoid the masts you had to see them in time.

"No sooner were we airborne with wheels up than Group identified the aircraft circling Felixstowe as friendly. We turned round and, flying slowly at 120 mph and some 60' above the ground, I waited for North Weald to re-appear, which it did in a few minutes. I signalled to Jack to 'break'; to my horror he broke upwards and commenced an upward roll. In a Hurricane it was impossible to carry out such a manoeuvre at that low speed. As I saw him start his right-handed roll, I screamed "Don't, Don't" down the R/T, but it was too late. Jack stalled and hit the ground upside down.

"I was on the ground and beside him within seconds. Jack had had his hood open to improve visibility in the awful weather conditions, and this had caused massive head injuries. I was devastated."

Shortly afterwards the Hamar family received the standard telegram informing of their son's death, and letters of condolence from North Weald began to arrive at "Hillcrest", the family home. Wing Commander Victor Beamish wrote:-

"It is with the deepest sympathy and regret that I write concerning the death of your son. He was one of the bravest of our officers, beloved and respected by all - I can say no more.

"Three days ago he had been awarded the Distinguished Flying Cross - a signal honour which he knew of before his death.

"May I again convey my very deepest sympathy on a sad loss to us all."

In a letter of July 26th, 1940, mainly concerning funeral arrangements, 151 Squadron's adjutant also commented:-

"It has caused considerable grief to all the Officers of the squadron that they are unable to be present with you to pay their last respects to a brother Officer to whom they were so attached. However, the reason is that they are constantly on patrol and continuing that work which your son has heretofore carried out with such honour and distinction.

"Finally, I would close by expressing on behalf not only of the Officers, but also the NCOs and Airmen who belong to this squadron, their deepest sympathy to you at this time. The loss to us all is a grievous blow, but his name and record will remain with us through the times which may come to us."

Pilot Officer Hamar's funeral took place on July 28th, at Knighton, and the twenty-five year old was laid to rest at an impressive military funeral, receiving over one hundred floral tributes. The firing party from North Weald, attending at their own request, fired three volleys over the grave, as the haunting notes of the "Last Post" faded across Radnorshire.

On September 4th, 1940, as the Battle of Britain approached its climax, the Hamars received a letter from Buckingham Palace:-

"I have the honour to inform you that your attendance is requested at Buckingham Palace at 10.30 o'clock a.m. on Tuesday, 17th September next, in order that you, as next of kin, may receive from the King the Decoration of the late Pilot Officer Jack R. Hamar, which he would have received personally had he survived."

In due course, in the plainly furnished air raid shelter below Buckingham Palace, the wives, mothers and fathers of thirteen brave men received from the King the decorations their loved ones' courage had won. In its setting the ceremony was unique in history. At the King's side was Lord Clarendon, the Lord Chamberlain, who called out the names of the heroes and then of the relatives to receive the decoration. As their names were called, these men and women filed quietly into the shelter and from their King received the sympathy and honour of the nation. Mrs Hamar proudly accepted her son's Distinguished Flying Cross, in its shiny black Royal Mint presentation box. As she did so, high above London, young men of Britain, the Commonwealth and the occupied lands still fought the young men of Germany, each fighting for their respective country and beliefs; many more sacrifices would be made, and equally as many medals won before Nazi Germany would eventually be defeated, the globe consumed by conflict.

Nearly fifty years later, whilst researching for the Malvern Spitfire Team's 1990 exhibitions, *"Fighter & Bomber"* at Hereford Museum, and *"Their Finest Hour: No Piece of Cake"* at Tudor House Museum, Worcester, I first learned of Pilot Officer Jack Royston Hamar DFC. Having traced Jack's brother Fred to his Knighton home, a quaint bungalow appropriately called *"Royston"*, in October 1989 myself and Andrew Long had the great pleasure of meeting Fred and his wife, Enid. Talking to Fred, a wise old native of Radnorshire, was an experience, as we were transported back in time to the old Knighton, the times of *"bone setters and wise women"*, and the faraway days of Jack Hamar's all too brief life. I remember Fred saying casually, *"I've got one or two things to show you"*, and there I saw an historian's dream, a veritable treasure trove of photographs, letters, Christmas cards, Jack's private flying licence, hundreds of newspaper cuttings, a glittering DFC in its presentation case, campaign medals, including the Battle

A display case in the Malvern Spitfire Team's exhibition "Their Finest Hour: No Piece of Cake", commemorating the fiftieth anniversary of the Battle of Britain at Tudor House Museum, Worcester. Amongst the items on display are Pilot Officer Jack Hamar's Commission, funeral notice, DFC, mess uniform and calling cards.   Andrew Long.

of Britain Bar, all still in their greaseproof paper wrappers and Jack Hamar's Commission, but perhaps most incredible of all was his mess uniform, in immaculate condition, buttons shiny bright, still hanging on the same coat-hanger on which he had left it, and in a waistcoat pocket was a small box of calling cards, each stating simply in copper plate: "*Mr JR Hamar, Royal Air Force.*"

The four of us later enjoyed a superb lunch at the "*Horse and Jockey*" in Knighton, a 16th century inn selected for our visit by Fred as Jack and his friends from 151 Squadron often visited the pub when on leave. He remembered particularly Allen Ives, who was killed at Dunkirk, and a South African, "*Poppy*" Pope, the latter being "*sweet on the landlord's daughter.*" Fred also vividly remembered six 151 Squadron Hurricanes giving a flying display over Knighton whilst Jack was on leave, Allen Ives even "*dive-bombing*" the family home !

I was interested to read the up-date in the "*Battle of Britain Then & Now Mk V*" (see bibliography) regarding Jack Hamar's story, and how the editor, Winston Ramsey, had been similarly fascinated by this young man from Knighton. I was especially interested to read that the 151 Squadron diary had not recorded the true facts of Jack Hamar's crash, stating instead that Pilot Officer Hamar was killed in a landing accident, and how Mr Ramsey had also received the true facts from Air Commodore Donaldson. Having contacted Jack Hamar's former friend and CO myself, I was also fortunate to receive from him a considerable amount of first-hand background information, some of which has been quoted in this chapter. Jack Hamar's death had so deeply affected Squadron Leader Donaldson that Wing Commander Beamish decided he must be rested; in the event Donaldson was shortly promoted to Wing Commander and left North Weald on August 5th, 1940, to become Chief Flying Instructor at Sealand. After visiting the USA in 1941, organising gunnery schools and teaching tactics, Donaldson commanded several RAF stations prior to taking over the post-war RAF High Speed flight in 1946. With that unit he broke the World Speed Record flying a Meteor jet. Retiring from the RAF in 1961, with the CBE, CB, DSO, AFC and US Legion of Merit to his credit, he became the air correspondent for the Daily Telegraph, a post which he held until his retirement in 1979.

In March 1993, I was sad to stand at Air Commodore Donaldson's graveside, at Tangmere, the accomplished aviator having died the previous year. True friendship is a precious commodity, especially that forged in circumstances likely to make that bond even stronger. Perhaps the special friendship between Jack Hamar and his Commanding Officer has been rekindled since the latter more recently crossed the great divide. One thing I am certain of is that to his dying day Air Commodore Donaldson's regard for Jack Hamar was as high as on that fateful day in 1940 when the *Strong Man* lost his life.

Chapter Three

STÖRFLUG TO HUCCLECOTE

Pilot Officer Alec Bird.
Via Allan White.

The critical aerial conflict now known as the Battle of Britain officially commenced on July 10th, 1940. The first phase of the sixteen week struggle consisted of attacks on Channel convoys and thrusts against Fighter Command to discover weaknesses in Britain's defences. Thursday, July 25th, saw a further escalation of German attacks along the south and east coasts and a fierce skirmish over a heavily protected convoy in the Dover Strait. Portland harbour also attracted several raids, three fighter squadrons flying over a hundred sorties in its defence. The day's combat had drawn fifteen Fighter Command squadrons into action for a cost of six Spitfires destroyed and four pilots killed.

There was another action fought that day, in a remote area of Gloucestershire, that does not fit into the overview of the day's fighting as previously recorded by historians, and a correct account of which has only now been published.

By this date during the summer of 1940, although large German formations attacked convoys, inland forays were actually seldom undertaken except by single aircraft when cloudy conditions prevailed. Such sorties were known as *"Störflug"* (harrassing attacks). The 5th Staffel of Kampfgeschwader 51 *"Edelweiss"* was equipped with Junkers 88 bombers and based at the Paris/Orly airfield in occupied France. One crew comprised Unteroffizier Friedel Dörner, the pilot, aged twenty-five and from Gruiten in the Rhineland, Unteroffizier Wilhelm Hügelschäfer, the navigator and observer, aged twenty-three years from Kleinlangheim, Unteroffizier Walter Theiner, the flight engineer aged twenty-six from Breslau, and Gefreiter Gottfried Treue, the wireless operator, aged nineteen from Bielefeld.

Three crew members of the Oakridge Ju 88, from left to right: Unteroffizier Wilhelm Hügelschäfer, Geffreiter Gottfried Treue and Unteroffizier Friedel Dörner.

Via Allan White.

Hügelschäfer, the aircraft's captain, had previously made eight operational flights over France and three over England. At the beginning of the war he was serving with a Luftwaffe Air District Command HQ at Munich but volunteered for operational duty as an observer, which embraced the duties of both navigator and bombardier. He trained at Fassberg and Wiener-Neustadt before being posted to KG51. At that time his staffel was based at Stuttgart/Echterdingen airfield, from where operations were flown during the Battle for France. In June his unit moved to Orly.

On the morning of July 25th, 1940, Unteroffiziers Dörner and Hügelschäfer attended a briefing and received orders for a "*Störflug*". The crew were to intrude English airspace, making a landfall over the Isle of Wight, proceed due inland and attack the Gloster Aircraft Factory at Hucclecote in Gloucestershire. Alone over England, the crew would be relying on their aircraft's speed, agility and relatively heavy armament to get them out of trouble along with cloud cover, the German bomber's natural defence.

Having boarded their aircraft, coded "9K + GN", Dörner took off and headed towards England. Wilhelm Hügleschäfer recalls that his crew were in high spirits, perhaps not surprisingly as at that time the world appeared Germany's oyster, and sang aloud as their bomber cruised towards their Midland target. Passing over the Isle of Wight at some 18,500', he also remembers that the day was a splendid one with actually very little cloud either above or below. East of the target, over Hucclecote in Gloucestershire, the Junkers 88 commenced a turn to take it directly over the aircraft factory. Hügelschäfer remarked to his pilot that if they flew around in such a manner they were bound to attract the attention of enemy fighters. Hardly had Hügelschäfer uttered his misgivings than Walter Theiner shouted "*Achtung, jager!*"

The progress of Hügelschäfer and his comrades had not gone undetected by the defenders. Lying sprawled out on the airfield at RAF Kemble in Gloucestershire, home of No 5 Maintenance Unit, Pilot Officer EW "*Bertie*" Wootten, a pilot with No 4 Ferry Pilots Pool, heard the unmistakable *umph, umph* of the raider's unsynchronised engines, and then saw the Junkers pass high overhead. Kemble's response was the immediate scrambling of two station defence flight Hurricanes piloted by Pilot Officers Alec Bird and Richard Manlove. Rapidly climbing northwards to 12,000', then turning south, the pilots spotted the "*bandit*" 500' above them and flying north. Bird's Hurricane, P3271, was equipped with a Rotol airscrew and rapidly overhauled Manlove's inferior De Havilland bladed aircraft in the pursuit.

As Bird closed in Theiner had spotted the Hurricanes and shouted the warning. Hügelschäfer immediately jettisoned the bombs and Dörner turned SSW to race for the far-off coast. Anti-aircraft fire then began bursting between Manlove's Hurricane and Pilot Officer Bird. The former could see his comrade at 18,000', level with the enemy aircraft, and closing in for an astern attack. Whilst converging from the enemy's port side, Manlove saw Bird "*close right in and deliver his attack from very close quarters before turning away upwards and to port.*" At the top of the break-away Manlove saw Bird's Hurricane suddenly go into a spin.

As Hügelschäfer jettisoned the bombs, Dörner had changed course and dived into the nearest patch of thin cloud. No sooner had Dörner done so than Hügelschäfer felt *"a severe jolt in the back"*. He believes that his aircraft was actually rammed.

With Bird's Hurricane rapidly tumbling out of the sky, Manlove delivered a further attack from long range, some 500 - 600 yards. The enemy aircraft's starboard engine flew to pieces and a parachute left the doomed bomber. Inside the Junkers was chaos. As Friedel Dörner gave up the hopeless struggle to retain control of his *"Edelweiss"* bomber at 12,500', he gave the order for his crew to bale out. One by one the white parachutes blossomed over the patchwork English countryside.

Manlove had followed the bomber's downward spiral and observed Alec Bird's fighter still in a spin at 500'. At that point he saw *"a flock of Spitfires arriving"* which appeared to circle the burning Hurricane. Seeing that Alec Bird's fate was sealed, he returned to Kemble.

The other fighters were from nearby 5 Operational Training unit at Aston Down, and actually consisted of a Spitfire, P9501, flown by Flight Lieutenant Peter Prosser Hanks DFC, and a pupil in a Hurricane. The pair had been undertaking dogfight practice when informed of the enemy aircraft's presence by ground control. Hanks was already an *"ace"* with eight confirmed victories to his credit, all scored during the Battle of France when he flew Hurricanes with 1 Squadron. In 1985 Hanks recalled the action:-

"When I first saw the Ju 88 he was well above me but being chased by a Hurricane, presumably Bird's. I went after them, leaving my pupil a long way behind. When the '88 entered cloud, Bird's Hurricane was about 800 yards astern of it and followed the bomber into cloud. I was still about 1,000' below. I carried on below cloud in the general direction of the Ju 88 and after only a short while it broke cloud about 1,000 yards ahead of me. It looked to be flying quite normally and I saw no damage to it or pieces falling off.

Flight Lieutenant P.P. Hanks DFC during the Battle of France whilst flying Hurricanes with 1 Squadron.

Via Allan White.

48

I managed to close with it and started firing. I must admit to having been surprised not to receive any return fire and almost immediately the crew started to bale out."

Floating down on his parachute, Hügelschäfer was perturbed as British fighters passed quite close to him. Although it seemed an eternity as he floated earthwards, the young German was surprised at the force of his landfall in a cornfield. For some time he just lay there, no doubt the prospect of imminent captivity uppermost in his mind, but eventually he released his parachute harness and made towards a nearby road, although not without difficulty as a flying boot had been lost during the descent and his right thigh was quite painful. He remembers events well:-

"After only a short time I saw some people, land workers carrying scythes and pitchforks, hurrying towards me. At the same time a car containing some policemen also arrived. They spoke to me but I could not understand the language. They put me in the car and drove me to a nearby airfield. Upon arrival I was taken to a barracks and inside were two of my crew, Dörner and Treue. A nurse gave us some tea and gave me an old gym shoe to replace my lost flying boot. We sat for a few hours but it was difficult for us to converse. In the evening a lorry came to take us away. It was a frightening moment - we were led to the lorry along an aisle of soldiers with fixed bayonets.

"We spent that night in a prison in single cells. We were in some sort of basement and on the ground was an old, dirty mattress and a single blanket. The window was covered by an iron plate with small holes in it. In the iron door there was a peep-hole through which a guard would peer every hour or so.

"The next morning we were taken to London by train, guarded by armed soldiers. I was placed alone in a room at a building in Hyde Park and remained there for about a week. Throughout I was handled in a very correct manner. Eventually I was taken to a prisoner of war camp at Oldham where I remained until January 1941 when shipped to Canada, returning to England in the spring of 1946 and remaining until repatriation in 1947."

Gefreiter Gottfried Treue had also baled out and landed in the garden of Mrs le Bailley. In a contemporary interview she stated:-

"For a moment I thought that the airmen would strike the holly tree but he missed it and came to ground on the lawn, striking his mouth on the sundial."

Mrs le Bailley had told her maid, nineteen year old Mavis Young, and her brother Roy, the gardener's boy, to go to the shelter. However, they approached the German airman with their mistress. Propping the shaken Treue against a wall, Mavis Young handed the German a glass of whisky. With Teutonic manners he said *"Thank you"*, and kissed the maid's hand. The schoolmaster, Mr Watson, a neighbour of the le Bailley's, took charge of the wireless operator and called the police.

"Edelweiss" on the Cotswolds; Ju 88 "9K + GN" of 5/KG51 down at Oakridge, Gloucestershire.
Via Allan White.

As the alarm bells rang at Miserden parish church, the local Home Guard unit was mobilised, arresting both Hügelschäfer and Dörner, the latter having landed practically on top of a house. Captain Guise, the unit's commanding officer, later reported that *"He seemed very frightened. I think that the Germans must have told their people that we ill treat or kill our prisoners, but he cheered up when we gave him a cigarette."*

Walter Theiner was not so lucky. Hit by machine gun bullets (presumably) during Bird's attack, he was thrown out of the aircraft as the Hurricane crashed into it. Several hours later his body was discovered by members of Brimscombe Home Guard who had formed a line to comb the hillside after previous attempts to locate the bomber's fourth crew member had failed. Only ten yards into Oldhills Wood Unteroffizier Theiner was found hanging head down from a tree, his

The shattered cockpit of the "Oakridge Junkers".

Via Allan White.

50

parachute not having opened. He was subsequently buried with full military honours at Brimscombe Church in Gloucestershire, later being reinterred at the Soldatenfriedhof at Cannock Chase.

At 2.15 pm Mr Albert Stephens had the shock of his life whilst hedge cutting when the Junkers 88 crashed into Bidcombe Bottom between Oakridge and France Lynch. Pilot Officer Bird's Hurricane, with him sadly still at the controls, impacted at Bournes Green, Oakridge, on the Bisley Road. Soon afterwards a car-load of special constables arrived on the scene to find the fighter burnt out and the remains of the pilot being removed by Mr P. Handy of Painswick.

The funeral of twenty-six year old Unteroffizier Walter Theiner at Brimscombe Church, Gloucestershire.
Via Allan White.

No account of this action would be complete without relating the biography of Alec Bird. A native of Kirkstall, Leeds, as a young boy his only ambition had been to fly, no doubt stimulated by the stories of his father, who had been an observer in the Royal Flying Corps during the Great War and had the Military Cross to his credit. So strong was this desire that he later undertook flying lessons privately at Yeadon but without the knowledge of his parents. Having been educated at Leeds Modern School and Leeds Technical College, in October 1938 he joined the air force, passing out as a Pilot Officer. On September 2nd, 1939, he married Miss Marjorie Wilmshurst of Colton; the following day the storm broke and, as Britain and France declared war on Hitler's Germany, the globe erupted in conflict. On his wedding day Pilot Officer Bird was posted to No 2 Ferry Pilots Pool at Filton near Bristol and commenced the ferrying of Hurricanes and Blenheims to the Advanced Air Striking Force based in France. On May 18th, 1940, during Hitler's blitzkrieg across the low countries and France, Alec Bird was at Glisy, having ferried a Hurricane, when Heinkel 111 bombers attacked the airfield. Immediately he took off and attacked the enemy formation, shooting one down with its port engine ablaze. Without oxygen he was obliged to discontinue combat at 22,000' by which time his aircraft had sustained three bullet holes in its wings. Bird was later posted to No 4 Ferry Pilots Pool and flew from Cardiff before being stationed at Kemble. On July 24th, 1940, the day before his death, whilst shopping with his wife in Cheltenham he spotted a poem in a magazine and said to Marjorie *"when I am killed put that on my gravestone and take me back to Yorkshire."* The following day he drove down the driveway of their home, off to the airfield, but stopped, returning to his wife saying *"I don't want to leave you today, somehow."* Whether twenty-three year old Alec had a premonition of death we will never know. As he had requested, they took his body back to Yorkshire and buried him in Adel churchyard.

More than fifty years after this action was fought, controversy still rages. Who was responsible for the demise of the Junkers 88, Bird or Hanks ? If Bird, did he shoot it down or ram it ? In his subsequent report, Pilot Officer Manlove does not account for Bird going into a spin. He does not describe having witnessed a collision. However, Wilhelm Hügelschäfer, an experienced combat flyer, believes to this day that he and his comrades were *"rammed"*. Another question then arises, did Bird deliberately ram the bomber or collide with the enemy accidentally whilst flying in cloud ? From evidence available it appears clear that the fate of the Junkers was sealed prior to the attack made by Flight Lieutenant Hanks, who, in fairness, retracted his claim for its destruction once he learned of Bird's fate. In Manlove's opinion, *"there is no doubt that the aircraft was destroyed by Pilot Officer Bird."* Whatever the truth of the matter, Pilot Officer Alec Bird died in the defence of his country during our Finest Hour. But that raises another issue.

As has been stated, the official dates of the Battle of Britain are from July 10th to October 31st, 1940. To qualify as one of the immortal *"Few"*, and therefore eligible to wear the coveted Battle of Britain Bar to the 1939-45 Star, the aircrew applicant must have flown at least one operational patrol between the specified dates and with one of the accredited units designated as having participated in the battle. As neither 4 Ferry Pilots Pool or 5 Operational Training Unit fall into that category, the names of Pilot Officer Alec Bird and Flight Lieutenant Peter Prosser Hanks DFC will not be found included amongst the *"Few"*. Having actually seen action during the Battle of Britain period it is ironic that this should be the case as some of those actually included saw no action at all, and qualified merely by making an uneventful operational patrol with an accredited unit. For a variety of reasons too complicated to examine here, historians have also long questioned the relevance of the official dates governing the start and finish of the Battle of Britain; perhaps the criteria for the *"Few"* should also be seriously questioned and possibly amended to allow pilots such as Bird and Hanks, who actually fired their guns in anger during the period in question, to be similarly immortalised ?

Chapter Four

THROUGH PERIL TO THE STARS

Pilot Officer Herbert Laurence Whitbread.
Mrs Sally Stubbs.

Herbert Laurence Whitbread was born in Ludlow, Shropshire, on August 21st, 1914. Known to all as *"Laurie"*, he lived with his parents and sister, Vera, at 4 Linney View, Ludlow, and attended the local primary and grammar schools. At the latter he was a popular pupil and an oustanding sportsman. Laurie became house captain of Wright's in 1933. Later a former master, George Merchant, wrote a series of articles for the *"Ludlow Advertiser"* regarding his teaching memories. In Episode 19, Merchant describes a Wright House photograph with Laurie *"sprawling in his majesty, flanked by his henchman and surrounded by his minions."* Whitbread's name at Ludlow Grammar became synonymous with boxing, rugby and hockey and he even represented the county in the latter. His best friend was Charlie Knight, a fellow pupil of Ludlow grammar, and son of the Rev. and Mrs Lacey Hulbert of St Mary's. Charlie's younger sister, Margaret, to whom Laurie was as a second brother, still remembers him with deep affection and humorously recalls when Laurie dressed up in her father's cassock and went out walking in Ludlow. After leaving school he obtained an apprenticeship at the Birmingham firm of Fisher & Ludlow which manufactured sheet steel for making car bodies. Ken Brown, another Ludlovian, also worked for the company and travelled with Laurie. He remembers his friend leaving Fisher & Ludlow in 1939 to take up a Short Service Commission in the Royal Air Force.

Like the other young men of his generation, Laurie Whitbread had grown up in the shadow of the Great War and had watched the storm clouds gathering once again over Europe during the 1930s. No doubt having accepted that a war with Hitler's Germany was inevitable, like many others of his social and educational background, Laurie volunteered for aircrew training. On Thursday, 12th January, 1939, he sat for interview at the Air Ministry and by March was undertaking his ab initio flying training at Desford. Our best record of his training days is actually recorded in Laurie's own hand, in his diary, and some entries are reproduced below:-

March 9th: *"Flying lots in afternoon - instructor to myself from 1.30 - 4.30. Managed okay. Stalling, gliding, turning, taxying."*

March 11th: *"Looking forward to first solo."*

April 25th: *"RAF test after 45 hours solo, passed okay."*

Having successfully won his "wings", Pilot Officer Whitbread then joined the Flying Training School at Kinloss in Scotland. There he commenced flying the Airspeed Oxford twin-engined training aircraft. Again his diary tells its own story:-

May 19th: *"Airspeed Oxford. Splendid instructor."*

May 25th: *"Went solo on Oxford okay, rough wind."*

June 9th: *"Solo, forty minutes, N6289."*

June 19th: *"Definitely difficult to land with closed throttle. Two bad landings."*

June 22nd: *"Someone's going to get hurt before long. Oxford aircraft not being maintained in very good condition. Petrol gauge and undercarriage lights all wrong. Not good enough."*

July 3rd: *"Night flying. Suicide, but made perfect first landing, solo second not so hot."*

On Sunday, 3rd September, 1939, the British Prime Minister, Neville Chamberlain, broadcast to the nation that as Hitler had ignored the ultimatum issued by Britain and France to remove forthwith his forces from Poland following Germany's invasion on September 1st, this country was at war with Germany. For Laurie Whitbread's generation the bubble had burst at last. On

November 26th, Pilot Officer Whitbread completed his training and was posted to 222 "Natal" Squadron at Duxford near Cambridge.

222 Squadron was a new unit having been formed on October 13th, 1939, at Duxford under the command of Squadron Leader HW "Tubby" Mermagen, who had already enjoyed an interesting career. Having initially joined 43 Squadron in 1931, he later served as a flying instructor and actually test flew all new fighters and bombers prior to them entering squadron service. At the Hendon Air Display in 1937, Mermagen led the Inverted Flying Formation and the following year performed individual aerobatics before the King.

"Tubby" *Mermagen (centre) pictured in 1945 whilst an Acting Air Commodore and with the Commanding Officer and a flight commander of a Tempest squadron at RAF Gatow.*
Air Commodore H.W. Mermagen.

Air Commodore Mermagen, now eighty-two, recalls:-

"*I formed this squadron as a 12 Group night fighter unit equipped with Bristol Blenheim twin-engined aircraft. As I was previously an A1 qualified flying instructor on the staff of the Central Flying School, to convert pilots to this type I was supplied with a dual Blenheim.*

"*Whitbread was one of the earliest postings to the new squadron, straight from flying training school. I can remember him as a pleasant, well-mannered, quiet individual. A shortish, stocky, cheerful character whom I instantly liked - a good mixer.*

"My flying log book records that on December 12th, 1939, at 1200 hrs, I took him up in the dual Blenheim, L6712, for a test/conversion to Blenheim Mk Is. The flight lasted twenty-five minutes and I must have been suitably impressed by his flying since since so far as my log book shows he had no further instruction and went solo immediately afterwards. I understand that he had trained on twin engined Oxfords, but even so he displayed a good standard of flying. The squadron subsequently conducted a very large number of flying hours and we were soon operational, with no accidents."

Throughout December 1939, 222 undertook convoy protection patrols over the North Sea without incident. As winter's grip strengthened, the weather for flying deteriorated to the extent that due to heavy snow there was no flying at all during the first nine days of February. On Wednesday, 14th February, Laurie recorded in his diary "Narrowest escape to date, nearly spun in whilst night flying."

222 shared Duxford with the Spitfire equipped 19 and 66 Squadrons. To every fighter pilot in 1940 the dream was to fly a Spitfire. For 222, flying their lumbering Blenheims, the dream unexpectedly became reality when on March 9th, 1940, five Spitfires arrived at Duxford signalling the squadron's conversion to this type. The following day the Blenheims were flown to, and deposited at, RAF Wittering.

Air Commodore Mermagen remembers the sudden change vividly:-

"To our delight the A.O.C., Air Vice-Marshal Leigh-Mallory, decided to re-equip us with Spitfires. The already enthusiastic pilots faced this conversion from twins to singles with great excitement. To help me with the conversion of all pilots from twins to singles, I was supplied with a Miles Master dual training aircraft, N7570. My log book records that on March 18th at 1600 hrs I took PilotOfficer Whitbread up for forty minutes conversion-to-type flying. I did the same the following day for another thirty minutes and he must have then satisfied me completely because he went solo on a Spitfire with no further instruction immediately afterwards."

The squadron then commenced an intensive flying training programme on Spitfires, involving much formation flying. Laurie's diary relates:-

March 20th: "Spitfire solo."

March 24th: "Spitfire. Try guns at Sutton Bridge."

April 6th: "Practise attacks."

April 10th: "Buy Wolseley Hornet, 1932, not bad!"

April 14th: "Squadron formation of twelve aircraft. Height climb 26,000'."

April 15th: "First accident, nose in Spitfire, but CO exonerates me from blame."

On April 17th, 222 Squadron was declared fully operational in the day fighter role. Subsequently 222 took over 19 Squadron's recently vacated dispersals at the eastern end of Duxford aerodrome, 19 having that day moved to Horsham St Faith. The training continued, however, with night flying being added to the programme as from April 23rd. Pilot Officer Whitbread's diary continues:-

April 21st: *"Pilot Officer Vigors almost writes off both of us overtaking at 60 mph and missed by five'!"*

April 28th: *"Formation flying."*

May 1st:: *"Formation flying. Bad weather."*

May 3rd: *"Formation flying."*

May 4th: *"Night flying."*

May 9th: *"Squadron shabbles. AOC very pleased. 12 minutes for refuelling and reloading the entire squadron - a record."*

On Friday, 10th May, 1940, the *"Phoney War"* came to an abrupt end when Hitler suddenly, and with great ferocity, swept into Belgium, Holland, Luxembourg and France. 264, a Defiant equipped fighter squadron based at Martlesham Heath in the Debden sector, received orders to move to Duxford and anticipate operating from forward bases in support of the Dutch. To make room at the airfield, 222 were posted north to Digby in Lincolnshire. Laurie wrote in his diary: *"At 12 mid-day we are told to go to Digby at 9pm! What a scramble packing. Arrived safely."* Two days later he wrote: *"More formation flying. Oh to be abroad!"*

On May 23rd, 1940, the squadron moved again, this time to Kirton-in-Lindsey in Lincolnshire. On the continent the military situation for the Allies was grim. The rout ended at the port of Dunkirk, from where the British flotilla of *"Little Ships"*, comprising military and civil craft of all descriptions, commenced the evacuation of some 338,226 Allied troops.

Obviously such an operation, codenamed *"Dynamo"*, required air support to prevent the Luftwaffe from pounding to a pulp the defenceless soldiers awaiting evacuation from the beaches. The troops did suffer terribly and the RAF's prestige sank to its lowest ebb in the eyes of the army. The soldiers had, they believed, been strafed and bombed for weeks without protection from their own fighters. In reality Fighter Command's squadrons were operating continuously between their airfields and Dunkirk, attempting to prevent German air attacks actually reaching the beaches. The distance was such that the RAF fighters were operating an extreme range across the English Channel and each squadron had only fifteen minutes fuel endurance at combat speeds before having to return home. Most air battles were fought unseen by those on the ground, at very high altitude above cloud cover or actually behind German lines. Fighter Command's squadrons flew 4,822 operational hours during the evacuation, destroyed 258 enemy aircraft and damaged 119, offset against their own losses of 87 machines.

On May 29th, 1940, 222 Squadron flew to Hornchurch and remained at that station for two days whilst participating in Operation Dynamo. Air Commodore Mermagen recalls:-

"On May 28th, 1940, I led the squadron and wing on its first patrol over the Dunkirk beaches, at 0630 hrs. The sortie lasted two hours and forty-five minutes, a long flight for a Spitfire. The squadron carried out several further sorties, ending on June 3rd when the wretched evacuation appeared completed - no life could be seen either on the beaches or in the country behind. I lost four pilots killed and one 'missing' whilst flying from RAF Hornchurch. Pilot Officer Whitbread must have taken part in most if not all of these sorties. I know that I had previously recognised him as a good, reliable and sound Spit pilot."

Indeed Pilot Officer Whitbread did fly on the majority of the squadron's patrols from Hornchurch, in Spitfires P9318, P9360 and P9378.

It is worth recording that although Pilot Officer Whitbread was in 'B' flight, Flight Lieutenant Douglas Bader was commander of 'A' flight and flew with the squadron during the Dunkirk patrols. Like Mermagen, Bader was a pre-war aerobatic expert but had lost both legs in a flying accident during 1931 whilst attempting a low-level slow roll in a Bulldog. Discharged from the air force due to his disability in 1933, incredibly he overcame his loss of limbs and shortly after the outbreak of war argued his way back into Fighter Command and the cockpit of a Spitfire. He was first posted to 19 Squadron at Duxford as a Flying Officer in February, 1940, but joined 222 as a Flight Commander upon promotion to Flight Lieutenant the following month. During 222's Dunkirk sortie of June 1st, with Pilot Officer Whitbread flying Spitfire P9318, Flight Lieutenant Bader destroyed an Me 109 over the beaches, the first of twenty he would *"score"* before being taken prisoner in 1941. By that time, however, the man was already a legend in the service and remains so today, ten years after his death.

Over Dunkirk Fighter Command had tried to put into practice the months of training in textbook attacks comprising smart, tight formations, which proved disastrously unsuitable for modern air fighting. Due to the tight formations specified by the accepted Fighter Command area attacks, of either vics of three aircraft or sections in line astern, with each aircraft in close proximity to its neighbour, the RAF pilots were unable to search the sky for enemy aircraft without fear of collision with their neighbour. Thus in the early days many British pilots went to their deaths totally unaware of their assailant's presence. The Luftwaffe, however, was more fortunate in having already evolved its tactics during combat in the Spanish Civil War and the Polish campaign. Werner Mölders, the *"father"* of German air fighting, developed the

"Schwarm" tactical formation of four aircraft flying loosely in line abreast, stepped up, each aircraft covering the other, and spread out like the four fingers of an outstretched hand. Each member of the "Schwarm" was therefore protected and able to search the sky for the enemy without fear of collision. When battle was joined the "Schwarm" broke into the "Rotte", a fighting pair of two such formations comprising leader and wingman. Eventually this tactic was also used by the RAF and remains the basic fighter formation to this day. Pre-war tactical thinking in Britain hinged largely on the mistaken theory that "the bomber would always get through." The Fighter Command "book" foresaw orderly queues of fighters in line astern peeling off one by one to attack lone enemy bombers flying straight and level. What was not predicted was fighter versus fighter combat, particularly that which became a reality in 1940 with many aircraft involved, all moving in excess of 350 mph and in which situation tight formations were clearly suicidal. The Great War adage "look for the Hun in the sun" again became well used as pilots rapidly realised that he who had height controlled the battle. Wing Commander George Unwin, in 1940 a Flight Sergeant with 19 Squadron, elaborates on the thinking of the time:-

"The tacticians who wrote the book really believed that in the event of war it would be fighter versus bomber only. What they could not foresee was Hitler's modern ground tactics that would take his armies to the Channel ports in an unprecedented period of time, thus providing basis for his fighters putting England within their limited range. Our tight formations were all very well for the Hendon Air Pageant, but useless in combat."

With experience gained at no small cost, the "book" would eventually be re-written, but for the time being, and well into the battles ahead, the tight formations persisted in most squadrons.

The late Flight Lieutenant Reg Johnson, who tragically passed away during the course of this research, remembered this period of the squadron's history when he was a sergeant pilot:-

"I was posted to 222 Squadron in April 1940 at RAF Duxford. I arrived there only to be told that the squadron had moved to Digby. I arrived at Digby to learn that 222 had moved to Kirton-in-Lindsey. Such was the level of administration in the conditions of 1940. On joining the squadron no-one was unkind to me but I was the first RAF Volunteer Reserve pilot (recognisable by my badges) to join this regular squadron. After about a week I was shown the 'knobs and things' by Sergeant J.I. Johnson, an ex-Halton apprentice, and sent solo. After a successful landing my engine failed and I was collected in a green MG sports car by Flight Lieutenant Douglas Bader, commander of 'A' flight (I was a member of 'B' flight).

"I soon learned that 222 Squadron was addicted to tight formation flying for which

Sergeant Reg Johnson pictured with Spitfire P8318 at Kirton-in-Lindsey; this snapshot was actually taken by Pilot Officer Whitbread. Note this aircraft's unusual rear-view mirror fitted inside the cockpit.

The late Flight Lieutenant R.B. Johnson.

I had no training whatsoever. A study of the pre-war flying career of our CO, Squadron Leader Mermagen, might explain this addiction, particularly in respect of flying so tight that our wing tips overlapped. From Kirton he led us off in squadron formation; at times we landed in squadron formation. In three behind three we even looped in formation. We even rolled as a squadron on one occasion. Mermagen was an exceptional pilot, but such training was to prove unsuitable for the Battle of Britain that lay ahead, although of course at that time he was not to have the benefits of hindsight."

Reg Johnson went on to relate his recollections of Laurie Whitbread:-

"Pilot Officer Whitbread was an established member of the squadron when I joined it in April 1940. During the following weeks and months he proved himself to be a pleasant and friendly young man. We spent many hours together in conversation at dispersal point and I have a photograph of him beside "my" Spitfire at dawn readiness about 4 am on a June morning. We each took each others' despite the light at that early hour being poor as we were forbidden cameras so had to take our snaps in secret. He was also a very good hockey player and spent long periods of time with his hockey stick dribbling around the aircraft and running around bouncing a ball on the shaft of his stick. We also spent many hours together flying in squadron training, often wing tip to wing tip. He was much more skilled at tight formation flying than I was at that time.

"In our squadron there was definitely an RAF social barrier between officer and

Pilot Officer Whitbread photographed by Sergeant Johnson with P9318, the fighter flown by the young officer during most of the Dunkirk sorties. The cap he is wearing survives to the present day and is seen in the introduction to this book.

The late Flight Lieutenant R.B. Johnson.

NCO pilots. Pilot Officer Whitbread, however, whom I never knew as 'Laurie' but always 'Sir', overcame this with his natural charm and was at ease with all ranks. He never lost face because of it and we became firm friends. We enjoyed a number of squadron flying adventures together at Kirton and would later suffer a number together during the Battle of Britain."

Another former NCO pilot, (now Squadron Leader) Iain Hutchinson, also recalled Pilot Officer Whitbread:-

"In general I remember him as an unassuming, approachable person, without affectation. You will understand that during the time we served together in 222 Squadron I was a Sergeant pilot whilst Laurie Whitbread was commissioned. Therefore there was only a very limited opportunity for an association between each group. Nevertheless there was less 'side' in Laurie's relationships than there was with other officers. I should emphasise, however, that within the constraints imposed by differences in rank there was still an excellent spirit in the squadron.

"The only incident in which I was involved with Laurie occurred on August 10th, 1940, at Kirton-in-Lindsey. An intruder was detected by the forward radar station and he and I were scrambled to intercept. We taxied out at speed, Laurie leading and I following. I was swinging the nose of my Spitfire from side to side according to the relevant rules, to ensure that I could see ahead of me as the nose blocked out a large sector of the view ahead, when as I swung the nose right I suddenly saw the tail of Laurie's *machine ahead of me, stopped. Despite heavy braking and evasive action I was unable to clear his aircraft and my wing demolished Laurie's tail.*

"*I also recall that one night a raider attacked the Scunthorpe steelworks and Laurie was sent up to intercept. Unfortunately the fighter controllers were apparently unable to get their act together and we watched frustrated as we heard the bomber droning on a western approach to its target whilst Laurie was vectored in the opposite direction.*"

Iain Hutchinson, a Sergeant Pilot with 222 Squadron during the Battle of Britain, who later retired from the RAF as a Squadron Leader. Squadron Leader J.I. Hutchinson.

Whilst the flying from Kirton remained monotonous during the first half of summer 1940, the same could not be said of southern England. As we have seen, the Battle of Britain commenced with fierce skirmishes over Channel bound convoys, and radar stations, before the conflict moved into its second and most critical phase; a concentrated attack on Fighter Command's airfields. Throughout August heavy fighting took place and airfields such as Biggin Hill, Hornchurch, Kenley and Tangmere were all severely damaged - nevertheless none ceased to remain operational.

The photograph that says it all; 222 Squadron at readiness, Kirton, 1940. Left to right: Sergeant John Burgess, Flying Officer Van Mentz, and Pilot Officer Hillary Edridge await the call to "scramble!"

The late Flight Lieutenant R.B. Johnson.

On July 31st, Squadron Leader John Hill replaced Squadron Leader Mermagen as CO of 222. Mermagen subsequently temporarily commanded 266 Squadron at Wittering prior to being promoted and posted as station commander to RAF Speke near Liverpool. The apparent lack of enemy activity on the morning of Friday, August 29th, 1940, gave Fighter Command the opportunity to rotate several of its squadrons. The Defiants of 264 Squadron had been decimated in action during preceding weeks whilst flying from Hornchurch, so Squadron Leader Hill and 222 Squadron were ordered to replace them in the battle zone of 11 Group.

The following day the squadron was ordered to patrol Gravesend. 'B' flight soon received its first sight of the enemy when contact was made with ten Me 109s north-west of Dover. No general combat ensued but Sergeant

Squadron Leader John Hill, Commanding Officer of 222 Squadron throughout much of the Battle of Britain.
Mr Joe Crawshaw.

Hutchinson was shot at from behind and forced landed a mile from the aerodrome. It is interesting to note that the squadron was still flying in the standard tight vic formations as stipulated by the Fighter Command *"book"*, with a *"weaver"* or *"tail-end Charlie"* whose job it was to guard the squadron's rear. Clearly the lessons learnt by the southern based squadrons were not being passed on to those fresh to the battle. Reg Johnson remembered:-

"Our squadron went south to Hornchurch and in the first 48 hours we lost eighteen aircraft and a number of pilots. We proceeded to go into action in tight formation and our losses were heavy. Eventually we evolved a weaving "tail end Charlie" section, which weaved about above, below, and to the rear of the squadron (still in tight formation). It helped. I was made a permanent member of Green Section, with Pilot Officer Whitbread and one other, and we were given the job to do."

According to the squadron diary, on August 30th *"the squadron was very positively engaged in operations and flew three patrols during the day. Sergeant JI Johnson was killed. Flight Lieutenant Matheson and Flying Officer Edridge were wounded."* During the three separate actions fought that day 222 lost six Spitfires destroyed and three damaged. In response, Flight Lieutenant Robinson had probably destroyed an Me 109, Pilot Officer Vigors claimed an Me 110 destroyed, Pilot Officers Davis and Cutts an He 111, and Squadron Leader Hill an Me 109 damaged.

August 31st saw Fighter Command suffer the heaviest losses of any day during the battle. During the day's first patrol, between 0821 and 0940 hours, Pilot Officer Whitbread flew Spitfire L1010 and patrolled base at 25,000' without contacting the enemy. On the next sortie, flown from the forward airfield of Rochford, between 1245 and 1415 hrs, ten aircraft of 222 Squadron, including Whitbread in L1010, were ordered to intercept bombers at 26,000' over Gravesend. Two formations of the Me 109 fighter escort were attacked, each comprising thirty machines, Pilot Officer Vigors claiming one destroyed and a second as a probable. Pilot Officer Whitbread and another ten aircraft of 222 later patrolled Canterbury at 20,000'. Over Maidstone they saw twenty-four Me 109s protecting a formation of He 111s. A dogfight developed which ended very much in 222's favour; Flight Lieutenant Robinson claimed one Me 109 destroyed, despite being shot down and wounded himself in N3233, and another was claimed by Pilot Officer Broadhurst. Two 109s were probably destroyed by Pilot Officers Carpenter and Cutts, and three more damaged by Flying Officer Van Mentz, Pilot Officer Whitbread and Sergeant Hutchinson. Pilot Officer Davies was also shot down but escaped with burns. Pilot Officer Whitbread made out the following report on his combat which took place at about 1330 hrs, 16,000' over Sittingbourne, Kent:-

"I manoeuvered until the Me 109 appeared in my sights, the enemy aircraft climbing slowly away not having seen me. I fired at about 400 yards and rapidly closed to within 50 yards when I could see the bullets entering the fuselage from tail to cockpit. The 109 half rolled onto its back and remained in that attitude, flying quite slowly with a little white smoke issuing from it. It eventually nosed down slowly when I was obliged to lose sight of it having noticed an aircraft approaching my tail which turned out to be a Spitfire."

This Me 109 was possibly an E-1, 4068, of 1/JG77 that crashed between Walderslade and Boxley, in Kent, timed at 1320 hrs. The pilot, Unteroffizier Keck, baled out and was captured.

On September 1st, Laurie again soared aloft from Hornchurch in L1010 at 1023 hrs, returning to Rochford at 1125. That day the raiders had advanced over England along a five mile front from Dover at 1055 hrs. The main balbo split into two formations of thirty bombers, each escorted by a similar number of fighters, and these formations again split, the targets being airfields at Biggin Hill, Detling, Eastchurch, and the London Docks. 222, patrolling in the Manston area, sighted two formations of bombers and attacked their fighter escort at 25,000'. Subsequently, Squadron Leader Hill, and Pilot Officers Vigors and Carpenter each destroyed an Me 109. No contact was made with the enemy during the day's next two sorties.

Between 0838 and 0915 hrs the next day, again in L1010, Laurie patrolled Chatham, Hawkinge and Manston with eight other Spitfires of 222 Squadron. However, it was over Hornchurch aerodrome itself that the squadron contacted the enemy. In the resulting mêlée, Flight Lieutenant Robinson destroyed an Me 109 and damaged an He 111, Sergeant Baxter destroyed an Me 110, damaged another and a Do 17, Sergeant Chipping damaged an Me 110 and Sergeant Scott a Do 17. Flight Lieutenant Robinson was wounded in the leg and forced landed back at base following a head-on attack by an Me 110. Two other Spitfires were damaged but with both pilots safe.

On September 3rd, 1940, Pilot Officer Whitbread flew Spitfire N3023 between 1440 and 1605 hrs when the squadron patrolled Rochford and Canterbury. The enemy were not encountered. During the morning, however, Spitfire L1010 met its end when a glycol leak developed forcing Sergeant Reg Johnson to part company with this particular machine which impacted at Canewdon.

Pilot Officer Whitbread flew N3023, his regular mount from now on, for the first patrol over Canterbury on September 4th but the sortie passed without incident. During the afternoon patrol, between 1235 and 1410 hrs, seventy He 111s and Do 17s, escorted by 200 Me109s, had crossed the Kent coast before splitting up to attack Canterbury, Faversham, Reigate, Redhill and Eastchurch. Nine 11 Group squadrons engaged, 222 intercepting the raid approaching Canterbury and became embroiled with the Me 109 escort. Twenty-four year old Sergeant John Ramshaw, who had joined the squadron straight from training school just five days before, was shot down and killed by an Me 109 over West Malling. Twenty-year old Pilot Officer John Cutts also fell victim to the German fighters and remains *"missing"* to this day. Pilot Officer Carpenter attacked an Me 109 but whilst breaking away his Spitfire was hit by anti-aircraft fire which blew him out of the cockpit. Fortunately he made a safe parachute descent. Pilot Officer Assheton claimed two Me 109s destroyed and Sergeant Chipping one. A III/JG3 Me 109E that fell victim to 222 Squadron was actually that flown by the *"experte"* and Geschwader Kommodore, Hauptmann Wilhelm Balthasar who was wounded.

On September 5th, Laurie flew two patrols. During the second, between 1420 and 1600 hrs, the squadron patrolled Maidstone without encounter before returning to Rochford. The airfield was then attacked whilst the Spitfires were being refuelled. Frantically scrambling, the squadron intercepted the raiders but was unable to do so as a cohesive unit. Pilot Officer Scott destroyed two Me 110s and Sergeant Chipping probably destroyed one before being shot down and killed over Dover, possibly by anti-aircraft defences.

The next day saw Pilot Officer Whitbread participate in three sorties. During the last, between 1730 and 1900 hrs, the squadron patrolled Hawkinge at 15,000' and encountered a large force of Me 109s escorting bombers. Battle was joined and Sergeant Hutchinson and Pilot Officer Vigors both destroyed Me 109s.

Saturday, 7th September, 1940, saw the turning point of the Battle of Britain when Goering changed the course of his tactics and commenced the daylight, indiscriminate bombing of London and its environs. The pyschology was to destroy morale amongst the civilian population, but in fact the opposite was achieved; Britain's resolve to beat the enemy was strengthened and the capital proclaimed *"London can take it."* For Fighter Command the raids on London gave the airfields, shattered and on their knees after several weeks of sustained attack, time to repair and return to *"Top Line"*. If the Luftwaffe's airfield assault had continued in its ferocity just a little longer the outcome of the Battle of Britain might well have been very different. Goering's tactical blunder became Britain's salvation. The day was a successful one for 222 Squadron, who with 603, at 1650 hrs intercepted a large force of enemy aircraft over London. In fact the German armada launched against London that afternoon consisted of some 348 bombers and 617 fighters, thus representing the largest aerial raiding force ever seen. Virtually the entire strength of five Kampfgeschwader (bomber wings), 1, 2, 3, 26 and 76, were launched against the ancient capital, escorted by the fighters of Zerstörergeschwader 2, Jagdgeschwader 2, 3, 51, 52, 54, I/JG77, and I and II/Lehrgeschwader 2. The enemy formation numbered nearly 1,000 aircraft and advanced along a twenty mile front over the Thames Estuary towards London. By 1630 hrs all twenty-one squadrons based within seventy miles of London were in the air. For once the combat against overwhelming odds ended very much in 222 Squadron's favour; Sergeant Scott destroyed an Me 110, Sergeant Johnson and Flying Officer Van Mentz claimed two more probably destroyed, Van Mentz and Pilot Officer Whitbread two Do 215 bombers probably destroyed, and a Do 17 by Pilot Officer Vigors. Pilot Officer Whitbread attacked his bomber 27,000' over London:-

"We engaged an enemy formation of Me 109s. I became separated from the rest of the squadron so I climbed back to my original altitude and flew round looking for a target. I found one in a formation of 25-30 Do 215s which appeared to have no fighter escort. Keeping in the sun I dived down on the last aircraft which was straggling behind some 100 yards at the rear of the formation and flying at 20,000'. I carried out a quarter attack from the port side (formation was flying westwards along south bank of the Thames at Dartford). I opened fire at 300 yards, range closing rapidly. The starboard engine set on fire and I broke away, the return fire from the rear three gunners and my closing range making it advisable."

The aircraft attacked may have been a Do 17Z, "5K + FN" of 5/KG3 which subsequently forced landed in Calais. Leutnant Leitner and an NCO were both wounded.

The close of day saw 306 civilians killed and 1,337 wounded in the capital, with a further 142 wounded in the suburbs.

222 received a respite the following day when the enemy were not encountered. On September 9th, however, the squadron took off from Rochford and 27,000' over Ashford in Kent attacked a formation of Do 17s escorted by Me 109s. Pilot Officers Whitbread and Vigors destroyed an Me 109 each, and Flight Lieutenant Dartford, Pilot Officer Broadhurst and Sergeant Scott damaged two more. Whitbread reported:-

"Whilst on patrol over east Kent with 222 we sighted a formation of enemy bombers flying west at 20,000' above cloud. It had an escort of Me 109s, flying above and behind at 26,000', and also another formation of fighters flying to one side, at the same height as the bombers. The fighters were engaged. I had a combat with an Me 109. A burst of roughly four seconds from my guns appeared to shoot off the starboard aileron when the 109 went into a spin. It continued to spin downwards into the cloud layer when it disappeared from view. My flight leader stated that he observed the 109 spin down and also the baling out of the pilot."

In his diary, Laurie wrote: "One Me 109 claim. Confirmed by Van Mentz."

The enemy fighter was an Me 109E-1 (6280), 7 +, of 6/JG27 which crashed at Mounts Farm, Benenden at 6.15 pm. The pilot, Unteroffizier Rauwolf, baled out and was captured.

An Me 109E, 3+, of II/JG27, the geschwader to which Unteroffizier Georg Rauwolf belonged until shot down by Pilot Officer Whitbread on September 9th, 1940. Note that the unit badge is Berlin's coat of arms, and the aircraft behind which is in standard pale blue colour scheme.

Chris Goss.

Two days later 222 were scrambled and ordered to patrol base. Several engagements took place. The following claims were made by the Spitfire pilots, without loss to themselves; two Ju 88s destroyed by Flying Officer Van Mentz and Sergeant Baxter, two He 111s by Sergeants Scott and Baxter, one Ju 88 probably destroyed by Pilot Officer Broadhurst and an He 111 probably by Sergeant Hutchinson, and two Me 109s damaged by Flying Officer Van Mentz and Sergeant Spears.

On September 14th, Pilot Officer Whitbread and thirteen other Spitfires of 222 and 603 Squadrons were scrambled and patrolled Rochford. A large formation of enemy fighters were discovered which proved difficult to attack due to them having formed a defensive circle. However, Sergeant Hutchinson destroyed an Me 109 and Sergeant Marland damaged a 110. Flying Officer McMullen chased an Me 109 across the Channel and destroyed it over Calais. Sergeant Baxter's Spitfire, X4275, was severely damaged by an Me 110 and he was killed whilst attempting a forced landing at Rochford. Sergeant Hutchinson was more fortunate as he safely forced landed X4265 at Detling after also being shot down by an Me 110. Sergeant Reg Johnson was shot down in X4249 by an Me 109 and baled out with slight wounds. The same day, Laurie wrote to his mother from the Officers' Mess at RAF Hornchurch, giving no indication of the danger and possibility of very violent death that he faced on a daily basis:-

"Dear Mother,

Thank you for your letter, received this morning. How nice to have Rex and Doris, and Colin at home together. I am disappointed that I won't be there too. Fancy Ludlow having some bombs!

Everything is going fine down here. We get far less to do now that the weather has broken. There is no sign of us leaving this station yet, so I doubt that I will get any leave until things quieten down again.

I am keeping fit - except that I got a touch of frostbite in the left hand last week. It's better now except from a large blister on the thumb!*

Mother, would you see if I've left my RAF navy blue blazer at home. I don't want it but I can't find it here. Please tell me in the next letter. I do hope I haven't lost it.

Love to all, Cheerio, Laurie."

The generally accepted climax of the Battle of Britain came on Sunday, 15th September, 1940, now annually celebrated as *"Battle of Britain Day"*. The

---

*Footnote: Caused by intense cold whilst flying at high altitude, not from "sleeping in his Spitfire" as has previously been published - September nights are not that cold, even in England!

whole fury and might of the enemy was thrown repeatedly against London. By the end of the day the hard pressed and exhausted defenders had defeated the German daylight bombing offensive and these islands no longer stood under threat of German invasion and dominance. On the great day, Pilot Officer Whitbread did not participate in the bitter fighting over England as his Spitfire, N3023, "ZD-R", was for some reason unserviceable so he returned to Hornchurch from Rochford for the aircraft to be repaired. 222 Squadron itself was in action over London but again without suffering loss.

In Laurie's diary on Wednesday, 18th September, 1940, he has written "Seven days leave start ?" No leave was forthcoming. On that day instead of travelling home to see his sweetheart, Jane, he found himself scrambling in Spitfire P9878 and patrolling the Canterbury area. He did not fly the following day but for the sortie on September 20th, his usual mount, N3023 was serviceable.

Since the September 15th climax, the fighting had continued, but on a slightly smaller scale than the previous German assault. On September 17th, activity had mainly been confined to fighter sweeps, and on the 18th the few German bombers attacking oil targets in the Thames Estuary were decimated, nine Ju 88s of III/KG77 being shot down in just two minutes. The German bombers had now commenced operating en masse at night protected by darkness, perhaps making their presence over England even more sinister.

Throughout the preceding weeks, the German fighter pilots had been tied to the close bomber escort role, forbidden by Goering to leave their charges. With just enough fuel for twenty minutes flying time over London as it was, the fighter pilots had become even more frustrated, continually throttling back to keep pace with the slow bombers and thus burning up even more fuel in the process. The essence of the fighter pilot's ideology is of being a hunter, but the German fighter pilots were unable to operate in their natural environment due to their rigid instructions. With the failure of the German daylight bombing offensive, however, the Jagdwaffe (fighter Arm) were now in a situation where they could again become hunters and regularly engaged on "Freie Hunt" sorties over southern England looking for trouble. The German High Command had a surprise in store for their jagdflieger (fighter pilots), however.

Orders were issued for one Staffel (squadron) in each Gruppe (wing) to be converted into a "Jabo" (jagdbomber: fighter-bomber) unit. This represented one third of the entire German fighter force. The operational value of fighter-bombers could not be denied, but only by presupposing a surplus of aircraft. Adolf Galland, Geschwader Kommodore of JG26, felt strongly that to use a fighter as a fighter-bomber when the strength of the fighter arm was already inadequate to achieve air superiority was *"putting the cart before the horse."* The fighter pilots bitterly reflected this violation of their aircraft, having done everything possible to increase their performance to keep pace with a progressive enemy. Everything dispensable had been discarded to squeeze another ounce of speed out of their Messerschmitts. Ejectable fuel tanks had long been demanded to increase range, but instead they were given bombs and forced to see a third of their fighters drop out of air combat. The Me 109 was only able to carry one SC500 H.E. bomb, so could therefore cause little damage. The strategy was that whilst the RAF could ignore fighter sweeps, they would be unable to do so if some of the fighters carried bombs and were therefore capable of causing some damage to targets in England. The guinea pigs for this new idea were the pilots of the experimental unit, Erprobungsgruppe 210, and Lehrgeschwader 2. In mid-September these units were moved into the Pas-de-Calais to be escorted by Galland's JG26. The order for the Jabo conversion was issued simultaneously. The Jadgwaffe had an outspoken antipathy for the order to escort the Jabos. The Luftwaffe High Command sharply countered this negative attitude. Goering declared angrily that the fighter arm had failed to give adequate protection to the bombers and were now even opposed to escorting fighter-bombers, a situation having arisen out of their own failure. Goering cajoled that if the Jagdwaffe failed in this task perhaps it would be better to disband it. Such an insult was the limit to the German fighter pilots who were justly convinced that they had done their duty. They had accepted heavy losses in unflagging action combined with outstanding successes without once questioning either the final objective or the length of this murderous pressure. Their morale, already heavily taxed by exhaustion and heavy losses, only to be falsely accused, put military discipline to a stiff test. In the fighter units the leadership was bitterly criticised in this first serious crisis between the Jagdwaffe and the High Command.

At first the Jabos flew as a unit protected by unladen fighters, but later, as the British fighters detected this and attacked accordingly, they were interspersed amongst the main formation. Each geschwader provided escort for its own bombers. The disgusted fighter pilots, however, sometimes took to dropping their bombs at the first opportunity so as to revert their aircraft to the *"jaeger"* (hunter) role in unfriendly skies. The dropping of bombs in a level attitude proved so inaccurate that the technique of low-level diving attacks was developed, remaining the standard method of fighter-bombing even today.

The first of these *"tip n'run"* raids occurred on Friday, September 20th, 1940. Twenty-two Me 109 Jabos of II/LG2, protected by numerous fighters, made a sortie to London. Between Calais and the English coast they climbed to 25,000' before swooping down on the capital. The British ground controllers, believing that unless the enemy aircraft were carrying bombs they were of no interest, recalled the fighter squadrons scrambled to meet them. Thus the enemy reached London unmolested. Diving to 12,000', pressing the bomb release switch and pulling out, the Jabo pilots had already turned for home when twenty-two bombs exploded in the City of London and on a rail terminus west of the great bend in the Thames. Listening to the British radio frequencies, the German intercepting service reported a great confusion of orders and counter-orders after the *"fighters"* had dropped their bombs.

Fighter Command was about to receive a salutary reminder of the competence of the Jagdfleiger when released from the close bomber escort role. After the first wave of fighters and Jabos had caused confusion, the second wave of German fighters, crossing the Kent coast at 14,000', attacked the Biggin Hill and Hornchurch Spitfire squadrons in the Maidstone area and a fierce dogfight ensued.

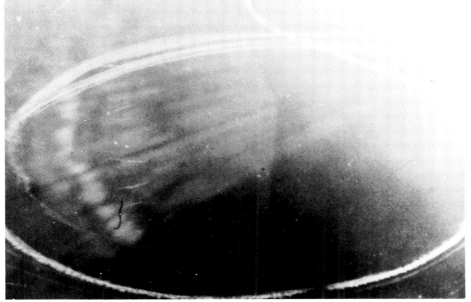

"Angels 33 over Hornchurch" *was the original and handwritten caption to this snapshot of a dogfight over that station during October 1940.*

Mr Joe Crawshaw.

222 and 603 Squadrons were scrambled from Hornchurch at 1055 hrs but as they desperately climbed for height at full throttle, the Me 109s fell on them.

Laurie Whitbread, in N3023, was the first British pilot to fall in action that day, as Reg Johnson remembered:-

"My vivid memory is that this sortie was a 'B' flight commitment only, led by Pilot Officer Broadhurst in Blue Section followed by Pilot Officer Whitbread, myself and another in Green Section. We climbed to the suicidal height of 14,000' and stooged around in tight formation with only one pair of eyes available to scan the sky in front perhaps over 200 degrees. I do not think that we deserved to be jumped upon, but we certainly invited it. We were banking gently to the left, which allowed me at No 3 to look over the top of No 1, and I shouted the warning "Bandits, 2 o' clock above - attacking!" I turned over and dived straight down. There is no way that Pilot Officer Whitbread could even have seen the enemy, formating as he was on the aircraft to his left and with three-quarters of his head and back to the attackers. When I left it was his right side facing the 109s which were already in firing range. I can only assume that having received my warning he too rolled to his right, exposing his left side to the enemy and was hit before he could commence his dive. It was a tragedy."

Pilot Officer Whitbread had been attacked by Oberleutnant Hans "*Assi*" Hahn of II/JG2 "*Richthofen*", himself just four months Laurie's senior. As N3203 plunged earthwards, Hahn noted with satisfaction his nineteenth victory; four days later he would destroy his twentieth and receive the Ritterkreuz (Knight's Cross) from a grateful Führer. Throughout the Battle of Britain Hahn was a leading Jagdwaffe figure, his jovial personality, love of life and self-confidence making him very popular amongst his fellow pilots. Such qualities were no doubt to sustain him in the trials that later lay ahead as a prisoner of the Russians after suffering engine failure behind Soviet lines in 1943 when his score stood at 108 kills and 36 probables.

N3203 crashed at 11.15 am in the garden of Pond Cottage, Hermitage Road, Higham, near Rochester, Kent. The occupant, Mrs Perry, wrote to Laurie's father on October 11th:-

"Your son died a great hero. He had three German planes firing all around him and his machine was riddled with bullet holes. It appears that he was trying to bale out as he was out of his seat. My husband, who was in the garden, ran to the Spitfire to see if he could be of any help, but the pilot was lying outside the plane. He must have been trying to bale out as the Germans caught him down his left side - he must have then fallen back into the cockpit and came down with the plane as it bumped across the ground, or maybe he got stuck in the plane whilst coming down. Either way he was thrown clear upon impact. He lay just outside the plane and must have died instantly. He did not suffer, so please tell his mother. I know this is very soon after your great grief but perhaps it will help you with a little relief knowing that he did not linger on and suffer after his injury. Will it help you if I say that if I have to lose one of my own

boys I hope that they go the same way. It would be awful if he had endured weeks of suffering only for the Lord to call. I hope God will give us the means to overcome these murderers. I feel sure that your son will not have given his life in vain. It was an awful feeling when the Spitfire was coming down. It gave me an awful shock especially as I thought that it was coming down on my house, but we felt more than sorry when we found that your son was dead. My husband covered him up until the ambulance arrived to take him to the mortuary. Where we live is between the Thames Estuary and the south-east, so if the Germans try to get to London from either direction we witness the full force of the fighting. We had another plane almost on us today, it crashed in the field just in front of our house."

Me 109E pilots of 4/JG2 "Richthofen". At second right is Hauptmann Hans "Assi" Hahn who shot down Pilot Officer Whitbread on September 20th, 1940. Note the Knights Cross, Iron Cross First Class and Pilot's Qualification badge (below the Iron Cross). At extreme left is Oberfeldwebel Siegfried Schnel, next an unknown pilot, and at extreme right Unteroffizier Rudolf Miese.

Chris Goss.

As twenty-six year old Laurie Whitbread lay dead outside the crumpled remains of his Spitfire at Pond Cottage, the killing went on high above.

222 Squadron's Flying Officer Thomas of 'B' flight managed to retaliate over Sittingbourne, Kent:-

"At 11.15 hrs I was climbing to patrol with five other aircraft when at 25,000' a *squadron of yellow-nosed Me 109s attacked us from the sun in a quarter attack. I saw tracer shells going past Pilot Officer Edsall and I broke away, getting on the tail of a 109. I opened fire from astern at approximately 200 yards and gave two long bursts of five seconds each. I then saw a trail of white vapour come from the enemy aircraft. I then broke away and carried out a deflection shot at two more Me 109s circling round in tight formation, but saw no result as I had to break away due to being attacked myself."*

At 1045 hrs Flight Lieutenant Ted Graham of 72 Squadron had led off from Biggin Hill the Spitfires of Pilot Officers Lindsay, Males and Holland. At 1025, Flight Lieutenant *"Pancho"* Villa and Sergeant Rolls also entered the fray. At 1120 hrs over Canterbury, twenty-three year old *"Dutch"* Holland was blasted out of the sky in Spitfire X4410. Although badly wounded he managed to bale out and was later admitted to hospital. Before he died, his last words to the doctor were

Flying Officer Thomas of 222 Squadron who damaged an Me 109 at 1115 hrs over Sittingbourne on September 20th, 1940. Note that his flying helmet appears to have been painted yellow, a practice adopted to assist in location if shot down into the sea. Flight Lieutenant N.H.D. Ramsay.

"I'm all right, old pal, Dutchy can take it." Pilot Officer Lindsay was also shot up in R6881 but although his Spitfire was seriously damaged the pilot was unhurt. 72's Pilot Officer Robert Deacon-Elliot, now a retired Air Vice-Marshal, recalls September 20th, 1940:-

"I recall this date vividly on which I flew Spitfire X4413. At the last moment before scramble, Operations HQ requested two pilots of 72 Squadron to proceed to Hawkinge and escort an Anson aircraft with army officers aboard spotting for shells landing on the French coast fired from big guns in the Dover/Folkestone area. Names were put into a hat and mine, together with Flying Officer Robson came out. At this point "Dutch" Holland, a very close friend of mine, approached me. He was worried about the hazardous nature of the mission and volunteered to take my place. Naturally I said "No", as my name had come out of the hat. Whilst escorting the Anson at very low-level, some 200/300', reports from Operations warned us of enemy aircraft in the area, but at much greater heights. However, the Anson pilot decided to get back to Hawkinge quickly, yes, very quickly. We saw him push his nose down to sea level and

beat it for base. He must have exceeded the Anson's speed limit because on seeing the aircraft at Hawkinge I noticed that the entire fuselage fabric was stripped to the extent that you could see through the aircraft. I did not meet the pilot or army officers involved. Mission accomplished it was back to Biggin Hill. There I learned of "Dutch's" death, which, at the time, was attributed to a direct hit by our own guns. A ghastly thought - had I accepted his offer to take my place we may both still be here today. I was also involved in a similar sortie three days later but on that occasion I was shot at and lost my tailplane and huge sections of my port wing. I crash landed at Detling having been escorted all the way down by Sergeant Norfolk. That was the end of X4413, relegated to the scrap heap!"

Over Maidstone at 11.30 hrs, Hauptmann Johannes Seifert of I/JG26, and Oberfeldwebel Heinrich Gottlob of II/JG26 each picked off a 253 Squadron Hurricane. Sergeant RA Innes successfully abandoned V6736 but Pilot Officer Barton was wounded and later admitted to Ashford Hospital after being shot down in R2686. Oberleutnant Erbo Graf von Kageneck of III/JG27 fired at a Hurricane, possibly P5179 flown by Sergeant Kee. Fifty-two years later former Pilot Officer John Greenwood remembered:-

"I remember being with Sergeant Kee and diving for our lives into cloud. As I recall he copped a little enemy fire and we landed together shortly afterwards having made no effort to locate the rest of the squadron. Kee's aircraft had a little fabric missing and a few holes. I think that I also stopped a .5 armour piercing bullet through my head armour, the core of the bullet lodging in my neck. It had only just penetrated but it was as sharp as a needle. I kept it as a souvenir for many years."

The 253 Squadron diary recorded:-

"Ten Hurricanes took off from Kenley at 1105 hrs to patrol base at 10,000'. Squadron was then vectored to Maidstone area where Yellow Section became separated in cloud, emerging to be attacked by twelve Me 109s approximately five miles east of Maidstone. Yellow Leader, Flight Lieutenant Duke-Woolley, reports at least three 109s painted light blue and yellow and were yellow nosed. Red and Blue Sections, flying in a vic at 14,000' with one aircraft in the box over Maidstone, were ordered to join up with friendly fighters above. The fighters then attacked at that moment and proved to be twenty Me 109s which dived from 16,000' onto the squadron and breaking up our formation. The squadron endeavoured to re-form but whilst doing so were dived on by Spitfires, the squadron again being separated whilst taking evasive action in cloud."

Also at 11.30 hrs, in the south London area, Gefreiter Gruber of III/JG 27 attacked and damaged a Hurricane, possibly V6722 flown by Pilot Officer Glowacki of 605 Squadron. The squadron diary relates:-

"A showery day with high winds. It appears that rough seas during the last few days have delayed German invasion plans. The moon is now well in the wane. Squadron did one patrol today and encountered only Me 109s which adopted different tactics to usual by flying alone in twos, threes or fours over a wide area which our pilots found very harrassing, never knowing when they would swoop down on them. No losses, but Pilot Officer Glowacki's aircraft damaged Category II from cannon and machine-gun fire."

At 11.35 hrs, Hauptmann Seifert struck again when he attacked Pilot Officer Edsall of 222 Squadron high over the Thames Estuary. Edsall's Spitfire, R6840, was seriously damaged and spiralled out of the fight to make a forced landing without flaps back at Hornchurch due to the pneumatic system having been wrecked by a cannon shell which had also punctured the petrol tank. Edsall subsequently overshot the airfield and crashed through the perimeter fence but was only slightly injured.

At the same time, Feldwebel Heckman of II/JG3 shot down 222 Squadron's Pilot Officer Assheton in Spitfire K9993. Assheton safely abandoned his aircraft high over Kent.

At 11.34 and 11.35 hrs, the German "Oberkannone" (Top Gun), Major Werner Mölders of Stab JG51, destroyed two Spitfires of 92 Squadron over Dungeness. The machines were X4417 flown by New Zealander Pilot Officer Howard Hill, and N3248 flown by Sergeant P.R. Eyles. The twenty-year old Hill was killed and his Spitfire crashed into tree-tops, only being discovered a month later. Twenty-four year old Eyles went down into the sea and his body was never found. These two victories were numbers 39 and 40 for Major Mölders and earned for him the Eichenlaub (Oak Leaves) to the Ritterkreuz, making him only the second Luftwaffe officer to receive the coveted decoration.

Group Captain Alan Wright, then a Flight Lieutenant, remembers how 92 Squadron were bounced by JG51:-

"The squadron was split in half due to oxygen failure. The first half were surprised by Me 109s. Howard and Eyles, both of Green Section, were lost. I have a vivid picture in my mind of me leading Green Section on that day. After the split, the front two sections, led by the CO, Squadron Leader Sanders, were left flying in a close formation of two vics in line astern. I happened to glance to my left and was amazed to see a 109 taking the place of the Spitfire that I expected to see there, a glance to the right showed another one! I immediately shouted "BREAK!" and pulled up and around in a tight turn. The others probably reacted similarly. I noticed that we were immediately above a coastal town. I cannot remember what I did after the break, when flying at 200-300 mph one can, in just a few seconds, find oneself quite alone and unable to re-join the action.

"At that time, many squadrons, including ours, would be vectored towards our targets in a close formation of nine, comprising three vics with two weavers criss-crossing overhead and safeguarding the blind area behind the formation. Its advantage was that the eleven aircraft as a whole were very manoeuvrable. The danger was that if anything happened to the weavers and they were unable to use their R/T, the rest of the squadron would be utterly vulnerable. On this occasion in the rush to scramble, one or more of the rear pilots could have failed to switch on their oxygen, or it may not have been working properly, so that in the confusion the first half were left unaware that no-one was guarding their tails. No oxygen at the height of Everest could put you to sleep without you even realising it. Very sad, especially about Howard Hill who had flown with our squadron since the previous October."

92 Squadron's Red Two, Pilot Officer TS "Wimpey" Wade in Spitfire P9544, attacked an Me 109 at 1145 hrs, 27,000' above Folkestone:-

"Ganic Squadron was split up due to attack by Me 109s. I got on the tail of one and after a short burst the enemy aircraft dived away steeply. At about 4,000' it pulled out and started evasive tactics. After 2-3 minutes it headed south-east at 5,000'. I fired a number of short bursts from astern at 100/150 yards range but was unable to close any further. After doing evasive medium turns for a short period he pulled up steeply into cloud at 2,000', 15 miles from the French coast after which I lost him. I had seen my ammunition going into the wings but without the desired effect."

92's commanding officer, Squadron Leader PJ "Judy" Sanders, also attacked an Me 109 at 1145, firing 2,450 rounds at it:-

"As squadron leader patrolling Dungeness I knew that there were enemy aircraft about and was weaving. At 27,000' Blue Section, behind me, was attacked, so I broke quickly to the left and saw an Me 109 also turning left behind me. I gave one short burst about 120 yards from above and from the right. The enemy aircraft at once half rolled to the right and dived steeply for about 10,000'. He then pulled up and I got a good deflection shot at him from above and slightly behind. He half rolled again and dived. I fired intermittently at him on the way down and he did not pull out. I came out of the dive at 500' and he crashed into the sea about five miles south of Dymchurch and disappeared. I tried to re- group the squadron and received instructions to return to base and land.."

Squadron Leader Sanders was also attacked during the combat and his Spitfire, X4418, was damaged, possibly by Leutnant Altendorf of II/JG 53. He subsequently returned safely to Biggin Hill, although soaked in petrol from a ruptured fuel tank, only to burst into flames when he lit a cigarette shortly after landing. Fortunately he survived but was out of the battle from then on.

No German fighter is recorded as having crashed into the sea as reported by Squadron Leader Sanders, but a machine of 7/JG53 forced landed at Boulogne due to damage sustained in combat over the Channel.

At 1210 hrs, 25-30,000' over the Ashford/Canterbury area, Biggin Hill's 72 Squadron Spitfires met fifty Me 109s. Sergeant Rolls submitted the following report:-

"I was Red Two in a section told to intercept the enemy fighters. We took off at 1040 and after having completed a patrol by ourselves were instructed to rejoin the rest of the squadron as the leading section. We did this and met the enemy near Canterbury. We were climbing up towards one batch of Me 109s when we were warned by our rearguard of another lot diving down on us. We kept climbing into the sun and the rest of the squadron had used evasive action to get rid of the Me 109s. I soon found myself over Ashford and unable to see any of my squadron near me. I was flying along at 22,000' when I saw what appeared to be a Spitfire or Hurricane diving down to 16-18,000' and then climbing again. I decided to have a look at it so I got into a position so that I had the sun behind me and could see the machine clearly. As it came up in the climb I saw plainly that it was actually an Me 109 with a yellow nose and fin. I let it climb up again and waited, thinking perhaps it would dive again. It did so and then I dived out of the sun onto its tail and waited for it to start to climb before I pressed the tit to fire. I let it have about three seconds fire and the 109 did a stall turn to starboard and I followed it. I saw a large black piece break away from the side of the cockpit on the port side. I got it in my sights again as it turned and let it have another four seconds burst. This time I saw smoke and what appeared to be oil and water coming from underneath it. It turned to dive and as it did I let him have a final burst when the whole back of the cockpit dropped away and the rest dropped down towards cloud. This was at about 12,000'. I flew through the cloud and made for the aerodrome as I had only 10 gallons of petrol left. I watched the spot where the machine went in and it was near Wye, between a wood and lake so far as I could make out from my own position. I landed back with three gallons of petrol and a leaky glycol seal".

Sergeant Rolls had shot down the only Me 109 to crash in England that day, an E-4, 2789, of 9/JG27. The machine crashed at Ospringe, Kent, killing the pilot, Unteroffizier Erich Clauser.

The skirmish over, the Jagdwaffe retired to their French bases leaving just Unteroffizier Clauser mangled in the wreckage of his fighter. Fighter Command, however, had lost four pilots killed and several others wounded. 222 Squadron's Sergeant Norman Ramsay makes an observation regarding his attitude to losses:-

"People missing or killed at that stage of the battle meant little to me. I had joined 222 from 610 at Biggin Hill after we had lost ten, yes ten, pilots, so I was well used to the disappearing faces. Having been shot down myself I had learned to survive, to get the experience necessary for survival."

92 Squadron's Pilot Officer Geoff Wellum:-

"On September 20th I flew two patrols in Spitfire K9998. After this length of time I can recall nothing of the action, but I do remember that during September and October 1940 Me 109s were always in the Biggin Hill sector in numbers and caused problems. I recall that they were always above us as we never seemed to be scrambled in time to get enough height. Our climb was always a desperate, full throttle affair, but we never quite got up to them. I did manage to get a crack at two Me 109s on one patrol but although I saw strikes I could only claim them as damaged."

Although the surprise attack of September 20th, 1940, had been successful, the Germans soon found, to their discomfort, that even the Hurricane could run rings around a bomb-laden Me 109 and the Jagdwaffe suffered further heavy losses. Eventually Jagdführer General Theo Osterkampf protested to Jeschonnek, chief of the Luftwaffe general staff, that it would not take long for the whole fighter arm to be grounded due to these "senseless operations." His protests helped. In November there were fewer such attacks and at the beginning of December they were halted altogether.

It is perhaps characteristic that Laurie Whitbread had arranged that in the event of his death on active service the official telegram giving such notification should not be delivered direct to his mother but to the Rev. Hulbert at St Mary's, whose duty it would then be to break the tragic news. On October 3rd, 222 Squadron's commanding officer, Squadron Leader John Hill, wrote to Mr Whitbread:-

"It is with deep regret that I have to write to you from 222 Squadron and offer our sympathy in the very sad loss of your son.

"He was killed instantly by a bullet from an enemy aircraft when doing his bit in the defence of his country. His passing is a great loss to us; he has been in the squadron since its formation and was always most popular, having a quiet and efficient disposition and charming manner."

Reg Johnson, Laurie's friend who was flying alongside him when he was shot down by "Assi" Hahn, remembered Pilot Officer Whitbread literally just before he himself passed away quietly in his sleep:-

"From my now very senior years I remember him as a brave young man of the highest quality. Naturally courageous, he was always prepared to give his life for his country, but it was taken away from him due to the practice of unsatisfactory tactics. For me personally it was a great privilege to be a member of 222 Squadron in which I completed 101 operational sorties. I was shot down twice and parachuted twice, and wounded once. From being the junior reserve pilot I soon became the senior NCO pilot due to my incredible good fortune."

Reg Johnson certainly was fortunate; during the Battle of Britain 222

Squadron lost a total of nine pilots killed in action.

Pilot Officer Whitbread was the first Ludlovian to lay down his life in the Second World War and as a mark of respect the town organised a full military funeral when Laurie was laid to rest in the local cemetery. Every year on the anniversary of his death, St Laurence's church is illuminated in his honour and a street has even been named after Ludlow's member of Churchill's Few. Perhaps it is fitting, however, to allow George Merchant, Laurie's old schoolmaster, who participated in the military funeral, to have the last word:-

"So we turned and went back and left him alone in his glory, with his name and rank on the gravestone and the proud badge of the Royal Air Force which he had carried through peril to the stars. For some reason I always think of him as typical of those fifty boys from the school who died in the same way, a kind of symbol of what they were and what they did and why. I hope nobody will think that as I have singled him out from the others, it means that I regard them as having done anything less or of deserving less to be remembered. He was just the kind of boy you noticed first and remembered afterwards if you saw him talking in a group of his fellows, though he was probably saying less than any of the others. He was the kind of boy one does not forget and is glad to have known."

Pilot Officer Whitbread's grave in Ludlow immediately after his burial.

Mrs Sally Stubbs.

Chapter Five

BLUE TWO

Sergeant Kenneth Clifton Pattison.
Mrs Joan King.

Originally built at a busy factory on the banks of the River Itchen near Southampton, it soon became apparent, however, that to meet the demand for Mitchell's fighter imposed by wartime, even taking into account the policy of sub-contracting work to dispersed locations, Spitfire production would have to increase beyond the capabilities of Supermarine. The new site chosen for a *"Shadow Factory"* was at Castle Bromwich, Birmingham. The theory was for the mass production line type operation of the automobile industry to adapt and instead construct Spitfires. Lord Nuffield, pioneer of the inexpensive, mass produced motor car, was chosen to oversee the project. The Castle Bromwich Aircraft Factory commenced production of the first Spitfire Mk IIs in June 1940, the test flying of these machines being conducted by a remarkable young man, Alex Henshaw, a distinguished pre-war civilian pilot and holder of the record to Cape Town and back. Determined that his flying skills should be put to their best use in time of war, Henshaw was appointed Chief Test Pilot at the new factory. Under his leadership the intensive flying programme continued from dawn to dusk, often in appalling weather conditions. To its enormous credit, ultimately the Castle Bromwich workforce, which included large numbers of women, produced the majority of Spitfires built.

Britain's wartime Prime Minister, Winston Spencer Churchill, pictured at the Castle Bromwich Aircraft Factory and in conversation with the Chief Test Pilot, Alex Henshaw.

Mr Alex Henshaw.

The Spitfire Mk IIa enjoyed a number of technical advantages over the Mk I, the type in service with fighter squadrons at that time. To many pilots the most important was the elimination of the large pump-handle and the fitting of a power-operated control for the undercarriage. A new Rotol or De Havilland Constant Speed Airscrew had also been fitted. The old two-position plunger type control was inadequate under certain conditions, particularly combat flying, but the new unit provided the pilot with a wide range of settings. The airscrew was driven by an improved Rolls-Royce Merlin engine, the XII, and this combination gave the Spitfire an extra 2,000' ceiling. The Mk II was also the first Merlin powered Spitfire to run on 100 octane petrol, previous engines running on 85, and was fitted with a Coffman cartridge engine starter. All Mk IIs were built at the Castle Bromwich Aircraft Factory, commencing with P7280, initially flown in May 1940. The first example delivered to a squadron was P7286, which joined 152, but the first to be fully equipped with the new Spitfire was 611 Squadron.

On August 10th, 1940, Alex Henshaw gave Spitfire Mk II P7323, the forty-third aircraft built at Castle Bromwich, its production test flight, which was successful. On August 28th, P7323, P7320, P7321, and P7322, were delivered by ferry pilots from No 9 Maintenance Unit to 611 Squadron at Digby in Lincolnshire. P7298, P7300 and P7301 also arrived from 6 Maintenance Unit, and pilots from 7 OTU at Hawarden near Chester collected the squadron's former type, Spitfires Mk Ia K9918, K9981, N3051 and N3052.

Flying Officer Peter Brown airborne in Spitfire Mk IIa, P8044, "EB-J" of 41 Squadron. This machine was a presentation aircraft, "1st Canadian Division", and eventually perished in a flying accident at Kirkbymoorside. This type and markings are representative of P7323, which was coded "FY-P" with 611 Squadron.

Squadron Leader M.P. Brown.

611 *"West Lancashire"* Squadron was a unit of the Auxiliary Air Force and had become a fighter squadron early in 1940, receiving a mixture of Hawker Hinds and Hurricanes, and Fairey Battles. These were soon replaced by Spitfires and the squadron became fully operational on this type. Based at Digby and commanded by Squadron Leader Jimmy McComb, 611 had participated in Operation Dynamo, flying from Hornchurch, during the Dunkirk evacuation. For the first half of the Battle of Britain, the squadron remained at Digby in 12 Group to provide protection to coastal convoys. The squadron did taste action

occasionally, such as during an interesting combat fought on Wednesday, August 21st. The poor weather over England on that day prevented any massed raids by the Luftwaffe, but as it was important not to give the RAF even the briefest respite, both Feldmarschalls Sperrle and Kesselring ordered scattered raids over a wide front, each conducted by formations of three aircraft. One such sortie was flown by three Do 17s of II/KG3, and which struck inland across Norfolk as far as the airfield at Horsham St Faith before being detected. Two sections of 611 Squadron were scrambled from Digby, but owing to the apparently aimless behaviour of the raiders, the controller experienced difficulty in accurately vectoring the Spitfires. Consequently it took more than an hour to find and destroy all three enemy bombers. Red Section of 'A' flight, comprising Pilot Officers Watkins, Brown and Lund, destroyed one near Burnham Market at 1235 hrs. Squadron Leader McComb's section dealt with the other two, which actually collided, near Mablethorpe. However, four of 611 Squadron's fighters suffered damage from return fire during the engagement, amongst them Pilot Officer Peter Brown's P7304, the twenty-fourth Castle Bromwich built Spitfire. Brown's combat report states:-

"After sighting the enemy aircraft for the second time I attacked with leader in

Pilot Officer Peter Brown pictured during training with a Hawker Fury biplane fighter.
Squadron Leader M.P. Brown.

echelon port. *The enemy aircraft were rather close and Red Three was not quite in position. I attacked No 3 of the enemy formation. After firing for some seconds black smoke came from the port engine. After finishing my ammunition black smoke was pouring from both engines. I saw my ammunition entering the enemy aircraft and consider that a number of hits were made. After breaking away I saw the enemy aircraft diving towards the sea, two of the crew baled out."*

Damage sustained to Spitfire P7304 as a result of enemy action whilst flown by Pilot Officer Peter Brown on August 21st, 1940. Note the unusual style of lettering and position of the serial number.

Squadron Leader M.P. Brown.

Brown's Spitfire suffered bullet holes in the spinner cap, rudder, and the wings, the latter bursting a tyre. He lived to tell the tale, however, and later photographed the damage to his machine after returning to Digby.

As the fighting in the south intensified, later in August the squadron began operating from Fowlmere, in the Duxford Sector, as a part of Squadron Leader Douglas Bader's *"Big Wing"* that would ultimately comprise five Spitfire and Hurricane squadrons, 19, 616, 611, and 242 and 310, respectively (see *"Spitfire Squadron"* also by this author).

P7323's first flight with 611 Squadron was made by one of the squadron's senior pilots, Flight Lieutenant (now Sir) Kenneth Stoddart, on August 27th, 1940, when the entire squadron flew south to Duxford. Throughout the remainder of August "FY-P" was flown by Pilot Officer David Scott-Malden, a Cambridge graduate who had joined the RAF in November 1939, successfully won his *"wings"*, converted to Spitfires at 5 OTU, Aston Down (see *"The Invisible Thread: A Spitfire's Tale"* also by this author), and subsequently joined 611 Squadron in June 1940. Scott-Malden ultimately retired from the RAF as an Air Vice-Marshal. A patron of the Malvern Spitfire Team, he now lives in Norfolk.

Scott-Malden flew P7323 on August 31st, 1940, the day of Fighter Command's heaviest losses during the entire sixteen week battle. Although 611 did not meet the enemy that day, the squadron Operations Record Book mentions that the unit's total flying time of 61 hours on August 31st was *"easily a record"*, and therefore indicative of the hectic time faced by fighter squadrons during the summer of 1940.

September saw the tempo of battle increase, and P7323 was flown on a number of patrols early in the month by Flying Officer Barrie Heath, and Pilot Officers Walker and Adams. Between 1530-1615 hours on September 11th, Pilot Officer Dennis Adams flew P7323 on a Wing patrol over London. The Operations Record Book tells the story:-

"At 1530 hrs 611 Squadron left G1 (Fowlmere) and went into position as the second squadron of a Wing formation which was ordered to patrol in a southerly direction towards the Thames Estuary. At about 1550, when in the vicinity of SE London, 611 Squadron formed up in three sections of four aircraft in line astern. 100 plus enemy aircraft were seen coming in from the north in the direction of our fighters. Our aircraft were then at 20,000' with a large number of Me 109s behind them at 24,000'. Our aircraft altered course, making a left hand turn, attacking the enemy formation on the beam. 611 attacked the Me 110s. Pilots report that from the moment of contact with the enemy it was impossible to keep formation and a general mêlée ensued. Flight Sergeant Saddler, No 4 of Yellow Section, got separated from his section and attacked an Me 110, giving two long bursts closing from 500-100 yards range and using nearly all his ammunition. The fuselage was seen to catch fire and the enemy aircraft was losing height. Pilot Officer Lund, No 4 of Blue Section, dived on an Me 109 and fired a short burst on deflection but without visible effect. As another enemy aircraft appeared in his rear view mirror, he climbed and saw five Me 110s. Selecting the starboard aircraft, he delivered an astern attack closing to 100 yards. Black and white smoke was seen coming from the enemy aircraft which seemed to be losing height in relation to its formation. No evasive tactics observed and no enemy fire experienced. Sergeant Burt saw a single He 111 following a formation of Do 215s. Our aircraft managed to attack the enemy from 3,000' above. Sergeant Burt dived and opened fire at about 400 yards, closing to 200, giving a burst of about 5 seconds

which apparently put the enemy rear gunner out of action as return tracer fire ceased. Our aircraft had to take avoiding action and made a steep climbing turn, caught up with enemy formation again and found that the He 111 was missing. The squadron landed at Duxford at 1620 to refuel and rearm, and then left for Digby, arriving at dusk. Sergeant Shepherd and his Spitfire P7298, are missing. Sergeant SA Levenson forced landed near Kenley and is returning to Digby by train. Pilots report that R/T was working well during combat. Me 110s were very dark in colour. Me 109s were painted yellow from nose to cockpit. Combats took place in 1/10th cloud and in good visibilty."

A further report was submitted by the squadron's Intelligence Officer:-

"Sergeant SA Levenson was outclimbed by the rest of his section when pursuit of the enemy started. He flew round a formation of fifty plus Ju 88s and encountered two Me 109s circling in the opposite direction. Turning on to them he made a 60 degree deflection attack from the rear and allowed both aircraft to pass through his sights whilst firing at about 200 yards range. Both aircraft dived normally to start with but after 500' the second aircraft turned on its back, dived and began to spin. Sergeant Levenson lost sight of the aircraft and climbed up above the formation of Ju 88s. These aircraft were in a very tight formation and he made an attack on the starboard side of the bandits from the front quarter, allowing the entire formation to pass through his sights whilst firing at about 100 yards range. Two enemy aircraft broke away below the formation and an attack was made with a short burst from the rear quarter using the remaining ammunition. Smoke poured from the starboard engine and the enemy aircraft began to glide down losing height at the rate of 10,000 in 10-15 miles. Sergeant Levenson flew alongside for some time before AA guns opened fire. He broke away with black smoke pouring from below the instrument panel and attempted to make Kenley aerodrome. His engine then stopped and he landed with wheels up in a field not far away. A nearby searchlight post informed him that the aircraft he was following crashed in flames about 6-10 miles south of Kenley. Sergeant Levenson then returned to Digby by train on the following day.

"Flying Officer DH Watkins followed 19 Squadron into an attack on a large formation of Me 109s and 110s. Fired a short burst at full deflection into an Me 110 from less than 100 yards range, but, owing to his rapid approaching speed, he saw no result. He broke away, climbing towards the sun, and lost the formation. At 1615 hrs he sighted a formation of about forty Do 215s, his attention having been drawn towards them by exploding AA fire. As he was about to attack these aircraft, two AA bursts upset his aircaft in its dive and the engine stopped. He forced landed at Hornchurch, later returning to Duxford thence Digby. Squadron Leader McComb, followed by Pilot Officer Williams, were preparing to attack an Me 110 when they themselves were attacked by an Me 109, and climbed away from the formation to *evade. They did not fire at any other targets. Flight Lieutenant Stoddart attacked an Me 109 at long range, firing 1,784 rounds, without observing a result. He then returned to base, followed by Flying Officer Hay, who was covering him. The latter did not open fire on the Me 109 as he was not within range. Pilot Officer DH O'Neill fired 174 rounds into a Do 215 without result. The general confusion and AA fire prevented him from making a further attack. Pilot Officer Adams (flying P7323) made no attack for similar reasons. Pilot Officer Lund's stoppages due to a faulty feed chute. Flight Sergeant Sadler's to jammed transporter guides. Sergeant Burt had two stoppages, one after 180 rounds, and one after 4, both due to cross feed."*

The foregoing account is excellent, I think, and a credit to the clerk who compiled the Operations Record Book, that of some squadrons being appallingly lacking in detail, although as Supermarine's Chief Test Pilot, Jeffrey Quill, once remarked to me, *"Our minds were not focused on posterity in 1940!"*. The account, however, also gives some idea of the confusion of air fighting. There seems to have been confusion too amongst the Spitfire pilots regarding identification of the German bombers encountered. For example, Sergeant Levenson's victim was not a Ju 88 as reported, but actually an He 111H-3 of 3/KG26, "1H + ML". The raider is also believed to have been attacked by Spitfires and Hurricanes of several other squadrons. It crashed and exploded at Hoopers Farm, Edens Road, Dormansland near Lingfield at 3.45 pm. Oberleutnant Abendhausen and Unteroffizier Hauswold baled out, the latter wounded, but Felwebel Westphalen, Unteroffizier Herms and Gefreiter Zaehle were killed.

On Sunday, September 15th, 1940, came what is now generally accepted as the climax to the Battle of Britain. On that day the Prime Minister, Winston Churchill, visited Air Vice-Marshal Keith Park's Headquarters. As the WAAF plotters placed their coloured markers on the map of England, indicating enemy raids and intercepting fighter squadrons, the great man inquired of the Air Officer Commanding 11 Group what reserves he had; Park's answer was simple: *"None, Sir."* On the great day, 611 Squadron again flew at first light from Digby to Duxford and operated thereafter with the Wing. Throughout the day, P7323 was flown in action by Sergeant Sandy *"Stromboli"* Levenson. Again, the Intelligence Officer's report provides superb reference:-

"611 Squadron joined Wing of Hurricanes over Duxford at 15,000' at 1131 hrs, then climbed to 27,000' to the left and above the Wing which was at 22,000'. When SW of London fifty enemy bombers and thirty Me 109s, escorting above, were sighted coming in from the south. The Wing went into attack the bombers and escort turning SE. 611 Squadron kept beside the Me 109s which were to the west and above. After the Wing attack had broken up the bomber formation, the Me 109s did not come down. After waiting about seven minutes, Squadron Leader McComb informed Wing

Leader that he was coming down, and gave order "Echelon port". The squadron proceeded SE and up-sun of the enemy. The squadron in line astern, three sections of four aircraft, executed a head-on attack down onto a formation of about ten Do 215s and 17s flying at 18,000' in a SE direction. Squadron Leader McComb attacked a Do 215 head-on, hits observed but no result. Pulling up he made a beam attack on an Me 110 which turned on its back and went down. The squadron formation then broke up. Squadron Leader McComb chased an Me 109 which was in a dogfight with a Hurricane, but could not catch them up as he was too far behind. He then proceeded to the coast in the hope of attacking homing lame ducks before returning to base. Pilot Officer Williams, after making his attack with the squadron without observing results, saw a Do 215 attacked by six fighters crash into a wood near Bishopsbourne, Kent. Two of the crew baled out. Pilot Officer Lund dived into the initial attack but enemy aircraft passed through his sights before he could fire. Pilot Officer O'Neill attacked six or seven times a Do 215 which had fallen behind the main formation. Four Hurricanes also attacked at the same time. He chased this enemy aircraft as far as Dungeness where three other Spitfires carried on the attack. He then returned to base, being short of both petrol and ammunition. Flight Lieutenant Leather carried out a head-on attack on three Do 215s. No results observed. He then attacked a Do 215 at rear of a large formation using up the remainder of his ammunition. The port engine exploded and stopped. A number of other fighters also attacked this enemy aircraft and Red 2 reports seeing two crew members bale out and their machine also crash near Bishopsbourne. Pilot Officer Pollard, after firing a short burst in the initial dive, chased, in company with another Spitfire and a Hurricane, a Do 215 between Rochester and Herne Bay. Enemy aircraft lost height, some smoke coming from port engine. Crew of two baled out and aircraft crashed on the edge of a wood near Herne Bay. He landed at Detling at 1305 hrs having lost his bearings. Yellow 3, Pilot Officer Brown, after an initial diving attack, on pulling out saw no enemy machines. He developed engine trouble and had to forced land at West Malling at 1255 hrs. Flight Lieutenant Stoddart fired one quick burst during the diving attack, but then had to take evasive action to avoid attack from Me 109s. He circled for some time and then returned to base. Flight Sergeant Sadler, after the initial attack, saw 12 Do 215s going SE and executed two frontal attacks on the leader. The enemy aircraft was believed hit, although no results were seen. He abandoned the chase at Lympne, being short of both ammunition and petrol. Sergeant Levenson broke formation to attack an Me 109 but the enemy aircraft escaped. He then flew towards a large formation of Do 215s flying at 18,000'. After sighting one Do 215 alone at 14,000', he rolled over and carried out an old stern attack diving onto the enemy. Got in a long burst and both enemy aircraft motors were smoking when he broke away. He broke away when both engines and both mainplanes immediately behind them were on fire."

Having returned to Duxford in ones and twos, and indeed other aerodromes in south-east England, after the morning's fighting, 611 were off again at 1412 hours, Sergeant Levenson again flying P7323:-

"The squadron ran into several formations of bombers before sufficient height could be reached, and so ignored them, attempting to get height in a westerly direction to keep the Me 109s off the Wing. The squadron consisted of eight aircraft in three sections flying in line astern. It was not possible to outclimb the Me 109s, and the Wing appeared to be both attacking and being attacked simultaneously. When at 20,000' over West London, the Squadron Leader sighted a formation of twenty-five Do 17s proceeding south unmolested, and being by then separated from the Wing gave the order "Sections echelon right". The squadron dived down onto the formation, coming out of the sun. At the end of the general attack, Me 110s came down. Squadron Leader McComb attacked the rearmost enemy aircraft, the rear gunner of which ceased firing and smoke poured from its port engine. He then pulled up into a loop and dived again in an inverted position. Guns worked perfectly in this position and the enemy aircraft went down in flames. The result of this attack is confirmed by Yellow 2 and Yellow Leader. Squadron Leader McComb then blacked out badly and came to in the clouds. After looking around and seeing nothing he returned to base.

"Pilot Officer Williams carried out a No 3 Fighter Command attack on an He 111. A second burst at 80 yards was given but no result observed. Enemy aircraft returned machine gun fire. He was unable to return to the squadron, which had by now broken up, but upon observing two further enemy formations he made an astern attack on No 3 of the last section of the first formation of Do 215s. The formation turned north, but Red 2's target fell out, losing height. He then carried out another attack finishing up his ammunition. The enemy then descended into the clouds with one engine stopped, Red 2 following. Cloud was 2,000' thick and on emerging no enemy aircraft were visible, but two minutes later he saw enemy airmen descending by parachute. Latter landed on the edge of a wood in the corner of Hawkhurst Golf Club about fifteen miles north of Hastings. Flight Lieutenant Leather followed Red Leader into attack astern and took the machine next in line as his was already aflame. He fired all ammunition and when he broke away the Do 17 was in flames. He was then forced to land at Croydon at 1540 hrs.

"Pilot Officer Brown had first to evade enemy fighters before putting a short burst into the Do 215 already attacked by Red Leader and which had one engine out of action. Oil or glycol from the enemy aircraft covered up his windscreen and so he had to break away. Then he attacked another enemy aircraft which had broken away from the formation. That aircraft went into a steep spiral dive with escape hatch over pilot's seat open. No further results noted as a large gaggle of Me 110s suddenly appeared and Yellow 2 escaped in cloud.

"Pilot Officer Lund attacked a Do 215 which was also being attacked by several other aircraft. He saw flashes of fire and smoke coming from the enemy aircraft. Whilst climbing back to the main formation of bombers, one Me 110 came down on him so he fired one short burst before turning away and down. As the enemy aircraft passed his port side, black smoke was pouring from an engine.

"Flight Sergeant Sadler, after attacking with the squadron, saw a Do 215 break away and begin losing height. He made two attacks on this machine, his second at 50 yards. A Hurricane also attacked after him and the enemy aircraft disappeared below clouds at 3,000' badly disabled.

"Pilot Officer DH O'Neill lost touch with Blue Leader but after circling for about six minutes had to evade eight Me 110s into cloud. Up again out of cloud saw Me 109s attacking one Hurricane, so he attacked one of these over Faversham without observing any result although the enemy fighter took no evasive action. After being attacked by another Me 109, he returned to base, landing first, however, by mistake at Debden.

"Sergeant Levenson attacked without visible result an Me 109 and a Do 215 before finding himself at 10,000' over Brooklands Aerodrome. He then saw about fifty Do 215s guarded by twelve Me 109s flying above. He climbed to 1,000' below the bombers and delivered a quarter frontal attack, opening fire first at 100 yards developing into a normal quarter attack at about 200 yards until all of his ammunition was exhausted. He observed ammunition hitting the leading enemy aircraft and the leading vic of 4 aircraft broke away to port, smoke coming from the engines of No 1 and 2. No further result was seen but it was assumed that at least No 1 was out of action."

For no loss in either action, the squadron "bag" claimed was three Do 215s, two Do 17s, one He 111, and a Do 215 shared with 310 Squadron, and one Me 110 and three Do 215s probably destroyed. Two Spitfires had received bullets in the wings, but both were repairable.

Stephen Austin Levenson had actually been a regular officer before the war, but was cashiered over what would now seem a relatively minor matter. Rejoining the service when war broke out, he became a Sergeant pilot. When he was killed during the night of September 16th, 1942, flying a Stirling bomber of Stradishall's 214 Squadron when attacking Essen, he had still only risen to the non-commissioned rank of Warrant Officer. I think that there can be little doubt, however, of the quality and courage of this fine Scotsman.

Over the next few days, P7323 was flown by Pilot Officers Adams, Walker, Scott-Malden, Williams and Watkins, on a variety of patrols. During this time, to afford some protection to the north-west, in particular Liverpool, 'B' flight of 611 Squadron moved north to operate from Ternhill in north Shropshire, whilst 'A' flight continued to operate as a part of the Duxford Wing. At 1630 hrs on September 21st, Pilot Officer Dennis Adams was scrambled from Ternhill in P7323 to investigate a *"bogey"* at 20,000' over Liverpool. Having climbed through cloud he found a Dornier 215, *"VB + KK"* of 2(F)/121, engaged on a photographic reconnaissance sortie. The enemy aircraft flew west but after a fourteen minute long chase Adams opened fire, seeing his victim crash land at Trawsfyndd, Merioneth, in North Wales. Mr RE Williams witnessed the dramatic incident:-

"I was an eye-witness to the crash, and I will never forget that Saturday afternoon. It was about five o' clock in the afternoon and I was having a wash in the kitchen of our farm house when I heard the roaring of an aeroplane. Looking through the window I saw a German bomber approaching, the big black crosses being clearly visible. I shouted to my mother and ran outside to see it just miss the house. Flying very low, it also just missed a fence near the house. I could see that one propeller was still and a Spitfire hovered above. As the damaged bomber had passed overhead the crew were throwing maps out of the window. I then saw the plane catching telephone wires, splitting one pole, before crashing down in Bomer field, part of it lying on a road to the farm. The Spitfire then emitted a cloud of smoke and turned back.

"My father and brother, with a farm helper, came running towards our house having seen the plane before me flying low through a valley called Cwm Prysor, with the Spitfire firing at it. As I was in the Home Guard and my father in the Observer Corps, we jumped in the car and were first on the scene. I think that there were five crew members, some with blond hair, and I think that they brought out one body. There was an army camp about a mile away and soon some soldiers came and shepherded us away from the crash site. I also remember a machine gun in the plane going off accidentally, but fortunately no-one was hurt."

Unteroffizier Peizer was killed but Leutnant Book, and Feldwebels Jensen and Kühl were captured. Dennis Adams survived the war a Squadron Leader and now lives in South Africa. However, he is in regular correspondence with the author and recalls the following of the action:-

"The Dornier 215 was at about 30,000' when I caught up with it. I climbed a couple of hundred feet higher on the starboard side before attacking. When I did so my third and fourth starboard guns fired two rounds each before jamming. Apparently the armourers believed that the lubricant they used froze at such a height. One thing omitted from my official combat report was that I tried to get the Dornier to land at Hooton Park or Speke airfields. From that height the pilot could have made either easily but he seemed pretty single-minded, flying a straight course but losing height all the time. I think he was very lucky that he found a field in which to land in such rugged country."

Pilot Officer Dennis Adams, fifth from left, poses amongst other pilots with a wing section from Do 215 "VB +KK" of 2(F)/121 which he shot down over North Wales on September 21st, 1940. The trophy is in use as the 611 Squadron "scoreboard".

Andy Saunders.

As a matter of interest, along with several other 611 Squadron pilots, a few days later Dennis Adams was posted to 41 Squadron at Hornchurch. Many books detail that on October 7th, 1940, Pilot Officer Adams was shot down by return fire from a German bomber near Folkestone. The truth of the matter is somewhat different, as Dennis himself explained to this author in 1990:-

"I let the chaps think that I had been a clot and let the Dornier's rear gunner get me. In fact we had a new boy flying as my number three, and he was trying to get himself a squirt. As I turned to attack he let fly and took out my controls plus half the instruments, and also put bullets into the fuel tank ! When I got back to Hornchurch in a commandeered car I was just sobering up, having met a very friendly farmer who insisted that I share a flask of brandy with him. Oh boy, Kentish hospitality ! I had quite a talk with this young man the following morning."

On September 27th, 1940, 611 Squadron received three replacement pilots at Digby, Sergeants Thomas Harold Sadler, Kenneth Clifton Pattison and Jack Scott.

Ken *"Pat"* Pattison was twenty-seven years old and came from Nottingham.

He had joined the RAF Volunteer Reserve on November 11th, 1938, continuing to work full-time at the John Player cigarette factory in the city until called up on September 3rd, 1939. His training took place at No 1 Initial Training Wing, Hanworth, commencing on November 22nd, 1939, No 5 Flying Training School at Yatesbury on March 26th, 1940, and No 8 Flying Training School at Montrose on June 8th, where he achieved a final result of 61.3 per cent. On August 31st, 1940, Sergeant Pattison reported to 7 OTU, joining the unit's seventh course.

Pre-Fighter Course, Montrose, June 1940; Sergeant Ken Pattison appears second from right, rear row. The majority of these young pilots went on to fly in the Battle of Britain.
Flight Lieutenant K. Wilkinson.

On June 1st, 1940, the Air Ministry had decided to open a third OTU and expand the two existing units until collectively they could produce 3,000 fully trained fighter pilots per year. The new unit, 7 OTU, opened at Hawarden near Chester on June 15th, 1940, under the command of Wing Commander JR Hallings-Pott DSO. The unit was equipped with twenty Hurricanes, twenty Spitfires and seventeen trainers. The first course commenced two days later, and as we have already seen, courses lasted for two weeks at that time. This reduction actually made OTU training little more than a conversion to operational type. Each unit trained according to its own ideas and discretion.

During the lull between the Battles of France and Britain, the three OTUs worked intensively with two objectives, maximum pilot output and minimum wastage of single-seater types. The maximum pilot output was greatly assisted by the keenness of pupils. A New Zealander reached Hawarden one evening and spent the night on Spitfire cockpit drill by torchlight before flying at first light. The salvage of crashed aircraft also became a priority. If a Hawarden Spitfire forced landed near the Dee, every available man was rushed there from the station to drag the aircraft out of the tide's reach. When the Battle of Britain began, 7 OTU even added some private and unofficial sorties and destroyed several raiders.

Although the course was officially of two weeks duration, the timescale actually held little meaning as pilots were passed out only when they were considered fit, usually between ten days and three weeks. With an average of some 10-20 flying hours on Spitfires or Hurricanes, the pupils were unable to receive any tactical training. Half of the pupils sent to 7 OTU were not passed out at the end of the nominal fourteen days, but retained for a further week of instruction, as was Sergeant Pattison. This, however, had the effect of over-crowding the OTUs which were soon unable to cope.

Fighter Command then devised the *"Stabilising Scheme"* which divided fighter squadrons into 'A', 'B' or 'C' units. 'A' squadrons were those in the front line, largely comprising those in 11 Group covering the south-east of England, and 'B' were those that were being rested but which could be called upon if necessary. 'C' squadrons were those unlikely to be called into battle and these units gave their entire attention to finishing OTU training mainly by providing tactical instruction prior to passing pilots on to 'A' and 'B' squadrons. By November 1940, the 'C' squadrons held a total of 320 non-operational pilots in addition to their own. Corporate entity and unit morale suffered seriously. To reduce the flow of pilots from OTUs, the Air Ministry reverted to the four week course. Many of the non-operational pilots already with 'C' units were transferred to the Middle East. The Stabilising Scheme was eventually abandoned in December 1940.

Having spent three weeks at 7 OTU, Sergeant Pattison was posted to a 'C' squadron, 266, which he joined at Wittering on September 23rd, 1940, with just thirteen hours flying experience on Spitfires recorded in his flying log book. After four days with 266, Pattison was posted to 611 Squadron, a 'B' rated unit.

During October 1940, Spitfire P7323 continued being flown on routine patrols from Ternhill by Sergeant Burt, and Pilot Officers Peter Brown and Peter Olver. All three would survive the war, Burt remaining in the post war air force, retiring in 1955 as a Squadron Leader with the AFC to his credit, Peter Brown also as a Squadron Leader and similarly decorated, and Peter Olver a Wing Commander with five enemy aircraft destroyed and in addition a well deserved DFC and Bar.

Sergeant Pattison made his first flight with 611 Squadron in Spitfire P7374 on September 29th, when he flew from Digby and joined 'B' flight at Ternhill. The following day he returned to Digby in P7282, flying P7300 to Ternhill on October 5th. On October 8th he flew P7356 against a suspected raid approaching Coventry and Leicester, but landed without incident. Three days later he met the enemy for the first and last time.

By Friday, October 11th, 1940, the onset of autumn had seen the Indian summer conditions fade to grey, and that particular day was one of showers with an early mist turning to night fog. During the day the Luftwaffe had attacked the south coast towns of Weymouth, Folkestone, Canterbury and Deal, along with the Fighter Command airfields at Southend, Biggin Hill and Kenley. The previous night had seen London, Merseyside and Manchester attacked; on that Friday night raids were planned on London, Tyneside, Teeside, Merseyside and Manchester.

During the late afternoon and early evening German reconnaissance aircraft were active over the night's proposed targets, amongst them two Dornier 17 bombers of 1/Kustenfliegergruppe 606, *"7T + EH"* and *"7T + HH"*, and a machine of the second staffel, *"7T+EK"*, which probed the Liverpool area on an intelligence gathering and nuisance bombing sortie.

At 1730 hrs, 'A' flight of 611 Squadron took off from Ternhill to patrol Anglesey, North Wales. At about 1820 hrs, whilst the flight was making a wide orbit at 17,000' in search formation of line astern, Yellow Leader (Flying Officer DH Watkins) sighted three enemy aircraft flying in a vic formation about twelve miles away and approaching from the south-west at 14,000'. After informing Red Leader (Flight Lieutenant Jack Leather), Yellow Leader ordered his section *"Echelon starboard, Go!"*, and attacked out of the sun. From 2,000 yards the enemy leader's gunner opened fire, but only then did the other raiders break formation. Their No 3 turned sharp left and out to sea, whilst 1 and 2 turned right, inland. Yellow Leader was followed into the attack by Yellow 3 (Pilot Officer TD Williams), as Yellow 2's engine had cut out immediately prior to the enemy having been sighted and Flying Officer Hay therefore had to leave the formation. In the meantime 'A' flight had split, Red Section attacking enemy No 2, who had turned inland. Yellow Leader opened fire at 15 degrees deflection from 300 yards above, closing to about 50 yards astern. His target's starboard engine was hit and return fire ceased as Watkins broke away. Yellow 3 then delivered a Fighter Command No 3 Attack, but the enemy turned away before the manoeuvre was completed. Yellow 3 then went astern and carried out a No 1 Attack. Yellow Leader then attacked from above, closing from 250 to 50 yards, whilst Yellow 3 continued attacking from astern. Although the enemy aircraft was losing height, return fire had recommenced. On breaking away, Yellow 3 received an *"explosive bullet or shell"* in the bottom of his cockpit which rendered his Air Speed Indicator u/s. Yellow Leader, confident that the enemy bomber would not make it back to France, ordered Yellow 3 to return to base. Pilot Officer Williams, discovering that his engine still worked and his aircraft was flyable, despite both ailerons having been damaged, circled for a short while before returning to Sealand, landing at 1905 hrs but having to use his emergency undercarriage system. Yellow Leader, having followed the German bomber, saw it jettison five bombs into the sea at about 200' and crash into the water at 1835 hrs some fifty miles west of Holyhead. Watkins then drew the plight of the crew, who had taken to their dinghy, to the attention of a *"large cargo boat"*, before returning to Ternhill where he landed at 1907 hrs.

Watkins and Williams had destroyed Dornier 17Z-3 "7T+EH" of 1/606. Leutnant zur See von Krause, Feldwebel Arpert and Gefreiter Sudermann, thanks to Yellow Leader, were rescued by a trawler. Feldwebel Vetterl was not so lucky, however, and remains *"missing"*. Pilot Officer Draper Williams later wrote in his log book, *"it crashed in the sea about fifty miles out and three of the crew were picked up"*.

In the meantime, Red Section, Flight Lieutenant Leather, Flying Officer Pollard and Pilot Officer Sutton, had carried out two No 1 Attacks on the starboard enemy aircraft which stopped the machine's starboard engine. The raider was last seen to be losing height rapidly and was believed to have crashed in the hills ten miles south of Caernarvon. No such crash actually occurred, but it is believed that this Dornier 17Z-3 "7T+EK" of 2/606 also crashed into the Irish Sea at 1835 hrs. The bodies of the observer, Leutnant zur See Horst Felber, and wireless operator, Gefreiter Walter Hoppmann, were both washed ashore in Ireland on October 26th; that of the pilot, Oberleutnant Friedrich-Wilhelm Richter, came ashore at Amlwch, Anglesey on November 7th. Unteroffizier Weber remains *"missing, believed killed"*.

After destroying "7T+EK", Red Section then returned to attack the enemy leader. As the Spitfires closed in for their third attack, two of the enemy crew baled out. With both engines ablaze, the raider was believed to have crashed near Capel Curig.

This bomber was Dornier 17Z "7T+HH" of 1/606. Unteroffizier Johannsen baled out but fell dead at Capel Curig due to parachute failure, but Feldwebel Staas baled out safely and was captured at Marthalyn, North Wales. Their aircraft, however, managed to limp back to Brest despite being seriously damaged.

Other German bombers were also active over North Wales. At 1825 hrs, Red and Yellow Sections of 312 (Czech) Squadron based at Speke encountered a lone enemy aircraft shortly after having taken off, which was attacked without visible result by Flight Lieutenant Comerford. The squadron's Hurricanes then sighted another raider between Prestatyn and Chester, which they promptly attacked. Pilot Officer Jaske left the bomber smoking, but had himself received a damaged mainspar, fabric, and main and tailplane elevator and aileron. After the Hurricanes had expended their ammunition, the raider made off southwards. No German loss tallies with either of 312's targets, so it is therefore assumed that both returned to France.

At 1745 hrs that day, the Supermarine Spitfires of 611 Squadron's Blue Section also took off from Ternhill to patrol the Point of Ayr at 20,000'. Flying Officer Barrie Heath led his section, comprising Sergeant Ken Pattison (Blue Two) and Sergeant Robert Angus (Blue Three), to their patrol line. At 1830 hrs, whilst flying in line astern over Prestatyn, Blue Leader sighted two Dornier 17s approaching from the south-west, some 500' below the Spitfires and a quarter of a mile to port. The fighters, being in an excellent tactical position, higher than the enemy and up-sun, were immediately ordered to attack. By the time Heath had turned out of the sun and approached the Dorniers, the German airmen had already seen the Spitfires and both bombers commenced a shallow dive towards Speke. As Heath closed to within one mile of the raiders, both rear gunners opened fire on his rapidly closing fighter. As Blue Leader answered with a burst at the starboard intruder, the bombers divided, Heath's target turning right and the second machine left over Hoylake. After ordering Blue Two and Three to deal with the left-hand enemy machine, Heath closed from 400 to 100 yards range, attacking his target from astern with an eight second burst. After breaking away Heath attacked again with a short burst at fifty yards range, at which point return fire from the Dornier ceased. After a final attack from starboard, closing to 100 yards, Heath's ammunition was exhausted. During the combat the enemy aircraft had re-crossed the Dee and one mile west of Sealand, at about 10,000', it slowed down and glided south-west to Flint, dropping incendiary bombs on farmland. At that stage a Hurricane appeared and made a short beam attack before turning back towards Liverpool. Flying Officer Heath last saw the Dornier at 4,000' east of the North Wales coastal town of Denbigh, turning north into cloud. By that time dusk had set in so Heath set course for Ternhill.

When Heath Tally Ho'd the two Dorniers, Sergeant Angus went down to head off the port enemy aircraft, which had turned inland, firing a short burst at 400 yards. Bits flew off the bomber's underside, and Angus pursued his victim towards the sea, getting in another burst from 150 yards. The Dornier pilot managed to control his dive and was last seen by Angus heading seawards. Neither of the bombers attacked by Blue Section are believed to have crashed, but instead also managed to return to France in a damaged condition.

Both Heath and Angus landed at Ternhill at 1850 hrs, but of Blue Two, Sergeant Kenneth Pattison, nothing had been seen since the enemy was initially sighted.

Pattison's glimpse of the Dorniers was his first of the enemy, and in fact initially he had been unable to see the bombers. Heath and Angus, concentrating on their targets, last saw Blue Two turning late into the attack, after which time they were totally committed to combat. By its conclusion there was no sign of Sergeant Pattison.

Eventually word reached Ternhill that Spitfire P7323 "FY-P" had crashed at the village of Cooksey Green, between Bromsgrove and Kidderminster in north-west Worcestershire. In the fading light, lost and with no ground-to-air direction finding facilities to assist the relatively inexperienced pilot, Sergeant Pattison had wandered across North Wales into Shropshire, and then south into Worcestershire. Perilously short of fuel and with darkness rapidly falling, he had no option but to find a suitable field in which to land. Harry Turner, the blacksmith at Cooksey Green Forge, saw the Spitfire circling with its wing landing lights lowered. Selecting the field adjacent to Cooksey Green farmhouse, P7323 was almost down safely when a herd of startled cows stampeded in front of the descending Spitfire. The pilot heaved back on the control column but at such low speed could not find the lift required to go round again; with a splintering crash

Cooksey Green Farm, Upton Warren, Worcestershire, pictured in 1990, the scene of Sergeant Pattison's crash on October 11th, 1940.

Andrew Long.

the aircraft hit a pear tree, inverted, continued on its back along half the length of the field, hit the ground and bounced fifteen feet into the air before coming to rest on an ancient tree stump. Mr Turner ran towards the wrecked aircraft, finding the pilot hanging upside down in his straps. Cutting him out with a pen knife, the blacksmith gently slid Sergeant Pattison out of the cockpit and away from the dense black smoke produced by burning engine oil. Shortly afterwards an ambulance arrived on the scene and conveyed the mortally injured pilot to Barnsley Hall Military Hospital near Bromsgrove.

Sergeant Pattison was a married man, his wife Joan rushing to the hospital in time to see her husband suffer and linger on in this world until October 13th when he died of injuries sustained in the crash. Buried in Wilford Hill cemetery, Nottingham, Sergeant Pattison never knew his daughter Jean, born just seven months after his tragic death.

In happier times,Ken Pattison strolls through the seaside resort of Skegness with his young wife, Joan.

Mrs Joan King.

Set in the heart of the Midlands, Worcestershire saw little action during the war, and Sergeant Pattison was to be the only one of Churchill's gallant Few to lose his life on active service in that county during the Battle of Britain.

Another interesting fact is that on October 12th, 1940, the day after Blue Section intercepted the Dorniers, Hitler conceded that time had run out for a seaborne invasion of Britain that year. This decision was announced by Generalfeldmarschall Wilhelm Kietel who stated that the invasion was to be postponed until the spring or early summer of 1941, and that in the meantime *"military conditions for a later invasion are to be improved."* In reality, having discovered that his Wehrmacht were not to blitzkrieg into Great Britain as in the occupied countries of western Europe, Hitler had no doubt already turned his territorial ambitions eastwards towards the Soviet Union.

And what of the other players of 'B' flight in that drama high over Liverpool, now over fifty years ago? Robert Alexander Angus was born in Leith, Edinburgh on December 17th, 1919. Having completed his secondary education at Dumfermline High School in 1935, he commenced a course in civil engineering. An enthusiastic Boy Scout, Angus was selected as one of five Scouts to represent Scotland at the World Scout Jamboree in America in 1936. Joining the RAFVR in 1938, the young Scot travelled to RAF Grangemouth every weekend to learn to fly. Having soloed on Tiger Moths shortly before the declaration of war, Angus was called up and set off on the train to London on the evening of that momentous day, September 3rd, 1939. Having completed his flying training, Angus joined 611 Squadron at Ternhill on September 29th, 1940, just three days after Sergeant Pattison. The October 11th action was also Angus' first glimpse of the enemy. Sergeant Angus later served with 41 Squadron at Hornchurch, commanded by Olympic gold medal hurdler Squadron Leader Donald Finlay. On February 20th, 1941, 41 Squadron engaged enemy fighters over Dover; in the ensuing combat Sergeant Angus was shot down by the German *"Oberkannone"* Major Werner *"Vatti"* Mölders. The twenty-one year old Scot was seen to bale out over the sea but his body was never found. Sergeant Angus is remembered on the Runnymede Memorial to those British and Commonwealth airmen who have no known last resting place.

Sergeant Robert Angus, standing third from left, who flew as Blue Three on the sortie during which Sergeant Pattison was lost, whilst serving with 41 Squadron at Hornchurch. Also relevant to this story is Pilot Officer Dennis Adams, second from left standing on the spitfire.
The late Mr Don Angus.

Born on September 11th, 1916, the son of the senior director of Rootes Motors, Barrie Heath attended Cambridge University and learned to fly with the University Air Squadron, being commissioned in the RAFVR in 1937. Having transferred to 611 Squadron in June 1939, he was called up to full-time service in August that year. Later seeing action over Dunkirk and during the Battle of Britain, Heath was made a Flight Commander in November 1940, before being posted to command 64 Squadron between March and September 1941, during which time he was awarded the DFC. Following staff appointments, Heath led 324 Wing in Italy and later served on the staff of the Desert Air Force, eventually leaving the service as a Wing Commander in 1946. In the post-war world Barrie Heath became a prominent industrialist and was Knighted in 1978. Sir Barrie passed away in February 1988 at the age of seventy-six.

Looking back on Sergeant Pattison's tragic first encounter with the enemy, perhaps it is fitting to let the Few have the last word. The late Wing Commander Roger Boulding who flew Spitfires as a young Pilot Officer with 74 Squadron during the Battle of Britain, remarked in 1988: *"It is astonishing on reflection how many young pilots failed to return from their first sortie. To see was to live, and your 'eyes' only grew with experience."*

Squadron Leader Dennis Adams: *"Sergeant Pattison would have been better off making a wheels up forced landing, his intention was no doubt to save his aeroplane from damage. I blame the Flight Commander and CO for not briefing the new boy that his training was worth more than his Spitfire. In those days it was estimated that the cost of training a pilot to operational standard cost £40,000, the cost of a Spitfire £8,000. Under the provisions of Lord Beaverbrook's "Spitfire Fund", by the way, a donation to the Air Ministry gave you a Spitfire; Barrie Heath's father did just that!"*

Wing Commander Peter Olver: *"Your letter brought back many partly forgotten memories. I must also have been with Pattison at 7 OTU in addition to our short time together in 611 Squadron. The mention of him dying in Bromsgrove Hospital grabbed me rather strongly as I was at Bromsgrove School and once visited a sick friend in the hospital. The thought of Sergeant Pattison also being there I find very sad, not implying any criticism of the hospital but rather that at such a young age I was unduly impressionable. At that period I was strongly under the impression that the war would be won before I could get there, so I applied for a posting straight from OTU to a squadron in the south of England. Fortunately for me, however, I was actually sent to 611 at Digby, a 'B' unit, on September 30th, with whom I remained for sixteen days and received eighteen hours of flying, some of it operational, until my posting came through to 603 Squadron, an 'A' unit, at Hornchurch. On my first subsequent operational trip, on October 25th, 1940, I was shot down by an Me 109."*

On June 2nd, 1990, the Malvern Spitfire Team opened a major exhibition commemorating the Battle of Britain's fiftieth anniversary at Tudor House Museum, Worcester. The exhibition was entitled *"Their Finest Hour: No Piece of Cake"*. Dedicated in Sergeant Pattison's honour, the display was officially opened by his widow, Mrs Joan King, at a private preview attended by fifteen of the Few. On display were Sergeant Pattison's flying log book, medals and cap badge, all of which Mrs King had kindly donated to the Team's collection of memorabilia and to enable these important artifacts to be shared with the public. *"Their Finest Hour"* received over 18,000 visitors in just four months, and due to public demand was retained by Worcester City Council for over a year. These figures are a credit not only to the team, but in particular the curator, Brian Owen, and his technicians who have exhibited the team's research work on several occasions to dramatic effect. I hope that our collective efforts have gone some way towards ensuring that Sergeant Pattison's sacrifice is accurately documented for future generations.

Mrs Joan King, Sergeant Pattison's Widow, proudly displays her late first husband's Pilot's Flying Log Book and photograph.

Author.

Kenneth Clifton Pattison was one of only two pilots killed during the Battle of Britain with 611 Squadron, but one of five hundred and thirty-seven airmen lost in total by Fighter Command during that summer's conflict which actually dictated the destiny of the twentieth century.

Chapter Six

THE NEW BOY

Pilot Officer William Pearce Houghton
"Robin" *Rafter.*

Mrs Elizabeth Barwell.

William Pearce Houghton Rafter, more commonly known by his family as *"Robin"*, was born on July 17th, 1921, the son of Sir Charles and Lady Rafter whose home was at Elmley Lodge in Old Church Road, Harborne, Birmingham. Sir Charles was actually Chief Constable of the Second City's police force and was a serving officer for thirty-seven years. He died in 1935, but was survived by his wife, elder son Charles, Robin, and the boys' elder sister, Elizabeth. Robin was at Shrewsbury School when his father passed away, but the following year moved to complete his education at Cheltenham College. At school he was an enthusiastic sportsman, excelling at cricket, rugby, football, squash and swimming. His education complete by the end of 1939's summer term, Robin left Cheltenham and went straight into the RAF, receiving a Short Service Commission on June 26th, 1939. Having volunteered and been accepted for aircrew training, Robin commenced his ab initio flying on Tiger Moth biplanes at 6 Civilian Flying School at Sywell in Northamptonshire. There he obtained his civilian flying licence before moving to 12 FTS at Grantham in Lincolnshire on September 2nd, 1939, to complete his service flying training, but was transferred to 10 FTS at Ternhill just three days later. There he won his *"wings"*, being authorised to wear the coveted flying brevet from November 3rd, 1939, and passing his final exam with 64 per cent. Upon conclusion of the course, Rafter was assessed: *"Ground subjects a poor average. Navigation and airmanship weak. A safe pilot but lacks polish. A keen average officer"*. Personally I find it incredible to think of an eighteen year old, straight from school, even despite the fact that public schools prepared their pupils for leadership, being given such enormous responsibilties, especially perhaps when compared with the teenagers of today. In 1939, however, youths, and they were no more than that, like Robin Rafter, had to accept man sized jobs and responsibilities.

Between the wars, tactical thinking in Britain had remained stagnant since the trench warfare of 1918, and whilst the fighter aircraft was neglected, the role of army co-operation flying was considered essential. Fighter Command was responsible for the training of pilots to serve in such squadrons, and suitable instruction was provided at the School of Army Co-operation at Old Sarum in Wiltshire. The school had actually been in existence since the Great War and was arguably the forerunner of the OTU system. Its objective was to train replacement crews for tactical reconnaissance squadrons equipped with the Westland Lysander, a high-winged, single-engined monoplane, and the night and strategic reconnaissance squadrons flying the twin-engined Bristol Blenheim. Many of these units were called to France shortly after the outbreak of war with the Air Component of the field forces. At Old Sarum the school was reorganised and a reserve pool was added. The combined school and reserve pool proposed to train seventy-two pilots, thirty-seven observers and seventy-two air gunners on a six week course that included forty hours of flying. The aircraft establishment was increased to twelve Lysanders, twelve Hector biplanes, twelve Ansons and fifteen Blenheims. The unit soon became generally regarded as the Army Co-operation Group Pool. Old Sarum, however, was soon found to be too small, so the pool split, single-engined types there remaining, and twins going to Andover. Old Sarum therefore became the home of No 1 School of Army Co-operation, and Andover No 2. No 1 trained twenty pilots and twenty air gunners per fortnight on a two week course, but at No 2 the course remained of six weeks duration.

Pilot Officer Rafter was posted to No 2 Army Co-operation School at Andover on February 1st, 1940, and after completing the twin-engined course, reported to No 1 School on March 17th.

I have in front of me the flying log book of Pilot Officer Arthur Vokes, by coincidence of Erdington, Birmingham, who flew Spitfires throughout the Battle of Britain with 19 Squadron (see both *"Spitfire Squadron"* and *"The Invisible Thread: A Spitfire's Tale"* also by this author), before losing his life in a flying accident in 1941. However, during his training, after leaving 8 FTS at Montrose, Arthur joined No 8 War Course at No 1 School of Army Co-operation, Old Sarum, on June 1st, 1940. There he commenced flying on June 3rd, in Hector K9734 and received *"familiarisation of aircraft"* with Flight Lieutenant Hughes. Over the next few days Pilot Officer Vokes flew solo in Hectors K9711, K9740, K8121 and K9776 on a variety of air exercises and practice landings. On June 7th, he flew a Lysander, L1312, for the first time, supervised by an experienced pilot, Flying Officer Longley. During the next two days, Vokes flew Lysanders L6858 and L6870 on four more sorties, *"pinpointing ponds, photography, and vertical pinpoints"*. The course was then disbanded, in view of the serious calls being made on Fighter Command, and its pilots went on to 5 OTU and became fighter pilots. Those few entries, however, provide us with an idea of the type of flying that Pilot Officer Rafter would also have undertaken whilst at Old Sarum.

Rafter next reported to RAF Station Andover on April 26th, 1940, for flying duties, remaining there engaged on supply flying until May 7th, when he joined 225 Squadron at Odiham in Hampshire.

225 Squadron was originally formed at Alimini on April 1st, 1918, and thereafter operated the Sopwith 1 Strutter, Hamble Baby Convert and Sopwith Camel until being disbanded on December 18th, 1918. Re-formed on October 9th, 1939, at Odiham, the squadron was equipped with Lysanders and became an army co-operation unit. When Pilot Officers Rafter, McCandlish, Tuppin and Walsh together reported for duty from Andover, 225 Squadron's strength was twenty-four officers and three hundred and fifteen airmen. On June 10th, 225 moved to Old Sarum, from where its pilots conducted much dawn and dusk flying at what was the time of the Dunkirk evacuation. Pilot Officer Rafter's first flight was made on June 27th, 1940, in Lysander N1315, between 2030 and 2230 hrs in company with LAC Howes. The sortie was a *"coastal recco"* of St Alban's Head and Selsey Bill which was uneventful other than a destroyer being sighted six miles south of Ventnor and which gave no reply upon being challenged. No enemy movement was seen. On July 1st, 1940, the squadron moved to Tilshead. During that month Rafter flew a further six similar sorties with LACs Howes and Parr, all either dawn or dusk patrols and similarly uneventful. In August, Rafter and Howes flew just two sorties, on 12th and

13th, a *"photo recco"* and a *"coastal recco"*. It is perhaps worth noting that Pilot Officer Rafter's air gunner and observer was a Leading Aircraftman. Later in the war all aircrew were automatically given at least the non-commissioned rank of Sergeant.

By August 1940 the skies of Britain were being furiously defended by Fighter Command who were suffering such grievous losses that the provision of sufficient replacements went beyond the capability of the OTUs. Fighter Command appealed to other Commands, and even the Fleet Air Arm, for volunteers to become fighter pilots. For many young men like Robin Rafter, languishing in the comparative boredom of army co-operation and bomber squadrons, often flying types that barely captured the imagination, this exciting opportunity to fly Spitfires or Hurricanes into battle was their salvation. On August 22nd, 1940, Flying Officer Ian Hallam and Pilot Officers Rafter and Sanders left 225 Squadron and reported to 7 OTU, there joining No 6 Course comprising thirty-four officers, four NCOs, six American officers and three pupils having been re-coursed due to periods of hospitalisation caused by flying accidents.

By coincidence, in October 1987, a probationary police constable, Martin Hallam, who had recently left the army upon completion of a long period of service, arrived to work with me at Malvern Police Station. His father was none other than Ian Hallam. Squadron Leader Hallam's flying log books indicate that he joined the RAF in 1937, commencing his flying training at Reading Civilian Training School. Later, having also attended the School of Army Cooperation at Old Sarum, he joined No 2 Army Cooperation Squadron at Hawkinge on April 30th, 1938, flying Lysanders. On October 6th, 1939, Pilot Officer Hallam moved with his unit to France, returning to England in May 1940 during the Blitzkrieg. In July 1940 he joined the Photographic Reconnaissance Unit based at Heston, where he flew a Spitfire, R9309, for the first time. During the next few weeks Flying Officer Hallam flew Spitfires, Harvards, Hornet Moths, a Wellington and a Hudson on a variety of air experience gaining exercises. On August 7th, 1940, however, he returned to flying Lysanders with 225 Squadron at Tilshead. There he would have met Pilot Officer Rafter, compared with whom Flying Officer Hallam was a very experienced pilot indeed with over 500 hours flying time on single-engined aircraft. Just one week later, as we have seen, the pair reported to Hawarden for operational training on Spitfires. Hallam's log book would no doubt, therefore, be a mirror image of Rafter's, had the latter document survived, so it is interesting to examine the entries in detail. Between August 23rd and 29th, 1940, Flying Officer Hallam made fourteen Spitfire flights and two in a Miles Master. Spitfire training flights included local familiarisation, formation flying, aerobatics, map-reading, homing practice, No 1 and 5 attacks, and firing guns into the sea. Spitfires flown were K9942, P9361, P1071, P9391, P3238, P9501, P9445, P9386 and L1018. By the end of the course he had accumulated just fifteen hours flying time on Spitfires, but was more fortunate than Pilot Officer Rafter as he had already flown the type for six hours at Heston. After leaving Hawarden, Hallam and Rafter went their separate ways, Flying Officer Hallam being posted to fly Spitfires with 610 Squadron at Acklington, making his first flight on September 5th, in L1037, "DW-D". Based in the north of England at that time, the squadron was not heavily engaged with the enemy, so Hallam was fortunate in receiving a further 21.05 Spitfire flying hours before himself being posted to 222 Squadron at Hornchurch on October 1st. By the time he damaged an Me 109 seventeen days later, during his first clash with the Luftwaffe, Hallam had recorded in his log book a total of 78 hours on Spitfires, making him somewhat more fortunate than Pilot Officer Rafter, who, as we shall see, met the enemy for the first time during a ferocious dogfight with probably just fifteen such hours. At the end of the Battle of Britain, Hallam was posted to 73 Squadron, with whom he forced landed Hurricane V6725 near Redhill on November 3rd, 1940, due to poor visibility, and later also flew Hurricanes with 151 Squadron. In December 1940 he was promoted to Flight Lieutenant and briefly became a Flight Commander with 303 (Polish) Squadron, also flying Hurricanes, until commencing a period of instructing at various locations from the start of 1941. In July 1942, however, he returned to operational flying and was posted to 208 Tactical Reconnaissance Squadron in the Western Desert. On August 24th, 1942, whilst acting as *"weaver"* to the squadron, Flight Lieutenant Hallam was shot down in Hurricane BV156 and taken prisoner by the Germans. His period of captivity was also punctuated by excitement, due to his later involvement with the famous *"Wooden Horse"* prisoner of war camp escape. After the war Hallam remained in the RAF, again serving as a flying instructor, before taking command of the Aberdeen University Air Squadron on September 5th, 1950. Sadly on May 7th, 1952, he was killed as the result of a flying accident whilst instructing a pupil in Chipmunk WB724.

Flying Officer Ian Hallam. Whilst in Stalag Luft III, Hallam was actually leader of the room which planned the famous "Wooden Horse" *escape and is referred to in both the book and film of that name.*

Mr Martin Hallam.

Returning to the 1940 operational training process, we have already seen in previous chapters how hard pushed the OTUs were at this time to cope with the demands made upon them, and how courses had been reduced from four to two weeks. In reality pilots were passed out as and when considered fit, usually between ten days and three weeks, during which time they received, if they were lucky, between ten and twenty hours flying. The OTU therefore was merely only able to provide conversion experience to operational type. Incredible though it may seem, at OTU some lucky pilots were able to practise firing their guns into the sea, as proved by Ian Hallam's log book when he flew such a sortie of forty minutes duration in Spitfire P9386 on August 27th, 1940, but no air-to-air practice firing was conducted at this time. Many new pilots therefore only fired their guns for the first time with an enemy aircraft in their sights, and for all such an occasion would be the first experience of air-to-air shooting.

On Saturday, August 31st, 1940, Fighter Command lost thirty-nine pilots killed in action. On that day, at the height of Luftwaffe attacks on fighter airfields, Flying Officer BR MacNamara, also a former army co-operation pilot, and Pilot Officers FJ MacPhail and WPH Rafter reported for flying duties with 603 *"City of Edinburgh"* Squadron at Hornchurch, a front-line station in Essex.

603 Squadron was an Auxiliary Air Force unit whose pre-war pilots had civilian occupations and had flown for pleasure at weekends. Formed on October 14th, 1925, at Turnhouse near Edinburgh, the squadron flew the DH 9A, Wapiti, Hart, Hind and Gladiator biplanes before being equipped with the Supermarine Spitfire Mk Ia in September 1939, during which month the unit was also called to full-time service. 603 Squadron was soon deployed as a defensive facility to the north of Scotland, 'A' flight operating from Dyce to afford the RN some protection, and 'B' flight at Montrose to protect the FTS there against enemy attack. The squadron was therefore responsible for the great stretch of coastline between the Firth of Tay and Aberdeen. However, as the nearest Luftwaffe units were in Denmark and Norway, it was hoped that the long flight over the sea would mean that attacks in this area, although frequent, would not be heavy.

When Pilot Officer Richard Hillary, an Oxford undergraduate, joined the squadron in June 1940, 'B' flight and Red Section's commander was Flight Lieutenant *"Rusty"* Rushmer. Flying Officer Laurie Cunningham led Blue Section. Then there were Pilot Officers *"Ras"* Berry, *"Bubble"* Waterson, Boulter, and *"Broody"* Benson, the latter apparently possessed of but one ambition, *"to shoot down Huns, more Huns, and then still more Huns!"*. Another pilot, Don MacDonald, had an elder brother with the squadron, with 'A' flight, and twenty-three year old *"Pip"* Cardell, the most recent addition to the squadron prior to Hillary's arrival, was *"still bewildered, excited and a little lost"*. The flight also had two pilots from overseas, Flying Officer Brian Carbury, a New Zealander, and Pilot Officer *"Stapme"* Stapleton from South Africa.

Having destroyed a number of, largely, lone bombers unprotected by fighters, 603 Squadron's chance to join the Battle of Britain proper was soon to come. On August 20th, both flights were ordered back to Turnhouse. The pilots knew that such a move could only mean one thing, their being called upon to replace a front-line squadron in 11 Group. Nineteen year old *"Broody"* Benson was beside himself with excitement, hopping up and down like a madman shouting *"Now we'll show the bastards!"*

Flying Officer Richard Hillary drawn by Eric Kennington shortly before the disfigured pilot's death in a flying accident.

RAF Museum.

During their time at Montrose, 'B' flight's Pilot Officers Waterson, Stapleton and Hillary had formed a close affection for the children of Tarfside, a tiny hamlet near Invermark. News of the children soon spread, and no three Spitfires would return from a practice flight without first sweeping in low across the bed of the valley where the children would wave and shout in ecstasy. As Flight Lieutenant Rushmer led his entire flight of six Spitfires off from Montrose towards Turnhouse, he called his pilots on the R/T: *"Once more, boys"*, and the two sections of three banked to starboard, heading for the mountains. Even the children had heard the news, and as the flight went into line astern and dived one by one over the valley, they neither moved nor shouted. On the road, in white rocks, they had spelt out two words: *"Good Luck"*. Of the twenty-four pilots who eventually flew from Turnhouse to Hornchurch only eight would survive.

Squadron Leader *"Uncle"* George Denholm led 603 Squadron to Hornchurch on August 27th, 1940. In Scotland the squadron had been accustomed to just one section of three pilots being at readiness, ie available for immediate take off; at Hornchurch they were dismayed to find three squadrons at such a state. With the Luftwaffe intensifying attacks on Fighter Command's airfields, 603 Squadron were scrambled shortly after arriving. By the end of that day, Flight Lieutenant Cunningham, Pilot Officers Don MacDonald and Noel *"Broody"* Benson, the teenager who was *"going to show 'em"*, were all dead. In response, Squadron Leader Denholm destroyed an Me 109, and Flying Officer Waterston probably destroyed another. Denholm's victim on that occasion was a machine of I/JG54 engaged on a *"Freie Hunt"*. The pilot, Feldwebel Schöttle, was captured unhurt at 7.15 pm.

There was no respite the following day. During the first sortie, Flying Officer Boulter destroyed an Me 109, as did Pilot Officer Stapleton who also claimed a *"probable"*. Pilot Officers Hillary and Read also claimed Me 109s probably destroyed. Flight Lieutenant Rushmer, however, was shot down and forced landed slightly wounded at Bossingham. During the second, and final sortie, of the day, Flying Officer Carbury, Flying Officer Pinckney and Pilot Officer Hillary each destroyed an Me 109, whilst Sergeant Stokoe and Pilot Officer Stapleton probably destroyed one each. Flying Officer Pinckney, however, was also shot down but safely baled out. Pilot Officer Richard Hillary, however, became separated from his squadron and instead, although not in any radio contact, became attached to Squadron Leader Peter Townsend's 85 Squadron, criss-crossing the sky at the rear of the Hurricanes and searching for the enemy. Townsend, a professional airman and experienced combat pilot, was unimpressed with Hillary's behaviour. With his Hurricanes in open, or search, line astern formation, covered by a section of three *"tail-end Charlies"*, Hillary's Spitfire, the frontal view of which was not dissimilar to an Me 109, caused the Hurricane pilots momentary confusion in identifying an enemy attack when it came over Winchelsea. Immediately, Hillary's Spitfire, L1021, *"XT-M"*, was hit and he forced landed near Lympne. In 1989, Peter Townsend explained to me that *"Hillary might have known better. We lost Flight Lieutenant Hamilton, a Canadian and a super Flight Commander, purely because the Me 109s were identified a fraction of a second too late"*. In his excellent book, *"The Last Enemy"*, Hillary later described the incident as *"the most amusing though painful experience"*.

At this time, half a dozen of 603 Squadron's pilots would actually sleep in their dispersal hut so as to be ready for any surprise dawn attack. This entailed their being up by four-thirty, and having their Spitfires warmed up by 5 am. The first attack usually came at breakfast-time, and from then on until about 8 o'clock at night the squadron was almost continuously in the air. Baked beans, bacon and eggs were sent over from the mess and the pilots ate when they could.

On August 30th, 603 Squadron flew three sorties. During the first, between 1035-1137 hrs, in combat over Deal, Pilot Officer *"Black"* Morton claimed one Me 110 probably destroyed, and a second damaged. Squadron Leader Denholm, however, was forced to bale out of Spitfire L1067, "XT-D", which he had named "Blue Peter" after the famous racehorse of the time. The next sortie was flown between 1555-1712 hrs and the enemy was engaged over Canterbury. Flying Officers Carbury and Waterston each destroyed an Me 109, and Sergeant Sarre, who claimed one as probably destroyed, was himself shot down but baled out.

On Saturday, August 31st, 1940, the day that Pilot Officer Rafter reported to Hornchurch for flying duties with 603 Squadron, the Luftwaffe heavily bombed the airfields of Detling, Eastchurch, and Croydon, and attacked the vitally important sector stations of Hornchurch and Biggin Hill twice. Some of those airfields were subsequently rendered close to unserviceability. The Hornchurch Station Operations Record Book relates that:-

"Mass raids continued to be made against our aerodromes, again starting early in the morning. The first two attacks were delivered at 0830 and 1030 respectively and were directed at Biggin Hill, Eastchurch and Debden. The third attack was delivered at Hornchurch, and although our squadrons engaged, they were unable to break the enemy bomber formation, and about thirty Dorniers dropped some one hundred bombs across the airfield. Damage, however, was slight, although a bomb fell on the new Airmens' Mess which was almost completed. The only vital damage, however, was to a power cable, which was cut. The emergency power equipment was brought into operation until repair was effected. Three men were killed and eleven wounded. 54 Squadron attempted to take off during the attack and ran through the bombs. Three aircraft were destroyed, one being blown from the middle of the landing field to outside the boundary, but all three pilots miraculously escaped with only slight injuries.

"The fourth attack of the day was also directed at Hornchurch, and once again, despite strong fighter opposition and AA fire, the bombers penetrated our defences. This time, however, their aim was most inaccurate, and the line of bombs fell from then towards the edge of the aerodrome. Two Spitfires parked near the edge of the aerodrome were written off, and one airman was killed. Otherwise, apart from the damage to dispersal pens, the perimeter track, and the aerodrome surface, the raid was abortive, and the aerodrome remained serviceable. Our squadrons, which had a very heavy day, accounted for no less than nineteen of the enemy and a further seven probably destroyed. 603 Squadron alone were responsible for the destruction of fourteen enemy aircraft. Although we lost a total of nine aircraft, either in combat or on the ground, only one pilot was lost."

On that day of particularly bitter fighting, 603 Squadron were in action four times. By the end of the day, the squadron had actually claimed a further twelve Me 109s destroyed, and a Do 17, an Me 109 probably destroyed and one more damaged. The squadron suffered no losses itself until the day's final sortie. Then,

The Battle of the Airfields; a 222 Squadron Spitfire lies wrecked at Hornchurch following a raid on September 1st, 1940.

Mr Joe Crawshaw.

at 6.20 pm over the Thames, Pilot Officer *"Sheep"* Gilroy was shot down in Spitfire X4271, *"XT-N"*, but safely baled out. His doomed aircraft crashed into 14 Hereford Road, Wanstead, but fortunately only a dog was killed. At 6.30 pm, Flying Officer Waterston was killed in X4273, *"XT-K"*, when shot down by an Me 109 of I/JG3 over Woolwich. At the same time, Flying Officer Brian Carbury was slightly wounded when the compressed air system of his Spitfire, R6835, *"XT-W"*, was hit by 20 mm ammunition fired by an Me 109. Fortunately he was able to return to base safely. The Me 109 claimed by Flying Officer Carbury was also attacked by Flight Lieutenant Denys Gillam of 616 Squadron. The German fighter was engaged on a *"Freie Hunt"* and was flown by Oberleutnant Eckhart Priebe, Staffelkapitän of 2/JG77. Priebe baled out and landed near the village of Elham, where he was promptly captured. Preibe was well educated and the son of a famous churchman. Doubtless previously destined for high office in the Luftwaffe, having been a member of the elite *"Goering Kadetten"*, veteran of the Spanish Civil War and personal aide of Feldmarschall Milch, his career and war ended abruptly that summer's day, his immediate destiny being Grizedale Hall prison camp in the Lake District.

On September 1st, 1940, 603 Squadron were in action once, between 1545-1725 hrs. Sergeant Stokoe destroyed an Me 109 of III/JG53, but himself baled out wounded. Pilot Officer "Pip" Cardell, "bewildered and lost" in June 1940 but made a veteran during the last three days of fighting, forced landed L1020, "XT-L". The following day yet again dawned fine, the weather therefore offering no respite to the hard pressed defenders. 603 Squadron went up three times that day. The first raid was early, and between 0728-0830 hrs 603 was in action. Three more Me 109s were destroyed, but Sergeant Jack Stokoe, who damaged an Me 110, had the cockpit hood of X4250, "XT-X", shattered in combat over Hawkinge but managed to return to Hornchurch. During the next sortie, the squadron claimed two Me 109s destroyed, one Do 17 destroyed, and two Me 109s damaged for no loss. The last sortie was flown between 1604 and 1820 hrs. Pilot Officer Hillary claimed an Me 109 probable, as did Pilot Officer Dudley Stewart-Clark who was making his first flight with the squadron at Hornchurch since having returned from leave. At 1725 hrs, Sergeant Stokoe was shot down in flames over Maidstone in Spitfire N3056, "XT-B". Fortunately he baled out, and was later able to record in his log book that before having done so he had damaged two Ju 88 bombers.

During those first few days in 11 Group, 603 Squadron had to learn quickly. The pilots soon determined not to allow themselves to be "bounced" from above. Squadron Leader Denholm would fly on a reciprocal of the course provided by the ground controller, until at 15,000' when the squadron would fly back, climbing all the time. Flying in such a fashion the Spitfire pilots usually saw the enemy striking inland below them, and were then in a perfect position to deliver an attack. A very sensible system was also devised whereby two pilots would always fly together for mutual protection. The Spitfire and Hurricane squadrons, however, were always so outnumbered that it was virtually impossible for them to deliver any more than one concentrated attack as a squadron. The formation then split up, the sky immediately becoming a spider's web of intricate vapour trails. Group Captain Denholm remembers that "the squadron would then come home individually, or in ones and twos at intervals of about two minutes". As Commanding Officer, in addition to leading the squadron, which he did virtually without exception on every sortie throughout the Battle of Britain, and performing the various administrative duties, Denholm also had to check who was missing after each action. He usually did this an hour after the squadron had landed. Sometimes a telephone call would be received from a pilot who had perhaps forced landed elsewhere, or from a recovery team announcing the identity of a crashed aircraft and pilot. Richard Hillary later wrote that "at that time, the losing of pilots was somehow extremely impersonal; nobody, I think, felt any great emotion as there simply wasn't time for it".

Hornchurch, September 1st, 1940, showing Spitfires of both 222 and 603 Squadrons. The 603 Squadron machine "XT-M" is that in which Pilot Officer Richard Hillary was shot down two days later. Note the steam roller in the background repairing damage to the runway caused during a recent raid.

Mr Joe Crawshaw.

Tuesday, September 3rd, 1940, saw the first anniversary of war being declared. 603 Squadron's first sortie took place between 0915-1030 hrs. The main attack of the day was the first, which commenced formating behind the Pas de Calais at 0830 hrs. Raid 45, comprising 54 Dornier bombers, forged up the Thames Estuary at 20,000' escorted by eighty Me 110s. By 0940 hrs sixteen RAF fighter squadrons - one hundred and twenty-two Spitfires and Hurricanes - had been ordered into the air to patrol Essex and Kent. The ground controllers were unsure as to whether the raid would be continuing the assault of Kent's airfields, turn north into Essex, or continue on its course towards London. At 0945 the enemy turned northwards, slightly west of Southend, and headed towards the airfield at North Weald. As more fighters scrambled from the surrounding airfields, the bombers attacked their target successfully from 15,000' causing extensive damage. It was only as the raiders turned for home that the defenders obtained the necessary altitude and attacked. 603 Squadron's eight Spitfires joined in the mêlée with six Hurricane squadrons. An enormous dogfight then developed above the Thames Estuary and Channel. Pilot Officer Richard Hillary later wrote:-

"At about 12,000' we came up through the clouds; I looked down and saw them spread out below me like layers of whipped cream. The sun was brilliant and it made it difficult to see the next plane when turning. I was peering anxiously ahead, for the controller had warned us that at least fifty enemy fighters were approaching very high. When we sighted them, nobody shouted, as I think that we all saw them at the same

moment. They must have been 500 to 1,000' above us and coming straight on like a swarm of locusts. I remember cursing and going automatically into line astern; the next moment we were in among them and it was every man for himself. As soon as they saw us they spread out and dived, and the next ten minutes was a blur of twisting machines and tracer bullets. One Me 109 went down in a sheet of flame on my right, and a Spitfire hurtled past in a half roll; I was weaving and turning in a desperate attempt to gain height, with the machine literally hanging on the airscrew. Then, just below me and to my left, I saw what I had been praying for - a Messerschmitt climbing and away from the sun. I closed in to 200 yards and from slightly to one side gave him a two-second burst. Fabric ripped off the wing and black smoke poured from the engine, but he did not go down. Like a fool, I did not break away, but put in a three-second burst. Red flames shot upwards and he spiralled out of sight".

At that moment, hurrying to the assistance of his "kamerad", Hillary's Spitfire filled the Revi gunsight of Hauptmann Erich Bode, Kommandeur of II/JG26 "Schlageter" based at St Inglevert. The German thumbed the cannon button on his joystick, simultaneously squeezing the machine-gun trigger also thereon, and in an instant Hillary became, in fighter pilots' parlance, a "flamer":-

"At that moment I felt a terrific explosion which knocked the control column from my hand, and the whole machine quivered like a stricken animal. In a second, the cockpit was a mass of flames; instinctively I reached up to open the hood. It would not move. I tore off my straps and managed to force it back; but this took time, and when I dropped back in the seat and reached for the stick in an effort to turn the plane on its back, the heat was so intense that I could feel myself going. I remember a second of sharp agony, remember thinking 'So this is it!' and putting both hands to my eyes. Then I passed out."

Hillary was miraculously thrown clear of his blazing Spitfire and, despite being horrendously burned, managed to deploy his parachute. He drifted down and landed in the Channel, being rescued by the Margate lifeboat two hours later. Under the care of the famous surgeon Sir Archibald McIndoe, Hillary became one of the "Guinea Pigs" at East Grinstead's Burns Unit. Tragically his recovery and suffering was for nothing; on January 8th, 1943, whilst training to become a night fighter pilot, his Blenheim crashed and the gallant, disfigured, Richard Hillary was killed.

Minutes after despatching Pilot Officer Hillary from the fight, Bode next caught Pilot Officer Dudley Stewart-Clark in X4185, "XT-Z". Seconds later that Spitfire pilot too was descending seawards under his parachute. Stewart-Clark was somewhat more fortunate than Hillary as he was not burned, but was wounded and later admitted to Chelmsford Hospital. He later returned to operational flying but was eventually killed when a Flight Commander with 72 Squadron in 1941. Erich Bode had been a fighter pilot in the Rekalamestaffel Mittleldeutschland in 1934, which was even before the *"official"* formation of the Luftwaffe. It is possible that he went to Spain, flying in the Spanish Civil War with the Legion Kondor, and later became a Staffeloffizier in 4/JG26 before the Second World War. On July 25th, 1940, he succeeded Karl Ebbighausen as Kapitän of the 4th Staffel, and later succeeded Hauptmann Ebbighausen as Kommandeur of the Second Gruppe upon the latter's death in action on August 16th. Hillary and Stewart-Clark were Hauptmann Bode's first kills, and he made his third and last three days later. On October 3rd, 1940, Bode lost his command when the Geschwader Kommodore, Major Adolf Galland, replaced many of the older, pre-war officers who had been relatively unsuccessful. Bode did not receive another combat command and is believed to have survived the war.

Pilot Officer Dudley Stewart-Clark at the Edinburgh Races, early 1940.

Group Captain G.L. Denholm.

On September 4th, 603 Squadron was in action again, over Canterbury. Sergeant Sarre forced landed near Ashford in X4263 due to engine failure, but the squadron was otherwise unscathed.

Pilot Officer Rafter had yet to fly with 603 Squadron, and during the last four days since his arrival at Hornchurch on August 31st, 1940, he must have enviously watched the Spitfires taking off to assail the enemy, and later anxiously counted them back in, their wings stained with the soot from gunsmoke. He must have noticed too the frequently missing faces. Air Vice-Marshal Harry Hogan commanded 501 Squadron throughout the Battle of Britain, and when I interviewed him at his Worcestershire home in 1989, he told me *"some of our Hurricane squadron's replacement pilots were straight from OTU, and these we tried to get into the air as soon as possible to provide a little extra experience, but we were just too tired to give them any dogfighting practice at all. They were all very green, youngsters who were completely bewildered and lost in action".*

Another tale from a Hurricane squadron was of two replacement pilots who had arrived together in a car, their luggage squeezed within. They went into action virtually immediately, but failed to return, their luggage still in the vehicle, unpacked. It seems appalling now, from the safe vantage point of over fifty years hence, to send such inexperienced young pilots into action against such a determined foe who had not only studied his craft for many years, but had already used his experience to devastating effect in the aerial battlefields of Spain, Poland, Norway, Denmark, Holland, Belgium, Luxembourg and France. But desperate indeed was our Finest Hour.

Pilot Officer Rafter's first flight with 603 Squadron was operational, and occurred on Thursday, 5th September, 1940. At 0934 hrs, Squadron Leader Denholm led twelve Spitfires off from Hornchurch, a formation which included all three new boys, MacNamara and MacPhail in addition to Rafter. The German tactics on that day were an enigma to Air Vice-Marshal Park and his controllers. Two major attacks were launched by the enemy which crossed the coast at Dungeness simultaneously at 0945 hrs and set a north-westerly course. At that point the raiders were attacked by the Hurricanes of 501 Squadron which had taken off from Gravesend at 0910 hrs. The RAF pilots had sighted the oncoming enemy whilst patrolling between Canterbury and the coast. 501 later reported having seen thirty Dornier 17 bombers escorted by seventy Me 109s at 20,000'. It was the latter that the Hurricanes engaged. As the two formations of bombers and their fighter escort neared Maidstone, each separated into a number of small forces whose progress the Observer Corps found impossible to plot. One raid headed for Biggin Hill, and 6,000' above the bombers weaved their fighter escort, thirty Me 109s of II/JG3 "*Udet*". The Gruppe was led by its Kommandeur, Hauptmann Erich von Selle. Flying in his Stabschwarm were his two staff officers, Leutnant Heinrich Sanneman, the Technical Officer, and Oberleutnant Franz von Werra, the adjutant. Suddenly a warning shout came over the Germans' radio: "*Achtung! Achtung! Spitfeur!*", as 41 Squadron, for once enjoying the advantage of height over the enemy, "*bounced*" the Me 109s. Von Selle took control; "*Stella Leader to everybody. Keep formation. Wait! Stella Leader to Fifth and Sixth Staffeln: Stay put and watch out! Fourth - attack! Horrido!*" Von Selle and the Stabschwarm dived to port, the Fourth Staffel following. Battle had been joined.

41 Squadron had taken off from Hornchurch at 0915 hrs with orders to patrol Canterbury. However, when the enemy had crossed the coast at Dungeness and headed north-west, the squadron was vectored south. The Spitfires were flying high, at 27,000', and were above the German fighter escort, through which one flight crashed to attack the bombers between Maidstone and Romney. Several

of the Spitfire pilots later made combat claims, Flight Lieutenant Ryder an Me 109 damaged, Pilot Officer Bennions reporting having hit an Me 109 which he last saw *"streaming glycol and going down 8 miles south of Maidstone"*, and Sergeant Carr-Lewty whose victim crashed into a wood south-east of Canterbury. Flight Lieutenant Webster hit two Me 109s, one in the engine and one which burst into flames, but neither were seen to crash. He then attacked another Me 109 which rolled over and went in near Maidstone. Flying Officer Boyle set an Me 109 on fire that was attacking two of his comrades. That machine was possibly an Me 109 of 1/JG52 which crashed at Bethersden killing the pilot, Unteroffizier Kind. Squadron Leader Hood and Pilot Officer Wallens managed to get through to the bombers and both damaged Do 17s.

603 Squadron engaged the enemy formation seconds after 41 Squadron. Flight Lieutenant Ryder of 41 later reported having seen *"XT"* coded Spitfires during the combat. For Pilot Officer Rafter, who had previously experienced a handful of training flights and dull Lysander reconnaissance flights, the sight of a hundred fighters, whirling, twisting and turning, must have been incredible, stacatto radio transmissions punctuating the visual effect: *"Look out, behind you!"*, *"Jump, get out!"* *"Tally Ho!"*. As a schoolboy of seven I watched a similar scene in the *"Battle of Britain"* film with my heart in my mouth, but the real thing must have been terrifying. Flung into the fray, in Spitfire X4264, *"XT-R"*, Rafter lasted but matter of seconds after the squadron broke up. He later wrote to his mother from West Kent General Hospital:-

"I have received both your letters and thank you very much for them, but really you must not show quite so much worry about me as I came off very fortunately. But may be I had better tell you the whole story to satisfy your 'feminine curiosity'.

"Well, I was over Kent at a little over 25,000' on a lovely morning of the 5th September when I sighted a huge formation of Jerries. I very nearly shot a Spitfire down by mistake, but then saw on my starboard side, underneath me, an Me 109. I got all fixed and started my dive on to the Me 109 and was nearing it when I saw in my mirror a couple of Me 109s on my tail. Well, I took what evasive action I could, but found two a bit of a problem. I started to get away from them when my tail must have been damaged as all movement on the control column was of no avail, thus putting my machine out of control so far as I was concerned. Well, by this time I had a little piece of shrapnel in my leg, and probably owe my life to the fact that my machine was out of control as the Jerries evidently found difficulty in getting their sights on me as my machine was going all over the place. Luckily I was very high up and it then occurred to me to bale out. My oxygen tube had already become detached, but I had great difficulty in undoing the pin of my harness to loosen myself out of my seat. I eventually got the pin out, but could not get out of the aircraft. By this time the

Jerries had ceased firing at me, but I had no idea where I was over. The next part of my experience was rather a miracle. The machine's nose dropped violently thus having the effect of throwing me forward, the force so great that I went through the canopy, thus unknowingly injuring my head. You can't imagine my surprise. I was then at about 15,000' and floating about in the air rather like a cork. You will understand why when I explain that instead of diving at 400 mph, I had rapidly slowed down to about 180 mph as the human body never falls faster, that being the 'terminal velocity'. I then felt so light I had to look to ensure that I was wearing a parachute. Luckily I had given it a slight inspection that morning. I pulled the cord and the 'chute opened up and I breathed once more.

"Now the most terrifying experience happened, I floated down right through the aerial battle that was taking place. I came through it without a scratch, but then I noticed an Me 109 coming towards me, and you've no idea what a damned fool you feel suspended in mid-air with an enemy fighter buzzing around you.

"Well he never fired at me, as a Spitfire came along and drove him off; whether he would have done or not cannot be said. Next worry was where I was going to land as there were a lot of trees near. I avoided them and landed in a nice field. My Spitfire, which was new, crashed in a ploughed field some way away. The LDV accosted me with a shotgun as I was wearing my RAF battledress which must have confused them a bit. I was treated by a local 1st Aid post then taken to hospital.

"That afternoon they performed a slight operation stitching up the back of my head, which had a slight cut, and my right cheek, which is invisible now. They also took the piece of shrapnel from my right leg which entailed a rather deep incision, but I am okay now and had all of my stitches out yesterday. I have been up and about for the last three days. I am coming out at the end of this week and will soon be back to get my own back on the Jerries. There is a saying that you are not a fighter pilot until you have been shot down once. Well, you have nothing more to fret about and you've heard everything there was, and see how simple it all was, and how well I was cared for? I'm still as good as new, with no facial disfigurement. Might get a few days leave to see you. You must remember I got off lightly and many more have received worse than me."

I find that letter not only a first class account of the traumatic experience of having been shot down and wounded, but, having read similar testimonies by many other Battle of Britain pilots, it so typically exemplifies the tremendous spirit of the time, as if mother had no more to worry about than as if the writer were in the school team!

But it is at this juncture, thanks in part to Robin Rafter's letter home, that the story gets really interesting and makes a significant contribution to our knowledge of that particular action and an infamous German participant.

Two 603 Squadron pilots made claims after the action. Pilot Officer Morton reported that at 0950 hrs, south of the Thames:-

"*I was last to attack a formation of Do 17s and Me 109s at 20-25,000'. I was unable to engage the bombers so became engaged with the Me 109s. I attacked one from the port quarter and saw incendiary bullets striking the enemy aircraft which continued turning and losing height gently. I was unable to follow it*".

Pilot Officer Stapleton reported that at the same time he was also patrolling with the squadron at 20,000' near Biggin Hill:-

"*I was diving to attack them (the bombers) when I was engaged by two Me 109s. When I fired at the first one I noticed glycol coming from his radiator. I did a No 2 attack and as I fired I was hit by bullets from another Me 109. I broke off downwards and continued my dive. At 6,000' I saw a single-engined machine diving vertically with no tail unit. I looked up and saw a parachutist coming down circled by an Me 109. I attacked him (the Me 109) from the low quarter, he dived vertically towards the ground and flattened out at ground level. I then did a series of beam attacks from both sides, and the enemy aircraft turned into my attacks. He finally forced landed. He tried to set his radio on fire by taking off his jacket and setting fire to it and putting it into the cockpit. He was prevented by the LDV*".

I think it reasonable to assume that Stapleton went to Pilot Officer Rafter's assistance. This assumption is supported by the following facts, bearing in mind that the two pilots' written accounts were made totally independently and with each even unaware of the other's identity:-

1. In Rafter's letter, he mentions that his "*tail must have been damaged*" in the attack on his Spitfire by two Me 109s. His Spitfire spun out of control, but later plunged vertically, nose down, an attitude and sequence of events conducive to a damaged tail unit becoming detached from the aircraft. The single-engined fighter seen in a similar attitude by Pilot Officer Stapleton "*had no tail unit*".

2. Rafter states that an Me 109 came towards him which was driven off by a Spitfire. Stapleton reports having attacked an Me 109 that was behaving in an identical manner towards a parachutist and in the immediate vicinity of the tail-less fighter.

3. Rafter's Spitfire crashed at Marden in Kent, some twenty-four miles south-east of Biggin Hill. Three Me 109s forced landed in England as a result of damage sustained during this action, one of 1/JG3 at Wichling, some thirty-two miles east of Biggin Hill, and another, of 3/JG3, at Aldington, sixteen miles south-east of Wichling. At Loves Farm, Winchet Hill, Marden, however, near to where Rafter's Spitfire crashed, <+- of Stab/II/JG3, forced landed at 10.10 am. The pilot was captured in circumstances identical to those described by Stapleton. He was Oberleutnant Franz von Werra, who I am sure requires no introduction other than that he became the only German prisoner taken in

England to escape from captivity, and later made famous by the 1950s book and film, "*The One That Got Away*". The fact that both Spitfire and Me 109 crashed at Marden is also a salient point.

This, I believe, is the first ever accurate sequence of events ever published regarding von Werra being shot down. In their book, "*The One That Got Away*", Burt and Leasor incorrectly credit von Werra to Flight Lieutenant Webster of 41 Squadron. His report describes an Me 109 which "*turned over and crashed near Maidstone*", some ten miles north of Marden. Such a description hardly describes an aircraft making a controlled forced landing.

Other authors credit von Werra to Flight Lieutenant Pat Hughes of 234 Squadron, but this claim is similarly erroneous as that unit attacked the enemy over the Isle of Sheppey, some considerable distance away from where this action was fought.

Another historian correctly credits von Werra to Stapleton, but claims that when his Me 109 was attacked by the 603 Squadron pilot, it had already been damaged when 41 Squadron first bounced the German fighters. He also claims that Pilot Officer Bennions' description of having hit an Me 109 which was then "*streaming glycol and going down eight miles south of Maidstone*" describes the initial attack on and damage to von Werra's machine. He does point out, quite rightly, that the combat was reported in the right area for Marden, and suggests that the report aptly describes a crippled Me 109 going down under control. He then goes on to suggest that Pilot Officer Stapleton later attacked the same, already damaged, Me 109 which he pursued until it forced landed at Marden. This particular author has consulted Stapleton's combat report, but strangely fails to make any mention of the fact that the Spitfire pilot intercepted the Me 109 whilst the latter was "*buzzing*" a parachutist. That fact is an essential element in analysing this incident, because surely no German fighter pilot in his right mind, in an aircraft supposedly so damaged, would either be capable of, or stupid enough to, "*buzz*" an enemy parachutist. His thoughts would surely revolve purely on safely forced landing his machine or a safe return to France. Another salient point is that neither Rafter or Stapleton make any reference to the fact that the Me 109 involved was damaged in any way prior to the latter's attack. I assume that this author has used "*The One That Got Away*" for reference, in which von Werra's aircraft is described as having been damaged in 41 Squadron's initial attack and pursued to a forced landing by an attacking Spitfire. The book was based upon a transcript of von Werra's dictation relating his experiences upon his repatriation to Germany having escaped from Canada. Oberleutnant Franz von Werra was publicity conscious, and, frankly, a liar, as will be later discussed. I do not consider that any information supplied by von Werra, particularly from a morale boosting propaganda exercise, can be considered as being in any way credible for our purposes. I say this because:-

1. When captured I am convinced that von Werra would have omitted to tell his interrogators that he was intercepted by a Spitfire whilst *"buzzing"* a British pilot descending by parachute, his motive perhaps being murder. Far better, therefore, to claim to have been shot down in a clean fight.

2. Even when returning to Germany, von Werra stuck to this story as no doubt not even the German public would find such openly ungallant behaviour by a national hero in any way acceptable.

3. The written testimonies of both Rafter and Stapleton clearly indicate a different sequence of events from those claimed by von Werra.

The correct sequence of events, I believe, was as follows:-

1. II/JG3 attacked from above by 41 Squadron between Ashford and Maidstone. German formation splits and battle is joined. It is interesting to also note here that both Stapleton and Rafter describe having been attacked by two Me 109s, two machines being the standard German tactical formation in combat of leader and wingman, the *"Rotte"*.

2. 603 and other squadrons join the huge dogfight between Maidstone and Biggin Hill.

3. Pilot Officer Rafter shot down by two Me 109s, loses control of machine when tail is damaged, is catapulted out of his Spitfire when tail subsequently becomes detached and aircraft plunges vertically. Whilst descending by parachute through the aerial battle taking place, is *"buzzed"* by an Me 109 in a fully serviceable condition and which is then driven off and attacked by Pilot Officer Stapleton.

4. Stapleton pursues the enemy fighter which forced lands and its pilot taken prisoner. Confirmed as Oberleutnant von Werra due to location, time, and description of events leading to capture after forced landing by both soldiers and Stapleton being identical.

The only supposition not supported by fact that I would be tempted to add to the debate is how, unless he shot him down, von Werra knew that Rafter was a British pilot, although this may have been due to Luftwaffe parachutes being a sky blue colour and the RAF's white silk. Oberleutnant von Werra is not believed to have claimed any RAF fighters shot down in the action, and judging by the sort of character he was, this author has no doubt that had he done so then the German would have made much of this fact in both his interrogation when made a prisoner and on the occasion of his heroic homecoming. To understand this viewpoint, it is necessary to examine von Werra himself in more detail.

Hauptmann Franz von Werra whilst Gruppenkommandeur of I/JG53.
Goss/Rauchbach Collection.

Of Swiss origin, François Gustave de Werra was born in Leuk in 1914, the eighth child of Leo de Werra who became bankrupt shortly after Franz's birth. François and his younger sister were then adopted by a family friend, Baroness Luisa von Haber, and went to live with her in Southern Germany. Baroness von Haber was married to Major Oswald Carl, a cavalry officer. Soon François became *"Franz"*, and *"de"* translated to *"von"*. The two children grew up looking upon the pair as their parents. From an early age Franz had displayed the tremendous vitality and restlessness that would remain his two most pronounced characteristics throughout his life. Relations between the Baroness and her husband became strained, and they eventually divorced. As the result of a domestic crisis, Franz later ran away to Hamburg, was taken on as a cabin boy by the Hamburg-Amerika Line, and just before he sailed sent his foster-mother a letter giving her the news.

When the ship docked in New Orleans, Franz was taken off and returned to Germany. He was welcomed back at school as a hero, and was called upon there to give an account of his experiences. It was his first taste of fame and popularity. Already convinced that he was special, von Werra received a rude awakening when he left school in 1932. There was mass unemployment and Germany was a social and political disaster in the wake of defeat in the Great War. In order to live, he had to take whatever casual work he could find. In 1933 Hitler and the Nazis came to power, and the following year conscription was introduced. In 1935 the formation of a new air force was undertaken, previously forbidden by the Versailles Peace Treaty of 1919. To Franz von Werra the picture of a swashbuckling life in the new air force, as portrayed by the propagandists, was a dazzling vision.

He volunteered as a private, but after two years' basic training was selected as an officer candidate and for flying duties. His character made him an obvious choice for training as a fighter pilot. Commissioned as a Leutnant in September 1938, von Werra was given his first posting - to JG3.

The ambitious von Werra soon realised that it was useless to wait patiently for his potential to be recognised, and instead tried to impress at every opportunity, even though in peacetime such occasions were rare. His mind's eye created a picture of what a young German fighter pilot should be like, and did his utmost to live up to that image. The young pilot saw himself as an exceptional human being, a highly romantic figure destined to play a part in life appropriate for such a character.

In June 1939, whilst performing low-level aerobatics over his unit's airfield at Königsberg, von Werra crashed in an accident reminiscent of that as a result of which Douglas Bader lost his legs. With spinal injuries, von Werra lay on his back in hospital for several weeks. Whilst in such a condition his commanding officer, Oberleutnant Wilhelm Balthasar, a national hero for a record-breaking flight and exceptional service during the Spanish Civil War, introduced Leutnant von Werra to a girl who gave him the will to overcome his injuries and whom he later married. The young Baron passed a medical board that enabled him to participate in the Polish campaign which commenced on September 1st, 1939. In the French campaign of 1940, von Werra destroyed two Potez bombers in one day, for which he received the Iron Cross II Class. Those victories were followed by the destruction of six British bombers, all of which were widely publicised by a war correspondent, Doktor Erhardt Eckert. Von Werra was becoming the national hero that he craved to be. When the Battle of Britain commenced in July 1940, the Germans, masters of half Europe, expected to cross the Channel and conquer the small island within a short space of time. Ambitious young pilots like Franz von Werra felt that time was running out for them to make their mark. On August 24th, 1940, von Werra appeared on the front cover of a popular German magazine posing by his Messerschmitt 109E with "Simba", the Staffel's pet lion cub. A few days later, the German High Command issued a statement rating Oberleutnant von Werra as their eighth top scoring fighter "ace" with eight victories.

On August 28th, 1940, JG3 flew a freelance fighter sweep between Dover and London. Von Werra returned late to his base in France, and his subsequent combat report accorded him recognition by the German press for *"the greatest fighter exploit of the war"*. Von Werra claimed to have become separated from his squadron over England during a dogfight, during which he had been attacked by a Spitfire which put his radio out of action. The German apparently turned the tables on the RAF fighter, attacked the Spitfire and shot it down. He then happened across an RAF aerodrome where he found six Hurricanes going in to land. Lowering his undercarriage, he joined the rear of the formation hoping to be mistaken for another Hurricane. The ruse worked, and von Werra shot down three of the British fighters in less minutes. He then performed a daring a single-handed attack on the airfield itself, in the process destroying five more aircraft and a petrol bowser. He then retired as his *"position became uncomfortable when a curtain of tracer bullets were drawn in front of me. I turned back and made off"*. When the valiant pilot returned late to his base at Grandvilliers, short of fuel and with a damaged aircraft, his kameraden had nearly given him up for lost. Fortunately a war correspondent was on hand, and a broadcast of Oberleutnant Franz von Werra's amazing feat of arms was immediately made to the German public. He had achieved his ambition, now being Baron von Werra, one of the greatest fighter pilots of all time !

Such an exploit should deservedly provide the exponent with recognition and respect from both sides of the Channel. If it were true, but von Werra's story was not. The RAF lost no aircraft in such circumstances on the day in question, and neither was any airfield so attacked. Having been captured on September 5th, 1940, von Werra was later interrogated at Cockfosters House by Squadron Leader Hawkes, during which time the fabricated claim was brought to his attention in a scathing interview. Any such exploit should also have been deserved of the highest gallantry award, in Germany that being the Ritterkreuz. Von Werra's problem was that no-one, obviously, had witnessed his daring. Unwittingly it was the British, however, who came to his rescue when they broadcast a sarcastic statement to the effect that Oberleutnant von Werra's capture insured that he would have no further opportunities to destroy their aerodromes. Across the Channel the statement was interpreted as confirmation of von Werra's incredible claim. His commanding officer, Hauptmann von Selle, therefore felt compelled to forward the Ritterkreuz recommendation, which he had previously retained, to the High Command. Oberleutnant von Werra consequently received a Knights Cross as the result of a totally bogus claim, and at a time when such decorations were highly prized.

Franz von Werra did, however, carve a name for himself in military history by becoming the only German prisoner of war captured in England to escape from captivity. Following several unsuccessful attempts to escape from camps in England, which included the genuinely daring and imaginative exploit of posing as a Dutch pilot and trying to steal a Hurricane from Hucknall, von Werra eventually escaped across the Canadian border to neutral America. Of course he returned to Germany and a welcome fit for such a national hero. On June 22nd, 1941, Germany invaded Russia, and soon the Luftwaffe fighter pilots' scores were increasing enormously. Von Werra, with thirteen victories, was being left behind, the top aces now having some sixty kills, and pilots that he had never even heard of were in the forties. He pulled strings and was soon in action over the Soviet Union as Kommandeur of I/JG53, the *Ace of Spades* Fighter Wing. By the time his unit was withdrawn in August, von Werra was credited with a supposed total of twenty-one victories. The following month his Gruppe was posted to Holland for coastal defence duties. Von Werra was prohibited from participating in operations over England in case he should once again fall into their hands as a prisoner. On the morning of October 25th, 1941, he led three Me109Fs on a coastal patrol. Twenty miles out from Vlissengen his engine failed, and *The One That Got Away* went down to a watery grave in the North Sea from which there was no escape.

So on September 5th, 1940, Pilot Officer Robin Rafter might have had a lucky escape from Oberleutnant Franz von Werra thanks to Pilot Officer Stapleton's intervention. Regarding the German tactics employed that day, it is difficult to understand what the enemy hoped to achieve by splitting into small forces once the English coast had been crossed. The ground controllers were confused at first as until reaching Maidstone the formations had headed north-west, towards London, before separating. It could be that the operation was a reconnaissance in force to test the reaction towards an attack on the capital, the decision to change strategy and commence bombing London two days later having surely already been made by the German High Command.

For Pilot Officer Rafter there followed a number of weeks recovering from his wounds. He was transferred from Maidstone Hospital to the Officers' Hospital at Torquay on October 2nd, 1940, and was eventually discharged from there on October 29th. After a week's leave, he returned to RAF Station Hornchurch on November 7th, although still categorised as *"non-effective, sick"*. On November 26th, he rejoined 603 Squadron, still at Hornchurch.

By that time the Battle of Britain was over, the onset of winter weather being unfavourable for a seaborne invasion, and the German bombers having been forced to attack en masse by night due to the losses inflicted upon them in daylight by the Few. After the war, Luftwaffe fighter *"ace"*, Adolf Galland, by that time General der Jagerflieger, was provided with a questionnaire by the

Pilot Officer "Robin" Rafter, top button undone in true fighter pilot style, photographed at home whilst attending his brother's funeral. His father, the late Sir Charles Rafter, who was the Chief Constable of Birmingham, looks on from the impressive canvas backdrop.
Mrs Elizabeth Barwell.

Senior Air Historical Branch Narrator. The reason for the switch to nightly attacks by the bomber force, he stated, was the failure of the Me 109 to provide deep fighter escort, and the German commanders having already recognised that the opportunity to destroy Fighter Command had passed. German historians argue, however, that the end of a battle can only be determined either by the total defeat of one belligerent party, which had not been the case, or by the attacker ceasing to do so, again which had not happened. The night blitz went on with some ferocity until May 1941, and it was only then that Hitler turned his military ambitions away from England and towards the Soviet Union. The Germans argue, therefore, that the Battle of Britain did not actually finish until that time. Whatever your opinion on the subject, one thing clear to me, having studied the period in some detail, is that the fighting did not just stop as at the conclusion of the *"Battle of Britain"* film. It was more a case of changing tactics, ie bombers operating under the cloak of darkness that initially afforded them some protection, and the German fighter units conducting *"freie hunt"* offensive sweeps by day over southern England to engage Fighter Command who had yet to go on the offensive themselves. The Few, however, had denied Hitler the aerial supremacy that he required over England before carrying out a seaborne invasion, so thanks to Fighter Command such an undertaking was impossible. On February 22nd, 1944, Hauptmann Otto Bechtle, the Operations Officer of KG2, gave a lecture at Berlin-Gatow airport regarding the air war against England between 1940-43. Regarding the *"Schlacht um Britannien"* of summer 1940, he stated that*"the enemy's power of resistance was stronger than the medium of attack"*, which I think says it all.

On November 29th, 1940, Pilot Officer Robin Rafter made his second and last flight with 603 Squadron. Squadron Leader Denholm led nine Spitfire Mk IIs south-east at 0950 hrs. Off Ramsgate the squadron sighted a lone Me 110 of Stab/StG.1. The squadron's Operations Record Book states that the Spitfire pilots, *"frustrated as being in search of bigger game"*, virtually used the lone twin-engined German fighter as target practice. Unfortunately the document is amongst the poorest that I have examined and in many places is both inaccurate and lacking in detail. In the case of this particular action there appear two completely different lists of pilots involved, but in both at least Pilot Officer Rafter's name remains constant. The aircraft type has also been incorrectly indentified as a Do 17.

The enemy aircraft, "A5+AA" was flown by Oberleutnant R. Pytlik, who was killed when it crashed into the sea. His gunner and radio operator, Oberleutnant T. Fryer, remains missing. Robin Rafter had at least achieved his ambition to get his *"own back on the Jerries"*.

As the squadron returned to Hornchurch, Pilot Officer Rafter's Spitfire, P7449, suddenly dived out of formation from 2,500' and crashed in a meadow at Kingswood, Sutton Valence, Kent. The nineteen year old pilot was killed. Such occurrences can often be put down to oxygen system failure, but at 2,500' Pilot Officer Rafter was not at sufficiently high an altitude for the use of oxygen to be required. It is possible that Rafter's aircraft had been damaged by return fire from the Me 110, or that the crash might have been caused as the result of the pilot suffering a black-out as a consequence of his still relatively recent head injury.

I contacted Group Captain George Denholm himself regarding the matter, but although he could remember Rafter, he could recall nothing of his demise. As he explained, "*after action the squadron never returned to base as a cohesive unit, but in ones and twos. Therefore the only witnesses to the crash would have been whoever was flying with him*".

Another pilot that participated in the attack on Pytlik's Me 110 was Pilot Officer Peter Olver, also mentioned in Sergeant Pattison's story. Peter wrote and told me "*I do remember Rafter, mostly I expect because of the horror I felt at his flying into the deck for no known reason. In those days if a pilot failed to return, you could usually be 100 per cent certain that an Me 109 had sneaked up unseen, but during this operation there had actually been no such enemy fighters in the area*".

Ironically, on the eve of Pilot Officer Rafter's unfortunate death, 603 Squadron held a dinner party at the Dorchester Hotel to celebrate its successes against the enemy. For Lady Rafter, already having to come to terms with widowhood, and her elder daughter, Betty, the death of "*Robin*" was a double blow; on October 11th, 1940, Pilot Officer Charles Rafter, the elder son, had been killed when the wing of his 214 Squadron Wellington touched a hangar shortly after take off from Stradishall. The bomber crashed and the entire crew was lost.

Peter Olver pictured whilst a Pilot Officer serving with 611 Squadron at Digby during the Battle of Britain.
Wing Commander P. Olver.

The two brothers were buried with their father in Birmingham. In more recent times their grave was seriously vandalised. Just how sick is the society that we live in fifty years later, that young men such as the Rafter brothers gave their lives to make possible?

Chapter Seven

AN UNKNOWN BRITISH SOLDIER

*Squadron Leader Thomas Henry Desmond
Drinkwater DFC.*

Mr Les Drinkwater.

The small coincidences of life never cease to amaze me, and it is one such illustration of what a small world we live in that led to the researching and writing of this chapter. My grandfather was a Grenadier Guardsman, captured during the Battle of France before Dunkirk whilst fighting a rearguard action. To me, as a young boy, he was as all ex-Grenadiers appeared, tall and dignified. I knew that grandad had *"been in the war"*, but my resolve to discover more of his experiences met with a stony silence. Bert largely refused to discuss his war, so it was with great surprise that the family discovered upon his death in 1983 that Guardsman 2611042 HH Smith had fought in the famous action on the banks of the River Scheldt during which Lance Corporal Harry Nicholls won the first Victoria Cross of the Second World War. They were, in fact, captured together, and I have several photographs in my possession of the two Grenadiers in Stalag XXB. I soon commenced researching the action involved, tracing and interviewing many survivors, including Guardsman Percy Nash who had fought alongside Nicholls himself, and Guardsman Les Drinkwater, one of 4 Company's stretcher bearers, who had actually rescued my grandfather's friend, Guardsman Arthur Rice, who had been seriously wounded. Les and I rapidly developed fascinating correspondence, through which I learned that his elder brother, *"Tommy"*, had been a wartime Spitfire pilot with the DFC to his credit.

Thomas Henry Desmond Drinkwater was born on September 26th, 1914, at Truro in Cornwall. *"Tommy"* was to travel an interesting road towards achieving his ultimate ambition of becoming a fighter pilot.

Formerly a butcher, on February 25th, 1936, Drinkwater enlisted in the air force as No 529527 Aircraftman 2nd Class/Aircrafthand under training and joined the Training Depot Squadron. On May 15th, 1936, he reported for duty at 3 School of Technical Training. That course successfully completed, he became a *"mate"* on June 26th, 1936, commencing training as a Flight Rigger on July 3rd, 1936, at 2 Wing, Henlow in Bedfordshire. As a fully fledged Rigger, on September 10th, 1937, *"Drink"* joined the ground staff of 9 Flying Training School, Hullavington. Two years later, on July 1st, 1938, he became an Aircraftman 1st Class, and on August 1st, 1939, a Leading Aircraftman. On September 1st, 1939, the day that Germany invaded Poland, Tommy became a Flight Rigger under Pilot Training. The period immediately after the outbreak of the Second World War saw Great Britain mobilise for war. At this time many squadrons either formed or re-formed, one of the latter being 219 which had initially served as a fighter squadron during the Great War. On October 4th, 1939, 219 Squadron reformed at Catterick, equipped with Bristol Blenheim Mk IF nightfighters. Two weeks later LAC Drinkwater joined the squadron. Later moving with the squadron to Redhill, Scorton and Leeming, *"Drink"* remained with 219 until August 19th, 1940, when he joined 4 Initial Training Wing and commenced the procedure that would lead to becoming a fighter pilot himself. He later returned to Hullavington, as a trainee pilot, on December 4th, 1940, and thereafter joined 57 OTU at Hawarden on April 23rd, 1941. The same month he also became a *"Temporary Sergeant"* to complement his aircrew status. Spitfire training completed, Sergeant Drinkwater joined 234 Squadron on June 9th, 1941. That long list of postings eventually leading to the ultimate goal of a Spitfire squadron must be unique, as I am sure that very few groundcrew, especially experienced pre-war regulars, actually made the transition to aircrew.

234 *"Madras Presidency"* Squadron had also been a Great War participant, disbanding in 1919, but reformed at Leconfield on October 30th, 1939. Having

flown Fairey Battles and Gloster Gauntlets, the squadron received Spitfires in March 1940. During the Battle of Britain, 234 Squadron had operated initially from St Eval in Cornwall, undertaking convoy protection duties, but later moved to Middle Wallop, inland of Southampton, during August 1940 and was soon heavily engaged defending the south of England. A month later, having lost five pilots, the squadron returned to St Eval. On February 24th, 1941, 234 moved to Warmwell, in Dorset, where Sergeant Drinkwater joined the unit four months later.

By this time the day fighter war over north-west Europe was changing significantly. We have already seen how the enemy's plans to invade England had been thwarted by the Few during the Battle of Britain, although

Sergeant "Drink" *Drinkwater pictured whilst flying Spitfires with 234 Squadron in 1941.*

Mr Les Drinkwater.

the fighters of both sides clashed over south-east England throughout the rest of 1940. During the autumn of 1940, Fighter Command already sought to seize an offensive initiative, to *"lean into France"*, a policy enthusiastically supported by its new Commander-in-Chief, Air Marshal Sholto Douglas. Between October 21st and December 20th, 1940, that policy was formulated. At that early stage offensive operations were referred to purely as *"Operation Rhubarb"*, which was to consist of a series of patrols over enemy occupied territory by single fighters, or formations of up to a flight in strength, utilising cloud cover. These sorties were impractical, however, unless cloudbase was 2,000' or less. According to the official narration, the primary purpose was to attack and destroy enemy aircraft, or if impractical suitable ground military objectives. The first *"Rhubarb"* was flown on December 20th, 1940, by Flight Lieutenant Christie and Pilot Officer Bodie of 66 Squadron. The Spitfire pilots later reported having successfully attacked an enemy airfield at either Berck or Le Touquet. As the tempo of Rhubarbs intensified, however, it was discovered that the intruding British fighters actually failed to induce the Luftwaffe fighters to battle. Imposing little threat otherwise, the German controller, like his RAF counterparts before him, refused to commit his fighters to combat under such circumstances. Fighter Command's immediate answer was to retain the Rhubarb as a purely fighter conducted operation for *"seek and destroy"* purposes under appropriate weather conditions, but to also introduce further tactics to draw the

Luftwaffe to combat. The recently late Wing Commander Peter Howard-Williams DFC RAF Rtd, a veteran of the Battle of Britain, having flown with 19 Squadron, found himself as a Flight Commander with 118 Squadron at Ibsley during 1941. Of *"Rhubarbs"* he recalled that *"I could initiate a Rhubarb if I thought the weather suitable. Some cloud cover at about 1,000' was what was usually required. We would often then seek out goods trains with the primary objective of holing the boiler. The danger was that there were sometimes flak guns at the rear of the train. Once the train was stopped, however, we shot it up. We even went as far as to send out more aircraft to shoot-up the breakdown gangs. Ops seemed to know how long it would take. Petrol lorries were also a favourite target."*

Whilst operating over England, the Germans had already discovered that although the enemy could ignore fighter sweeps, he could not fail to react to either bombers or fighter-bombers, as we have seen in the story of Pilot Officer Whitbread. Similar tactical thinking in Fighter Command led to the *"Circus"* operation in which a handful of bombers were escorted by large numbers of fighters to attack strategic targets in Northern France. The inclusion of bombers in the *"beehive"* therefore ensured that the German fighters were scrambled. The first Circus was flown on January 10th, 1941. By June that year the effort was intensified and by then the Circus had become a complex operation involving up to twenty squadrons of escorting fighters, some two hundred and forty aircraft. A Spitfire Wing would fly as close cover to the bombers, another as medium and a third as top cover. A further wing would sweep the target area before the bombers arrived, and a final wing would cover the withdrawal. It became a war of attrition for both sides.

Sweeps continued in use as a tactical initiative, comprising large numbers of fighters marauding over the enemy coastline. Also known as the *"Rodeo"*, Peter Howard-Williams recalled that *"the lowest aircraft would be down at 15,000'. To entice the German controller to committing his fighters to battle, we even resorted to the bluff of shouting "bombs away" over the R/T, hoping that the German 'Y' service would be listening and pass it on. Sometimes we took six Hurri-bombers to bomb Maupertus airfield, near Cherbourg, but they had no bomb sight and dropped from 15,000' relying on chance. I do not think that they ever hit the airfield"*. Another tactic was the *"Ramrod"* which were essentially fighter sweeps but directed against specific targets. The *"Roadstead"* concluded Fighter Command's offensive repertoire, being attacks on shipping by fighters and light bombers.

Fighter Command now faced a reversal of the Battle of Britain situation in which many of their pilots shot down either safely baled out over England or close enough to the coast to be rescued. At that time the Germans faced two sea crossings, possibly with a damaged aircraft on the return journey, and in any case their fighters having fuel enough only for relatively limited combat over London. The 1941 Fighter Command Offensive saw the RAF pilots contending with two sea crossings and combat over enemy territory far from home. RAF aircrew shot down over north-west Europe, however, did enjoy one advantage over Luftwaffe crews shot down over England; the Resistance could help them evade capture and return home via the *"Underground"* network. With Bomber Command waging war against the enemy by night, Fighter Command became the RAF's rapier. Squadron Leader Jack Stokoe DFC RAF Rtd, whom we met in Pilot Officer Rafter's story as a Sergeant pilot at Hornchurch in 1940, pointed out to me that *"the offensive operations were just as vital as the Battle of Britain, and certainly more nerve wracking as we were operating over enemy occupied territory"*.

"Leaning into France" became known as the *"Non-Stop Offensive"* by the RAF, but these operations turned out to be costly. The Germans therefore called it the *"Non-Sense Offensive"*. Already committed in the Balkans and the Mediterranean, during the early summer of 1941, many Luftwaffe Jagd and Kampfgeschwadern moved east ready for Hitler's invasion of Russia which took place on June 22nd, 1941. *"Operation Barbarossa"* was Hitler's largest singular strategic blunder the inevitable consequence of which was ultimately total defeat for Germany. The movement of units eastwards also saw the night blitz on Britain come to a close, its zenith having been reached on the night of May 10th, 1941, in the terrible firestorm on London. By that time too, the RAF night fighter defences had improved drastically, squadrons being equipped with the Airborne Interception radar-carrying Beaufighter which was exacting a significant toll of the raiders. With the war in the west no longer having priority, only two Me 109 equipped Jagdgeschwadern were left in the theatre, JG2 *"Richthofen"*, whose Kommodore was Major Wilhelm Balthasar, and JG26 *"Schlageter"* commanded by Oberst Adolf Galland. Between them Balthasar and Galland were responsible for defending the western European coast from the Netherlands to the Bay of Biscay. Many pilots of these two units were entering their most successful stage of the war. On June 21st, 1941, Oberst Galland scored his 69th victory. Within days, Balthasar and Seigfried Schnell of JG2, and *"Pip's"* Priller of JG26 all made their fortieth kills. In August JG2's Hans *"Assi"* Hahn also reached this score. General Theo Osterkampf, however, Jagdfliegerführer (Jafu) on the Channel Coast, briefed the Kommodoren of JG2 and 26, the *"Kanalgeschwadern"*, that they were to inflict maximum damage on the enemy but at the same time preserve their own limited forces.

In 1941 Fighter Command organised its front-line units into the offensive formation of *"Wings"*, each of three squadrons, based at such airfields as Biggin

Hill, Tangmere, Kenley, Ibsley, Northolt and Hornchurch. Several experienced Battle of Britain commanders were promoted to the new position of "Wing Commander Flying" at these locations, amongst them Douglas Bader, "Sailor" Malan, and Bob Stanford-Tuck. During the summer of 1941, however, Fighter Command was to lose many of its seasoned veterans; 74 Squadron's Commanding Officer, John Mungo-Park, was killed over France on June 27th, Wing Commander Bader was captured on August 9th, and early the following year Wing Commander Stanford-Tuck was also taken prisoner. The "Non-Stop Offensive" did indeed therefore become costly to Fighter Command. The Germans by no means had it all their own way, however; on June 14th, 1941, Leutnant Robert Menge, top scorer of the campaign in Norway and Denmark, was killed whilst flying as Galland's "Katchmarek", or wingman, by Wing Commander Jamie Rankin. Two weeks later Leutnant Gustav "Mickey" Sprick of III/JG26 was killed. On July 3rd, Hauptmann Wilhelm Balthasar himself went down with 47 victories to his credit. The latter's father had been killed in France during the Great War, and so father and son were buried side by side near Abbeville. Walter Oseau was recalled from the east to replace Balthasar. With the Ritterkreuz, Eichenlauben mit Schwerten, already to his credit, on October 26th, 1941, Oseau became the third German pilot to exceed the one hundred mark, 44 of these victories having been gained over Russia.

We have already examined the introduction to service of the Spitfire Mk II, and it was this type that Fighter Command operated until well into 1941. The Luftwaffe, however, improved upon its Me 109E of Battle of Britain days by introducing the classic Me 109F in early 1941. The "Franz" marque of the "Ein-Hundert-Neun" saw a major redesign of the previous angular airframe, dispensing too with the reinforcing tail struts. The 'F' was powered by the DB 601E engine which provided a top speed of 390 mph at 22,000'. The new fighter's ceiling was 37,000' and its range was 440 miles, cruising speed at 16,500' being 310 mph. The most important new feature, however, was the removal of all wing mounted armament. Instead, the F-1 had two 7.92 mm MG17 machine guns mounted in the upper cowling, and one Oerlikon MG FF/M 20 mm cannon mounted between the engine blocks and firing through the spinner at a rate of 550 rounds per minute. The drum-fed MG FF/M was replaced as from the F-2 with the new Mauser 15 mm MG 151 machine cannon, which was belt fed, firing at 700 rounds per minute. The new fighter carried 200 cannon rounds and 500 for each MG 17. This new armament became a major point of controversy, however. Adolf Galland felt that light armament was useless against contemporary aircraft, and that the two wing mounted 20 mm cannons of the Me 109E were more effective for the novice. Werner Mölders, on the other hand, favoured light armament because it reduced weight which therefore increased agility. The armament of the Me 109F was in fact a compromise, but whilst Walter Oseau was strongly opposed to this specification, other *"experten"* thought it sufficient. Some jagdflieger only used the rapid fire MG 151 cannon, rarely using the MG 17s. The 'F', nevertheless, was a brilliant aeroplane and undoubtedly the high point of Me 109 development.

During the Second World War, Fighter Command operated a system of resting its fighter pilots after a certain period of time and providing them with a break from operational flying, often by appointments as flying instructors. By mid-1941, therefore, apart from commanders, there were few experienced pilots in fighter squadrons, many Battle of Britain survivors having been rested. Across the Channel, however, the jagdflieger remained such until either killed or incapacitated through wounds. Therefore both JG2 and JG26 boasted many *"experten"* within their ranks.

Such, then, was the state of the day fighter war over western Europe when Sergeant Drinkwater joined 234 Squadron at Warmwell on June 9th, 1941.

The squadron was tasked with providing protection for convoys in coastal waters, an often monotonous sortie for the fighter pilot. It was on such a sortie that Sergeant Drinkwater made his first flight with 234 Squadron, in Spitfire P8194, between 0620-0650 hrs on June 18th, 1941. On July 5th, 1941, 234 re-equipped with the *"Long Range"* Spitfire which had a 70 gallon capacity external fuel tank attached to the port wing. The reason for this was to increase the range of squadrons which were operating against the enemy over the Cherbourg peninsular. On July 10th, flying P7984, Drinkwater flew his first offensive operation when the squadron undertook a sweep of Cherbourg. Squadron Leader Blake destroyed two Me 109s, and Sergeant Jacka probably destroyed another. Blake was actually shot up himself and forced landed in the sea with a damaged radiator, later being safely picked up by a Motor Torpedo Boat from Weymouth. Other sorties were made on July 14th, when 234 provided high escort cover for bombers on a Circus to Cherbourg, and on the 17th when more Me 109s were claimed during a search over the sea for a missing Blenheim crew.

On August 6th, 1941, Squadron Leader HM Stephen DFC, who had flown with 74 Squadron during the Battle of Britain, was appointed to command 234 Squadron. On that day Drinkwater flew Long Range Spitfire P7907 on a bomber escort sortie. Other participating pilots were Flying Officer Wootten, also a Battle of Britain veteran, Flying Officer Baynham, and Sergeants Fox and Jacka. On August 18th, the squadron flew from Coltishall, led by Wing Commander Boyd, providing low escort to eighteen Blenheims attacking shipping off the Dutch coast. A ship was sunk but one bomber crashed into the sea. On August

21st, the Long Range Spitfires, which were unpopular with pilots due to the loss of manoeuvrability, were replaced by Spitfire Mk IIas. Amongst these was P8046, "City of Worcester II", which was flown for the first time by Sergeant Jacka on August 26th, when 234 Squadron undertook a "beat up of Maupertus aerodrome", on the Cherbourg peninsular, between 1130-1225 hrs. During the attack, P8046 was hit by flak. Twenty-six year old Cliff Jacka, a motor racing enthusiast from Bournemouth, headed out to ditch off the French coast. His body was later washed up on the peninsular and buried in the town's cemetery.

September continued in similar vein, convoy protection patrols punctuated by offensive operations over Cherbourg. Sergeant Drinkwater flew P7543 on an uneventful sweep of Cherbourg on September 4th. On that day the squadron operated from Ibsley in Hampshire with 118 and 501 squadrons, and provided medium escort to six Blenheims on Operation Gudgeon VII ("Gudgeon" and "Blot" operations were attacks on fringe targets). The sortie was "uneventful". He next flew P7668 during a Channel sweep two days later, and P8366 on a similar sortie on September 20th. On that day, 234 Squadron again operated from Ibsley with 118 and 501, providing escort to six Blenheims attacking a whale oil ship in Cherbourg Harbour. Light flak was experienced over the target, but no German fighters were engaged. Ten days later he flew Spitfire Mk Vb AB186 during an attack by twelve Spitfires on nine ships off Cap-de-la-Hague. Black smoke was seen to issue from the largest vessel, and one had already been sunk by a previous attack. Return fire was experienced but only one aircraft was damaged when a single bullet passed through its port aileron.

Throughout September 1941, 234 Squadron had been re-equipped with the Spitfire Mk Vb. The Me 109F had outclassed the Spitfire Mk II, so the Mk V was introduced to restore the balance. Armed with four .303 Browning machine-guns and two 20 mm Hispano Suiza cannons, the new Spitfire neither lacked fire power nor experienced the tribulations of the experimental cannon-armed Mk Ib as operated by 19 Squadron during the Battle of Britain, and whose pilots regularly encountered cannon stoppages. At that time the cannons were mounted on their sides, so as to be accommodated within the thin wing section of the Spitfire, and it was this arrangement that led to jamming during combat. Eventually the Mk Ib was withdrawn (see "Spitfire Squadron" also by this author), but work on rectifying the problems continued. The cannons were eventually mounted the intended way up, and fed by an adjacent ammunition drum, with the addition of an aerodynamic blister to take the extra depth on both the upper and lower wing surfaces. The Mk Ib had been armed with cannons only, but X4231, also operated by 19 Squadron in 1940, was fitted with a wing capable of carrying four .303 machine guns and two 20 mm cannons. This combination was approved by 19 Squadron's Commanding Officer, Squadron Leader Phillip Pinkham AFC, prior to his death in action on September 5th, 1940, and it was such an arrangement that the Mk Vb enjoyed. The Mk IIb, basically a cannon and machine-gun armed Mk II, went some way towards rectifying the Spitfire's lack of cannon armament, but to compensate for the extra weight a new engine was required. The Merlin 45 was subsequently twinned with a more efficient three-bladed, wooden Rotol airscrew and the Mk V was born. The new Spitfire began reaching operational squadrons in May 1941.

By October 1st, 1941, 234 Squadron was fully equipped with the Spitfire Vb and flying from Ibsley as a part of the Wing with 118 and 501 Squadrons. On that day, Sergeant Drinkwater flew AB816 over Cherbourg seeking enemy shipping, but without success. Two Me 109Fs were sighted at 20,000' but were too high to intercept. On October 13th, the squadron operated from Redhill in Surrey and provided medium escort for six Blenheims with the Middle Wallop, Kenley, Tangmere and Biggin Hill Wings. The target was the airfield at St Omer. Light flak was experienced over Gravelines, and heavy anti-aircraft fire over Boulogne. Thirty Me 109Fs were intercepted in the St Omer area, and one of the enemy fighters destroyed a Blenheim. Two Me 109Fs were engaged by Flight Lieutenant Rose DFC and Sergeant Fox, the latter claiming a probable. During the sortie Sergeant Drinkwater had flown P8714 between 1230-1350 hrs. On October 15th, 234 Squadron flew on Ramrod 69 and operated out of Westhampnett, the Tangmere satellite, and with 118 and 501 provided high cover, whilst the Portreath Wing flew as close escort. The twelve Blenheims attacked the Le Havre docks. Battle was joined by the Luftwaffe and a number of Me 109Fs were claimed by the RAF pilots. Sergeant Drinkwater was a participant, flying AB816. On October 17th he flew the same machine when the squadron escorted twelve Blenheims on Roadstead 6, sweeping from Pas de Querqueville to Pas de Barfleur, unsuccessfully seeking enemy shipping.

The first sortie of November 1941 was on the 8th, when Drinkwater flew AA728 in Flying Officer Glaser's section. The Ibsley Wing, of which 234 Squadron was now a part, swept the Cherbourg peninsular providing cover for eight Whirlwind fighter-bombers of 263 Squadron. That day also saw Circus 110 launched against Lille, which was not a successful operation for a variety of reasons, and was the last such operation of the year (see *The Invisible Thread: A Spitfire's Tale*" also by this author). On November 11th, Sergeant Drinkwater flew W3937 on a sweep of St Saëns. The target was not located, however, so high tension cables were attacked and destroyed instead. On November 15th, each squadron of the Ibsley Wing attacked various distilleries. 234 Squadron, *"Drink"* again flying W3937, destroyed one at Bricquebec located on the Cherbourg Peninsular and another at St Saëns. On the same day, Flight Lieutenant Peter Howard-Williams of Ibsley's 118 Squadron, flying Spitfire Vb W3943, also participated in an attack on the alcohol distillery at La Meuffe. Three other similar targets were hit by 118, Flight Lieutenant David Fulford leading the attack on the most southerly target at St Lô. Shortly before his death in 1993, Wing Commander Howard-Williams remembered that *"it was a Fighter Command organised attack involving many other squadrons. Apparently the attack was co-ordinated to coincide with the distilleries being full of alcohol. A few weeks later I received a report from the French Underground that our attack had been successful. In the late 1950s I went to La Meuffe and could still see where our cannon shells had hit"*.

Still on the subject of attacking distilleries, I make no apology for recounting the following fascinating story of Rhubarb 87, not only an excellent wartime survivor's first-hand account, but one which clearly illustrates the danger faced by Spitfire pilots in operating over France. The sortie was conducted on February 2nd, 1942, again by 118 Squadron's Flight Lieutenant Peter Howard-Williams DFC, and Pilot Officer Ted Ames. Their target was the alcohol distillery at Eroudeville. In Spitfires Vb AA964 and AA741 respectively, the two pilots took off from Ibsley at 1120 hrs and set course for France. When twenty miles N.E. of Pointe de Barfleur, with cloud 8/10th at 1,000', at just 100' above the sea, Red One, Flight Lieutenant Howard-Williams, turned slightly west. The Spitfires bobbed along in line abreast just twenty-five yards apart. Five miles further on, at 1150 hrs, the Spitfires were suddenly *"bounced"* by four Me 109Fs of III/JG2 that *"swept out of the cloud, taking our aircraft completely by surprise"*. Red Two, Pilot Officer Ames, took evasive action by making a steep, hard climbing turn to the right, and Red One to the left, reaching 800'. Three hundred yards ahead an Me 109F overshot and passed across Red One's sights from east to west. As it did so Peter fired a short burst at it, but without effect. He then dodged into cloud seeking sanctuary, but upon emerging was immediately attacked by two Me 109Fs from behind. Turning tightly to the right, he managed to get on the tail of one of his assailants, firing a five second burst of both cannon and machine-gun fire from two hundred yards range. Following his victim down, the Spitfire pilot saw with satisfaction the enemy aircraft crash into the sea. Suddenly Red One was hit from behind, a 20 mm Oerlikon cannon shell entering the fuselage, smashing the wireless set and most of the machine's control wires. A 7.9 mm machine gun bullet also struck the Spitfire adjacent to the pilot's throttle hand, but fortunately did not penetrate the cockpit and ricochetted off. Peter again managed to reach the protective envelope of some 6/7 10ths cloud, but was attacked upon emerging and had a *"general dogfight"* with four Me 109s. He delivered four or five bursts of fire at the enemy during the mêlée and noticed De Wilde tracer bullet hits on two of them, one in the tail and fuselage by all machine guns from astern, and a second in similar circumstances. Three of Peter's attacks were made from astern, from 150-200 yards, and one from the beam closing to 75 yards. By this time the wind had carried the combatants far to the south. Being out of ammunition, and with a seriously damaged aeroplane, Red One found protective cloud and set course for base.

During Peter's return trip the weather closed in significantly. Fifty years later he remembered:-

"It is always difficult to recall the details of so long ago, but I always remember the trip back. I have written some notes but in fact the actual experience was probably more hairy and frightening than I have related it! Certainly the weather was bad across the U.K. and over the French coast. I think that it was marginal for a rhubarb.

"I started off in cloud, climbing after a while and found that I was actually flying between two layers of cloud. My radio had been shot up so I was unable to obtain a homing bearing. I continued to steer due north over 10/10ths cloud with no idea where I was. Suddenly I nearly hit a barrage balloon, not the wire but the actual balloon itself which suddenly appeared out of the haze. Visibility was very poor even between the cloud layers. I thought that it was either from a coastal convoy or part of the Portsmouth barrage. I turned onto a course due west, and after a while descended to try and discover my position. After getting down to below a thousand feet I decided that this was getting dangerous and climbed again until I was clear of cloud.

"I flew north for about five minutes before finally making the decision to bale out. I opened the hood and side door and undid my straps. I decided to climb out onto the wing.

"Looking out I suddenly saw a small gap in the cloud and a green field! I quickly resumed my seat, did up my straps and started to circle, descending into the hole. At about 500' or less, I found myself below cloud in poor visibility. I flew around for a few minutes and saw a golf course. Just the place for a wheels up landing, I thought, and selected one of the fairways. I made a couple of low passes hoping to clear the golfers away, but they only stood and waved!! I returned to cloud base and suddenly saw that Bournemouth was nearby. It was then a simple matter to fly to the coast, turn left to Christchurch and follow the river Avon to Ringwood and Ibsley. Cloud base was still low, so I waggled my wings in a low pass past the control tower, and prepared to land.

"I knew that my rudder and elevator trim wires had been shot away, so had to be

especially careful when landing. The wheels and flaps came down, and in spite of the lack of trim controls, I made an ordinary landing. I taxied in, but in view of the time that I had been airborne, people were getting a little worried, especially as control had been calling me on the R/T but receiving no response.

"I went into my Flight Commander's dispersal hut, but in spite of sitting in front of a fiercely blazing log fire, I could not stop shaking. There was only one cure. That evening we all went into Christchurch, to the Kings Arms, where I consumed more than my fair share of beer. Mary and Sidney Barker, who ran the famous inn, let me have a room for the night, even supplying pyjamas and a toothbrush. Next morning I drove back to the airfield and resumed normal flying".

Flight Lieutenant Peter Howard-Williams DFC of 118 Squadron poses with Spitfire Mk Vb AA964, "NK-D", following his lucky escape from JG2's Me 109s during Rhubarb 87. Note the cannon shell exit hole; the original photograph was captioned "Me looking very frightened".
The late Wing Commander P.I. Howard-Williams.

Sobering though Flight Lieutenant Howard-Williams's traumatic experiences had been, he was more fortunate than his number two. Of Pilot Officer Ames, nothing was ever seen again after the Me 109s pounced.

On November 17th, 1941, the weather prevented Sergeant Drinkwater conducting a scheduled Rhubarb, returning shortly after reaching the French coast, but Sergeants McCleod and Walker were more fortunate, destroying a building on the peninsular before returning to Ibsley. The last offensive sortie of the month was an uneventful Channel Sweep on the 26th, Sergeant Drinkwater flying his regular mount, W3937.

Flight Lieutenant Howard-Williams, returning from shooting up enemy shipping, taxies past the film set of "The First of the Few" *at Ibsley airfield. Note David Niven, centre foreground, and Leslie Howard in civilian clothing.*

The late Wing Commander P.I. Howard-Williams.

Throughout December the weather was bad, there being no operational flying at all by 234 Squadron between the 18th and 29th. The weather cleared the following day and the squadron flew from Predannack as close escort to Halifax bombers attacking the Brest naval base.

On January 1st, 1942, 234 Squadron was released for the day which heralded the third year of war. Again, throughout this month the weather closed in, the only flying being the constant convoy protection patrols. On January 26th, Squadron Leader Stephen left for the Far East, and three days later Squadron Leader Birchfield took over as Commanding Officer. On January 5th, Tommy Drinkwater had been discharged on appointment to a temporary commission as a Pilot Officer on probation.

On February 12th, 1942, Pilot Officer Drinkwater flew W3936 on an escort sortie, but this was one with a difference; *"Operation Fuller"*. The Joint Chiefs of Staff were aware that the Germans intended to break-out the battleships Scharnhorst, Gneisenau and Prinz Eugen from their base at Brest to a less vulnerable port. Contingency plans were drawn up to oppose any course that the ships might take when they reached the open sea. With any such break-out underway, the Royal Navy and the RAF were to execute immediate counter-action. The classified codeword to initiate these operations was *"Fuller"*. Unfortunately this information failed to filter through to 11 Group's fighter squadrons.

On that morning Squadron Leader Bobby Oxspring, Commanding Officer of 91 Squadron, received a telephone call from Squadron Leader Bill Igoe, the senior controller at Biggin Hill, informing him of considerable German fighter activity over the Somme estuary. Igoe was puzzled as to the Germans' intentions as they appeared to be staying roughly in the same area. He suspected that they were providing aerial cover to some sort of shipping, and asked Oxspring to have a look, adding *"but be damned careful as there are an awful lot of Huns about"*. Squadron Leader Oxspring and Sergeant Beaumont subsequently took off and flew just under the cloud base between 1200' and 1800'. Following the coast past Le Touquet towards the Somme estuary, the two Spitfires suddenly flew into a heavy barrage of flak. Banking into a turn, Oxpring and Beaumont saw a large formation of destroyers and 'E'-Boats protecting three much larger ships, all of which appeared to be travelling at speed. They then saw two Spitfires below them attacking 'E'-Boats on the periphery of the convoy. Being unaware of Operation Fuller, Squadron Leader Oxspring broke radio silence and reported to Igoe what he had seen. Returning immediately to Biggin Hill, Beaumont suggested that the larger of the three battleships was the Scharnhorst. Telephoning in his report to Bill Igoe, Oxspring was immediately put through to the incredulous 11 Group controller. Unfortunately the AOC, Sir Trafford Leigh-Mallory, was away at Northolt and Squadron Leader Oxspring got nowhere in conveying the gravity of what he and Beaumont had seen. Thirty minutes later the other two Spitfires, flown by Group Captain Victor Beamish and Wing Commander Finlay Boyd, landed at Kenley. They had maintained R/T silence, but their report both corroborated Oxspring's and, due to their senior rank, carried more weight. According to the late Group Captain Oxspring when I interviewed him at Duxford in 1988, the delay in alerting the various commands was both *"interminable and inexcusable"*. By the time that a response had been formulated, the Scharnhorst, Gneisenau and Prinz Eugen were off Dover and steaming into the North Sea.

Inclement weather had rendered the proposed powerful *"Fuller"* counter-action impotent, and the Navy had no sizeable warships based in the Channel capable of successfully engaging the German capital ships. Due to the low cloud base, Bomber Command was unable to attack using armour-piercing bombs which had to be dropped from a minimum of 7,000'. Nothing could detract, however, from the courage of smaller units to put an end to the "Channel Dash". The action climaxed with a desperate torpedo attack by six Swordfish biplanes, five of which fell victim to the murderous hail of flak belching forth from their targets before they even reached dropping range. The final "Stringbag" was destroyed by an Me 109. For what was a vain but gallant action undertaken against all odds, the formation's commander, Lieutenant-Commander Eugene Esmonde, received a posthumous Victoria Cross.

The Ibsley Wing had proceeded to West Malling from where it escorted aircraft of both Bomber and Coastal Command attacking the German battleships. German fighters were engaged, and Flight Lieutenant McKay hit an Me 109 which collided with another, both crashing into the sea. Pilot Officers McLeod and Pike failed to return, however, Pike having last been seen trailing black smoke over the target area.

The audacious German operation had been the brainchild of Oberst Adolf Galland, who by that time had replaced his friend Mölders as General der Jagdflieger following the latter's death in a flying accident. The movement of the capital ships from Brest to Germany had been ordered by Hitler himself. At staff conferences at the highest level, Galland argued that a nocturnal departure would bring the ships into the Straits of Dover in daylight. He was confident that the first part of the operation could be conducted in secret, and that in any case the Kanalgeschwader could fend off any attacks made by the RAF. The Führer agreed and placed Galland in command of the aerial aspects of the operation. All planning was conducted in his Berlin office. The plan called for continuous escort by four Schwarme, two at high and two at low altitude. Total radio silence was to be maintained until the codeword "Open Visor" was broadcast. With Group Captain Vincent having maintained radio silence upon sighting the enemy ships, Galland did not give the codeword following Oxspring's broadcast, correctly guessing that the British response would be to send out another reconnaissance. "Open Visor" was only given when Esmonde's Swordfish appeared with an escorting squadron of Spitfires. Ultimately, in addition to the six Swordfish, the British lost seventeen fighters and twenty bombers. The Germans lost seventeen fighters including eleven of their pilots.

Although assisted by the weather and the slowness of the British to respond, Galland later described the "Channel Dash" as the "greatest hour" of his career. Although the RAF had failed to directly inflict damage upon the three battleships, they did not reach their destination unscathed. At 2.30 pm

Scharnhorst struck a mine which arrested her progress, and after dark Gneisenau struck another air-laid mine, but although her speed was reduced she continued towards her destination on the Elbe. Scharnhorst then suffered substantial damage when she struck another mine. With over 1,000 tons of water shipped aboard, she eventually limped into Wilhelmshaven to join the other two battleships. Needless to say in Britain there was a public outcry and the Prime Minister, Winston Churchill, was furious.

Shortly after the *"Channel Dash"*, his first operational tour completed, on February 22nd, 1942, Pilot Officer Drinkwater was posted away to No 2 School of Air Navigation, with whom he remained until April 24th, 1942, when he rejoined 234 Squadron as a Flight Commander. On the same date he was appointed Acting Flight Lieutenant. Enthusiastically undertaking his new appointment, Flight Lieutenant Drinkwater led his flight on an escort mission to Hurri-bombers attacking enemy shipping off the September Isles. By the end of the operation, one German destroyer was at the bottom of the sea.

During this period the other 234 Squadron Flight Commander was Flight Lieutenant David Glaser, who recalled the following amusing story relating to *"Drink"* Drinkwater:-

"When we were at Ibsley for some reason we won a pig, but when we went to collect it the animal was still alive. We sent the flight van over to collect it and back at the airfield "Tommy" was in charge as he had been a butcher before the war. Combat was joined, the pig leaping all over the place, jumping in and out of the van pursued by "Drink" brandishing his service revolver. Then a shot was fired from within, and the pig came charging out - no sign of "Drink". We all peered inside to find him flat on his back, having been knocked over by the pig's charge, the round having fortunately caused neither injury nor damage. We then spent two hours trying to catch the pig!"

During May 1942, 234 Squadron moved to Portreath in Cornwall. Through-out that entire month the squadron's pilots flew a seemingly endless rota of convoy patrols.

June, however, was to see a return to offensive operations against the enemy. On June 2nd, 1942, Flight Lieutenant Drinkwater flew Spitfire Mk Vb AR383, between 1745-1845 hrs, on a *"shipping beat up, NNE of Ushant"*. On that occasion 234 Squadron had escorted Hurri-bombers of 175 Squadron. Later that evening the squadron flew an air-sea rescue sortie and another *"shipping beat up"*. The following day, 234 flew down to Middle Wallop and provided rear cover escort to 10 Group Circus No 6. The next day 234 operated from Warmwell and flew on a sweep over Maupertus airfield. Jannion airfield became their target on June 5th when the squadron escorted Whirlwind fighter bombers. An uneventful sweep of Le Tréport occurred on June 8th, the squadron pursuing its nomadic existence and operating from Redhill in Surrey.

On June 23rd, 1942, 234 Squadron flew low cover escort for six Bostons bombing Morlaix aerodrome, Flight Lieutenant Drinkwater in AA383 between 1825-2045 hrs. The conclusion of that sortie was to have an important future effect on the air war over western Europe.

German aircraft designer Kurt Tank had produced a lethal single-engined fighter, the Focke Wulf 190, which made its operational debut on the Channel coast in the hands of II/JG26 in July 1941. Tank had blended a BMW radial engine into the airframe of his new fighter which remained well proportioned and aesthetically appealing. The advent of *"Die Würger"* (Butcher Bird) caused great consternation amongst Fighter Command's pilots. Previously their Spitfires had at least maintained a staus quo with the development of the Me 109, but the Fw 190 was to prove a different matter entirely. This new warbird could out-perform the Spitfire Mk V in every respect excepting the two aircraft's turning circles. Descriptions of the new fighter's appearance and performance provided to Intelligence Officers by the first Spitfire pilots to meet *"Die Würger"* were treated with disbelief. Fighter Command felt it inconceivable that the Germans could have secretly produced such a machine and suggested that the pilots had encountered Curtiss Hawks which the enemy had captured and were now using operationally. The Spitfire pilots, however, who knew that the American Hawk was in no way comparable with their Spitfires, immediately rejected such a proposal. Although the first Fw 190 was shot down on September 18th, 1941, when the Gruppenkommandeur of JG26, Hauptmann Walter Adolph, failed to return from combat, the new fighter was only correctly identified by the RAF on October 13th, 1941, when clear cine gun-camera evidence was examined. Between June 14th and December 31st of that year, the RAF had lost 411 fighters over the Channel coast and the continent, whilst the Germans had only lost 103, including forty-seven pilots killed in action, seventeen in flying accidents, and three taken prisoner. Such losses, although serious, were tolerable for the Kanalgeschwader. Understandably, therefore, they were confident that during 1942 the Fw 190 would further increase their margin of superiority. By April 1942, as a direct result of the Fw 190, RAF losses on the Channel Front reached prohibitive levels. During the course of that month alone over one hundred Spitfires were lost in action. Inevitably the morale of the Spitfire squadrons suffered enormously. The desperate situation saw the hatching of various schemes to obtain an Fw 190 for evaluation, one such plan being a commando raid, to be led by Captain Philip Pinkney of E Troop, 12 Commando, on a Luftwaffe fighter base to steal a 190 which would be flown back to England by that great airman and Supermarine Chief Test

Pilot Jeffrey Quill. Fortunately, as an indirect result of the sortie to bomb Morlaix airfield on June 23rd, 1942, such a hazardous undertaking was not required.

Both the Portreath and Exeter Spitfire Wings, returning from France, had unbeknowingly been shadowed by Fw 190s of the Gruppenstab of III Gruppe and 7 Staffel of JG2, the German pilots coldly calculating the moment to strike. David Glaser recalls *"the Spitfires returned in battle formation. As we approached Start Point on the Devonshire coast, the Fw 190s attacked. As the Spitfires roared low over the town, someone shouted "For Chrissake Break!" as the Fw 190s hurtled down"*. In the ensuing mêlée, Unteroffizier Willi Reuschling's Fw 190 collided with Wing Commander Alois Vasatko's Spitfire. The German safely took to his parachute and was later rescued from the sea, but the Czech, Vasatko, remains missing. With both sides low on fuel the combat was short. Four Spitfires were scrambled by the Exeter Wing to intercept the escaping Germans, but in the process 312 Squadron's Flight Sergeant Mares collided with 310's Pilot Officer Strihavka. Only one Spitfire became airborne, BL517, flown by Sergeant Frantisek Trejtnar. As the combat had broken up over Start Point, Egon Mayer's fighters had returned to France; all, that is, except one flown by Oberleutnant Arnim Faber, who was heading north instead of south. Subsequently engaged by Trejtnar's Spitfire, Faber demonstrated the Fw 190's superiority once more by despatching the Czech after a protracted dogfight. Then the German again continued northwards, crossing the Bristol Channel. Every account that I have previously read regarding this incident states that Faber had made a navigational error and mistaken the Bristol for the English Channel, subsequently landing by mistake therefore at Pembrey airfield in South Wales. However, the Sector Station, RAF Fairwood Common, recorded the following in its Operations Record Book:-

"2028 hrs: One of Germany's latest fighters, a Focke Wulf 190, landed undamaged at Pembrey. The pilot's story is that after shooting down two Spitfires he was forced north, and, running short of petrol, landed at the first available aerodrome which happened to be Pembrey. He was escorted to Fairwood Common and was guest of the Officers' Mess for two days until he was sent to London for interrogation."

As the Fw 190 had landed off a steep turn, the quick thinking Duty Pilot, Sergeant Jeffreys, promptly jumped on the wing of the intruder, thrusting a Verey pistol into Arnim Faber's rapidly colouring face, and thus captured Fw 190A-3, Werk-Nr 5313, in a fully serviceable condition. Reichmarshall Hermann Goering, appreciating the Fw 190's value, had issued orders that the type must not cross the Channel, instead demanding that the new fighters returned to France when half-way across so as to avoid falling into British hands. Needless

Tommy Drinkwater with Oberleutnant Arnim Faber's Fw109 of Stab III/JG2 which was captured when the pilot landed at Pembrey on June 23rd, 1942.

Mr Les Drinkwater.

Close-up view of the cockpit area of Faber's Fw190.

Mr Les Drinkwater.

to say, when hearing of Faber's exploit, the Luftwaffe Commander-in-Chief was beside himself with rage. The following day several 234 Squadron pilots, including Flight Lieutenants Drinkwater and Glaser, flew to Pembrey and examined the captured "*Butcher Bird*". David Glaser recalls that he met Oberleutnant Faber himself on that occasion, and expressed to him his admiration for his Gruppenkommandeur, Hans "*Assi*" Hahn. JG2's badge was a cockerel's head, "*Hahn*" also translating to "*Cock*". The British pilots, however, thought that their German adversary's name was "*Cock*", so, not understanding the problem in translating his Kommandeur's name, Faber appeared evasive. David Glaser, who survived the war and retired as a Squadron Leader, stresses how much he and the other British pilots admired Hahn, whom he considered a brilliant aerial tactician and leader. After the war Squadron Leader Glaser traced Hans Hahn, whom he very much wanted to meet, but sadly before such an occasion could take place, the German ace died. At Pembrey Glaser also recalls Faber offering to "*take on a squadron of Spitfires. We all knew what his game was, of course, he would have just baled out to destroy his Fw 190.*"

The RAF rapidly took advantage of Faber's prize. The Fw 190 was promptly transported by road to the Royal Aircraft Establishment at Farnborough where it was completely dismantled and analysed. Allocated the RAF number

Faber's Fw109 at Pembrey. All of these photographs were taken by Tommy Drinkwater using his own camera.

Mr Les Drinkwater.

MP499, on July 3rd, 1942 the captured machine was test flown by Wing Commander Hugh Wilson. Ten days later the Air Fighting Development Unit took delivery of the invaluable prize and commenced intensive performance trials against the major Allied fighter types. The subsequent research confirmed what was already known about the *"Butcher Bird"*, but also eradicated the awe in which the RAF had held Tank's new fighter. Such new information was absorbed by the Spitfire development programme and taken into account in the production of later marques. In the meantime the stop-gap Mk IX had been produced to combat the Fw 190 menace. The new Spitfire was basically a Mk V airframe combined with the new Merlin 61 engine. The first Spitfire Mk IXbs were delivered to 64 Squadron at Hornchurch in June 1942. On July 30th, the new Spitfires destroyed four Fw 190s over France. The latter type, however, performed best between 14,000' and 22,000', at which heights the Mk IX did not. The Merlin 66 engine was then developed which operated best between 10,000' and 20,000'. It was a case of *"swings and roundabouts"*, but the Spitfire Mk IX undoubtedly met the Fw 190 on equal terms and restored the confidence and morale of Fighter Command. The deliverance of Faber's machine, therefore, saved the lives of countless RAF fighter pilots.

Oberleutnant Arnim Faber himself, also at Pembrey. Note his leather flying trousers.
Mr Les Drinkwater.

For 234 Squadron, July 1942 continued much as the previous month, monotonous convoy patrols punctuated by the occasional offensive sortie. August and September, however, were completely taken up by convoy protection duties. On October 25th, Squadron Leader Banning-Lover AFC arrived to command the squadron, on which date the squadron Operations Record Book also notes that *"only five more Huns are needed for our century"*. An interesting sortie took place on October 27th. The squadron diary records that:-

"The squadron joined 19 for an offensive sweep. Twelve Spitfire Mk Vbs of 234, including Wing Commander O'Brien, up at 1540 hrs, down, at Perranporth and Portreath, at 1700. The rendezvous was at 1545 hrs, 10,000' above the Lizard.

When climbing through layers of cloud the squadrons became separated. 234 flew to 23,000' and patrolled for three minutes, fifteen miles north of Ile de Batz, which was five miles north of the intended patrol line. 19 Squadron then received a warning from the controller that the bombers were climbing above the Spitfire squadrons. 234 Squadron turned right into the sun at the end of the patrol when three or four Fw 190s dived on them from behind. Squadron Leader Palmer (supernumerary) was seen by Flight Lieutenant Drinkwater to go down in flames and bale out fifteen miles north of Ile de Batz. At the same time flight Sergeant Drayton was seen in a spin. The formation broke up and three had a crack at the Huns but no claims were made".

On November 7th, 1942, another interesting sortie is reported in the squadron diary:-

"At 1313 hrs six aircraft of 'A' flight patrolled the Lizard at 5,000' as additional rear support to Ramrod 36. The flight was then directed to search for a pilot (Teacher 41) from the Exeter Wing who had called Mayday whilst returning from the operation. They found a patch of oil and a pilot in the sea. Flight Lieutenant Drinkwater and Red Section orbited at zero feet with two other sections at 1,000' and 2,000'. One Defiant of 276 Squadron was also sent out to search for Teacher 41, but its pilot called Mayday at a position twenty miles from the Lizard at 120 degrees. A second Defiant and a 406 Squadron Beaufighter were then sent to search, so when Flight Lieutenant Drinkwater saw these in the vicinity he left Teacher 41 to search for the Defiant crew. He instructed the rest of the flight to remain over Teacher 41, but owing to a faulty radio, the other pilots failed to receive the message and followed him. A second patch of oil was then seen in the sea some 6-8 miles west of Teacher 41, but no dinghy or pilot was seen".

Flight Lieutenant Drinkwater's second tour was completed the same month, during which he also received the Distinguished Flying Cross in recognition of his having flown fifty operations over France. On November 26th, 1942, the squadron diary recorded:-

"The popular Flight Commander of 'A' flight, Flight Lieutenant Drinkwater DFC, posted away to 57 OTU. He has been with the squadron for eighteen months and rose from Sergeant to Flight Commander. We are all very sorry to see him go and wish him the best of luck at OTU".

Drinkwater flew as an instructor with 57 OTU until July 6th, 1943, when he joined the staff of 52 OTU at Aston Down. Six days later, he reported for Flight Commander duties with 19 Squadron, who were still equipped with Spitfire Mk Vbs, at 122 Airfield, Gravesend.

By this time the United Kingdom had become a huge arsenal of men and machinery preparing to invade enemy occupied Europe. On December 7th, 1941, Japanese aircraft had attacked the American Pacific fleet at Pearl Harbour in Hawaii. That undeclared act of aggression led to America abandoning her neutrality and previous policy of isolationism from events in Europe, and declaring war on the Axis powers, Germany, Italy and Japan. Hitler's invasion of Russia had at first gone well, covering much ground in ideal weather conditions, but just four months later the German Quartermaster recorded that the invading forces were *"at the end of resources in both men and materials"*. Just a few miles outside Moscow itself the advance had been checked, and the German Army, unprepared and ill-equipped for the harsh Russian winter began to suffer the realities of their folly, just like Napoleon's Frenchmen a century earlier. On December 12th, 1941, Marshal Zhukov launched a general offensive against the Moscow Front. The Blitzkrieg and the German tide of conquest, which once appeared unstoppable, was over. By 1942 the Axis advance on every front had been halted, although the Germans remained deep in Russia and with the failure of the Deippe landings in August, the Second Front that Stalin demanded remained a long way off. By 1943, however, the Allies were on the move, the Russians rolling back the Germans, Stalingrad haunting Hitler as the most catastrophic and costly defeat so far. But it would ultimately be but one of many. The same year, Rommel left North Africa and advised Hitler that it would be *"plain suicide"* for German forces to remain on the sub-continent. On July 10th, 1942, Allied forces invaded Sicily, and on August 17th made the short sea crossing from there to land in Italy. For Hitler and Mussolini the sun was setting on their fascist monstrosities.

During this time Britain had really become a huge aircraft carrier. 1943 saw area, or indiscriminate, bombing at its peak. At Bomber Command Headquarters at High Wycombe, the Commander-in-Chief, Sir Arthur *"Bomber"* Harris, continued his nightly attacks against Germany on an ever-increasing scale. On August 17th, 1942, General Ira Eaker led the 8th Air Force's B17 Flying Fortresses on a major daylight raid attacking the Rouen-Sotteville railway marshalling yards, so signalling the start of the American Daylight Offensive. With the RAF bombing by night, and the 8th Air Force by day, the Ruhr was attacked from March to June 1943, Hamburg from July to November, and Berlin itself from November 1943 to March 1944.

By January 1943, 19 Squadron exchanged their Spitfire Mk Vs for Mk IXs. Throughout this time the squadron was heavily engaged upon offensive operations over France. These sorties invariably found the Spitfires escorting Hawker Typhoon fighter bombers, or the daylight raids by American bombers. Churchill had instructed the secret agents of the Special Operations Executive to *"set Europe ablaze"*; as the RAF fighter squadrons became fighter-bombers, attacking anything military that moved in France, the same directive could well have applied to the Allied air forces.

19 Squadron, 1943. Centre, sitting, is the Commanding Officer, Squadron Leader Vic Ekins (who passed away in 1993). Flight Lieutenant Drinkwater is seated to the Commanding Officer's right.

Squadron Leader Winston Dilks.

On November 11th, 1943, came a red letter day for 19 Squadron, and "Drink's" finest hour, flying Spitfire Mk IX, MH355. The squadron diary tells the story:-

"Clear fine morning. Briefed at 1115 hrs, role was a fighter sweep in the St Pol area as diversion for Marauders bombing construction work on Cherbourg Peninsular. Squadron up at 1155.

"The squadron had been over France for thirty minutes when 122 Squadron, on port side, were jumped by 14-16 Huns. 19 Squadron turned towards them and as we approached an Fw 190 turned away and dived down. Flight Lieutenant Drinkwater followed from 18,000' to 1,000'. He fired a number of bursts and saw strikes. The enemy aircraft eventually crashed in a field. This is the squadron's one hundredth confirmed victory and everyone is quite excited. Captain Johnson of 122 squadron also got one confirmed. The squadron was next airborne at 1505 hrs to sweep the same area, Marauders this time bombing constructions at Calais. Nothing doing, the squadron landed at 1635 hrs. The pilots attended a lecture at 1730 by Pilot Officer White of 485 Squadron who had just escaped from France. In the evening the Squadron Intelligence Officer, "Spy" Dilks, came down to congratulate us on our 100th victory when we all adjourned to the local and drank the health of Flight

Lieutenant Drinkwater".

Winston "*Spy*" Dilks "*surfaced*" in 1991 when his letter to a national newspaper was published concerning 19 Squadron having been disbanded that year. I sent him a copy of my first book, "*Spitfire Squadron*", which tells the story of 19 Squadron in action between 1939-41. In his eighties, "*Spy*" replied:-

"*Words cannot express my feelings of thanks and appreciation for your book. I will treasure it and no doubt read it again and again as 19 Squadron meant so much to me.*

"*Unfortunately, at the beginning of the war, I was in a reserved occupation and so was unable to join up until late 1941. After training, in 1942, I was posted to 313 (Czech) Squadron, but on June 20th, 1942, joined 19 Squadron a Perranporth. This was during their 'rest period' but I can assure you that there was plenty of activity. On most days there were sweeps over the French coast where many battles ensued, and many escorts around Brest where the enemy submarines were based. On one occasion the squadron was jumped by Me 109s and we lost Flying Officer Jackie Henderson, a wonderful pilot and a clever artist. Pilot Officer Réne Rogér, a Free fighting Frenchman, was killed at the very end of the war whilst flying to meet his parents at a French aerodrome where he crashed.*

"*The squadron was very good at spotting V2 ramps and as a result of the reports that I was able to submit to the Air Ministry the bombers had great success. When I arrived the squadron's total of victories was 99, and try as they could, as being engaged on a quiet sector of home defence German targets were few and far between, they could not get the 100th, although there were several probables. When Flight Lieutenant Drinkwater got the 100th kill there was a great party at a London hotel to celebrate. I attended with Squadron Leader Vic Ekins, our Commanding Officer, and Air Vice-Marshal Dixon was also there*".

Fifty years later, Wing Commander Vic Ekins, who sadly died in 1993, remembered:-

"*I knew Tommy Drinkwater very well and I had the greatest of respect for him. I always found him a quiet sort of man, respectful and a very hard worker. He reported to me as 'B' Flight Commander in 1943 and carried out his duties as a fighter pilot with courage and enthusiasm. 19 Squadron was proud of him. When I was away on leave he would often lead the squadron and did it very well. We had just changed over to Spitfire Mk IXs, a super aircraft with a four bladed airscrew. A lot of Drinkwater's time with us was spent at 83 Group airfields in SE England preparing for the invasion of Europe. I was so pleased that he got our 100th Hun. We certainly had a great party to celebrate*".

The 99th victim, a Do 217, had been shot down in February 1942 over the east coast. According to a national newspaper, the squadron had "*prepared the champagne bottles in preparation for the 100th, but they were to wait another twenty-*

one months for the 100th victory. Even the fierce air battle during the Deippe raid failed to provide a victim for the squadron". Apparently the pilots and groundcrew had since contributed sixpence each to a sweepstake before every sortie. The pot must have been substantial for the eventual winner!

The bomber escort sorties went on. On November 30th, 1943, 19 Squadron covered the withdrawal of 360 Liberators returning from the Rhineland.

On January 7th, 1944, twenty-four Spitfire Mk IXs of 15 Wing based at Gravesend, of which 19 Squadron was a part, took off at 1228 hrs on Ramrod 433. The Wing's objective was to provide cover for the withdrawal of American Liberator and Flying Fortress bombers. The rendezvous was made at Guise Villiers with the American 5th, 6th, 7th and 8th Fighter Groups. The first box of bombers passed out at Cambrai and Arras, escorted by four Thunderbolts. When SW of Arras, six Me 109s dived on a Liberator straggling on the port side. In the St Pol/Douvellers area, eight Fw 190s attacked the Fortresses but were chased away by 19 Squadron. Flight Lieutenant Drinkwater fired on an Fw 190 and had a second in his sights when another Spitfire jostled in front of him and shot it down. The pilot baled out. The Wing crossed out with the last box over

Squadron Leader Ekins holds the cake, being cut by Flight Lieutenant Drinkwater, at the party celebrating 19 Squadron's 100th kill and for which "Drink" was responsible.
Squadron Leader Winston Dilks.

the Somme Estuary and left them only when twenty miles off the English coast.

Flight Lieutenant Drinkwater reported:-

"*I was leading White Section and when at 19,000' in the St Pol area I saw eight Fw 190s coming in out of the sun from the port quarter and at our height. The enemy aircraft broke immediately they saw us and dived away in disorder. I picked out one and started to fire from 400 yards, but I could not close the range. The enemy aircraft went into a vertical dive and was lost in cloud which was 10/10ths at 4,000'. I saw no strikes but base my claim of one Fw 190 damaged on the assessment of my combat film, No TAF184*".

In January 1944, 19 Squadron began exchanging its Spitfires for Mustang IIIs, and over the next few weeks carried out numerous training and practice flights as the pilots familiarised themselves with their new mounts. 19 Squadron had been the first in the air force to receive the Spitfire, in 1938; so ended their association with Mitchell's fighter of over five years standing. The Mustang was produced by North American Aviation Inc and powered by an Allison engine. The first tested proved disappointing for high altitude combat and were thus allotted to army co-operation roles. In late 1942, the flying trials took place of a Merlin powered Mustang. The result was unquestionably superior in all respects. Within a year Merlin-Mustangs were operational in England with the USAAC. Fitted with extra fuel tanks they acted as "*Little Friend*" escorts for their "*Big Friend*" bombers, and were able to operate deep within enemy territory. For many pilots the Mustang became the best single-seater fighter to see combat in the European Theatre, its attributes surpassing even the legendary Spitfire and Fw 190.

On February 5th, 1944, 19 Squadron made its operational debut with the Mustang, flying two sweeps into Belgium and Holland, both of which were uneventful. That evening there was a party to celebrate the anniversary of 122 Airfield and at which the beer was free, no doubt a significant contributory factor to its success! The squadron diary also relates that "*there was screening of the airfield film, in which 19 Squadron figured prominently. Star of the show was undoubtedly "Ace" Drinkwater (terror of the Luftwaffe and hero of the squadron's century) who co-starred with "Spy" Ellis saluting the airfield flag which was the climax of the film*".

The squadron's duties, with the new Mustang, became more and more the escorting of American daylight bombers. An interesting sortie occurred on March 6th, 1944, when Flight Lieutenant Drinkwater's White Section shepherded a lone Flying Fortress which had to turn back but which they lost when it disappeared into cloud. On the same day, the squadron provided escort to 660 Fortresses withdrawing after bombing Berlin, the rendezvous with their charges being deep into the Reich, just ten miles east of the *"Big City"*.

On March 17th, 1944, the 19 Squadron diary humorously recorded:-

"It is with great regret that we have to announce today that 'B' Flight Commander, Flight Lieutenant Drinkwater DFC threw away his freedom and entered into holy matrimony. However, we really do wish both he and his wife very many years of happiness together. We were hoping to provide fighter cover for the happy event but as usual the weather washed out any likelihood of flying".

With the weather cleared a few days later, the escort missions continued. On April 11th, 1944, Flight Lieutenant Drinkwater's name comes to notice once more in the squadron diary:-

"Announced this evening that Flight Lieutenant Drinkwater promoted to Squadron Leader and to take over 122 Squadron. Whilst we are very thrilled to hear of his promotion, the squadron will miss one of its most capable and popular members whose efforts gained 19's 100th Hun. We all join in giving "Drink" our congratulations and extend to him our very best wishes and good hunting with his new squadron".

122 *"Bombay"* Squadron was another of the disbanded former Great War fighter squadrons, and had reformed in May 1941, equipped with Spitfires from then until January 1944 when it also received the Mustang III. It was this type that the squadron operated when Squadron Leader Drinkwater DFC took command at Gravesend. On April 19th, 1944, *"Drink"* led his new squadron on a Ranger to attack an enemy airfield. Aircraft were damaged on the ground by Wing Commander Johnstone and Flying Officer Minchin. These were the squadron's first successes flying Mustangs. Thereafter the unit flew an increasing number of Rangers and destroyed numerous enemy aircraft in similar circumstances.

On May 2nd, 1944, six Mustangs of 122 Squadron each carried two 500 lb general purpose bombs whilst another six acted as their escort. Railway marshalling yards between Nantes and Gassicourt were successfully attacked, but the Mustangs were the fleeting target for a heavy flak battery near Rouen. Six days later Lille aerodrome was successfully dive-bombed. When the Mustangs left, both barracks and a hangar were ablaze.

On May 14th, 1944, the squadron moved to Funtington in Sussex. On May 18th, Squadron Leader Drinkwater DFC, flying Mustang FZ164, led three other Mustangs off at 1800 hrs on a Ranger to the Tours - Nantes area. As the Mustangs bobbed along at low level, intense and accurate light and heavy flak was encountered from Chartres and Tours. *"Drink"* drew more fire that the others. A gaping hole suddenly appeared in his starboard wing and the gallant, recently married, twenty-nine year old Cornishman crashed in flames east of Tours. Flying Officer Cush, in FB118, was badly hit, his starboard ammunition box exploding, and a bullet through the cockpit nicked his neck. Flight Lieutenant Pavey, in FZ168, had his external fuel tank blown away, but Flight Sergeant Naish, in FZ118, was more fortunate and escaped without damage. The survivors returned to Funtington at 2030 hrs. Flight Lieutenant Peter Taylor, at that time flying Mustangs himself from Funtington with 65 Squadron, remembers the Mustangs returning, and that *"the boys were pretty shaken up"*.

Flying Officer Peter Taylor poses with his 65 Squadron Mustang at Gravesend, 1944. Note the whistle attached to his battledress collar.

Flight Lieutenant Peter Taylor.

Squadron Leader Drinkwater DFC was buried at St Symhorien cemetery at La Salle, as an *"unknown English soldier"*. After the war the RAF and other armed forces faced the massive task of identifying many servicemen so laid to rest, and collecting all such fallen warriors in communal war cemeteries. On June 22nd, 1946, Mrs Drinkwater received a letter from the Air Ministry:-

"I am reluctant to distress you by referring after so long an interval to the loss of your husband, Squadron Leader THD Drinkwater DFC, but I am compelled to ask for your assistance. Some information has now been received which may enable us, with your help, to trace his burial place. We have received an exhumation report concerning

a grave in St Symhorien Cemetery. *The cemetery records contain an entry: 'Unknown English soldier buried June 1st, 1944'. The exhumation found that the body was that of a Squadron Leader with the 1939-45 Star and DFC, wearing RAF battledress and a dark blue pullover. He had straight light brown hair. No means of identification could be found, but a cuff link was taken from the grave and has been forwarded here. The decorations and locality seem to indicate that this grave may be that of your husband and if you could identify the cuff-link, that would be conclusive. Unfortunately it is in a very bad condition but it has marks of diagonal coloured stripes on a background of pale blue enamel. I am sorry to cause you distress, but I should be most grateful if you could say whether you recognise the link from this description. I hesitate to send it to you because of its condition, but should you wish to see it I will do so".*

Mrs WD Drinkwater did indeed identify the cufflink. Squadron Leader "*Tommy*" Drinkwater DFC was subsequently buried at the Nantes (Pont-du-Cens) Cemetery at Loire Sinfereure: Plot L, Row B, Grave 21.

Squadron Leader T.H.D. Drinkwater DFC's grave showing the original marker shortly after the cessation of hostilities.
Mr Les Drinkwater.

Squadron Leader Drinkwater's career had truly been remarkable, considering his rise from Aircraftman to Squadron Commander and distinguished fighter pilot decorated with the DFC. His period of operational flying, from just after the Battle of Britain until a few weeks before D-Day, saw great variety, spanning from the tentative Circus escort sorties of 1941, to the escorting of massed American formations from 1943 onwards, and saw the role of the fighter pilot changing largely to ground-attack during the build-up to the Allied invasion of Normandy. This period of service also saw the introduction into service of Germany's lethal Fw190, and indeed many RAF squadrons converting from the Spitfire to the Mustang, the latter celebrated by many as actually the best fighter aircraft of the Second World War. "*Drink's*" flying career was virtually entirely operational, and such strain must eventually have told. To conclude this chapter, reproduced below is the last letter that he ever wrote to his wife, and which requires no further comment.

"*Darling, let me tell you again, I love you, This past weekend has made me so pleased that you are my wife because I am so in love with you, and I will love you for the rest of my life. And Darling, thank you for loving me. My sweet, I am sure that you have something belonging to me, because I am always so happy when I am with you, but as soon as we are apart I'm just as flat as can be. I am like a man with no brain, but only a memory of you. Oh Darling, it is terrible. Please do not think me sloppy or stupid, though I may be, but I just can't get over it. Perhaps I am a bit tired tonight, and after a good night's rest will be better and able to write you a nice letter. Anyway, I'll see.*

"*Darling, my operational flying days are nearly over. The Wing Commander has told me this evening that I can't go on so many shows, and he is very concerned about it. He said, 'out of fairness to you and your wife, I don't intend to let you stay on ops much longer, even if you want to'. You see, there was something in what I have said, but hell, I'm going to miss this life. I have had over three years of it and the trouble is that now I know nothing else. My sweet, I must off to bed now, I can hardly see what I am writing, I love you, my own precious darling, more than anything else in the world.*

"*Yours forever, Tom.*"

Chapter Eight

MISSING

Sergeant Eldon Howard Caldwell, RCAF.
Via Allan White.

The River Severn rises at its source high in the Welsh hills, rushing along its upper reaches through Shropshire until sedately meandering through Worcestershire and its cathedral city, downstream becoming tidal at Gloucester. Thereafter the river soon develops into an estuary, joined by the Wye, before discharging into the Bristol Channel. The Severn estuary is amongst the most dangerous in the world, respected and feared by both fishermen and sailors alike. During the Second World War its tidal reaches were to claim the bodies of a number of airmen.

For the young pilots of the Spitfire OTU at Aston Down in Gloucestershire, the Severn estuary held an attraction; the famous railway bridge under the arches of which many flew. Flying Officer Richard Hillary, who trained at Aston Down in 1940, describes in his book *"The Last Enemy"* how he and Pilot Officer Noel Agazarian engaged in a friendly feud which culminated in both of them flying underneath the arches. Air Vice-Marshal David Scott-Malden, who also trained there just before the Battle of Britain, recalled that *"I remember very clearly that we treated flying under the Severn bridge rather as a parting gesture when we had already been posted to a squadron and so reasonably safe from any complaints to the authorities. There were several large arches in the bridge, and two smaller ones on the Welsh side. I had long arguments with my great friend George Barclay about whether a Spitfire could get through one of the smaller arches. He decided that it could get through on the diagonal, ie with the wings at a 45 degrees to the horizontal, and we watched whilst he did so, with some relief at seeing him emerge safely the other side! Personally I played safe and used one of the larger arches."* One pilot who did not safely emerge the other side was a twenty year old Canadian, Sergeant Jack Pierce, who, on February 8th, 1942, was seen by Sergeant Foster to hit the water in Spitfire R7135 and disappear. A subsequent search failed to locate the aircraft and so it was presumed that Sergeant Pierce, of London, Ontario, had been killed. That presumption was proved correct when Sergeant Pierce's body was washed ashore near Chepstow some four months later. The estuary was also used as a firing range, the fledgling fighter pilots shooting at drogues towed by such types as the Fairey Battle. On July 23rd, 1942, twenty-two year old Sergeant Donald Machin, of Widnes, Lancashire, lost control of Spitfire P7509 after attacking such a target, and plunged into the river off Sudbrook, Gwent. His body was recovered the same day.

By January 1942, Fighter Command's squadrons were no longer desperate for replacement pilots, and a review of the OTU situation took place. It was decided to stabilise training and use Hawarden as an example. There courses were sub-divided into four squadrons working to a planned programme putting a steady load on flying, ground and synthetic aspects of training (such as cockpit drill in sectioned fuselages in the Technical Training Block). Courses were increased to nine weeks and the quantity of flying hours was raised to fifty-eight per pupil. Each course consisted of thirty-two pilots and commenced at three week intervals. By this time there was also a new link in the chain of pilot training with the advent of the Advanced Flying Unit. This meant that, coupled with the new OTU course, pilots would have over three hundred flying hours prior to joining their squadrons. Each OTU course was sub-divided into three phases of three weeks duration. During the first the students learned to fly the Spitfire, during the second they practised air-to-air gunnery, and finally tactical training operating from a satellite field. During the latter phase students lived as if actually on an operational squadron and flew mainly air firing, night flying and formation practice sorties in what was really a polishing and refresher period. The nine week courses were designed on a flexible basis, however, so as to allow the posting of students to squadrons after just six weeks in the event of an emergency. Courses also started and finished on a Tuesday so as to avoid weekend travelling. 1942 became the OTU's peak year of output, with 4,353 pilots trained and 390,000 flying hours conducted by the eleven units in operation by that time.

By March 1942 it had been acknowledged that eight day-fighter OTUs were sufficient to meet all UK requirements, even when offensive operations were at a maximum. By July, however, the lull in fighter operations meant that OTU output exceeded demand, so courses were frozen for three weeks with those in progress extended by the same period. When training recommenced, intakes were again thirty-two pilots every three weeks, but after the Dieppe operation in August 1942, when losses were higher than anticipated, the intake was increased to forty-four.

With the Russians on the offensive, rolling back Hitler's final eastern frontier, Stalin put increasing pressure on the Allies to open a Second Front in Europe to further drain German resources and thus alleviate the intensity of opposition encountered in the Soviet Union. The west was not yet in a position to invade enemy occupied Europe, but Stalin was appeased to some extent by the Torch landings in North Africa. As the British stood to at El Alamein, and the Russians surrounded their enemy at Stalingrad, there was a brief clash fought on the French coast; Operation Jubilee. On August 19th, 1942, some six thousand British and Canadian troops landed at Dieppe with inadequate air cover and few supporting destroyers. No German strongpoints were captured and the landing party suffered heavy casualties; of five thousand Canadians only two thousand returned. The RAF lost one hundred and six aircraft, including eighty-eight fighters, with one hundred and thirteen aircrew killed. In what was the most intense and greatest aerial combat since the Battle of Britain, the RAF flew a staggering total of 2,617 sorties. The operation did, however, prove a point; improvisation and inadequate forces would not conquer "Festung Europa". This lesson learned, there then followed eighteen months of detailed planning that would ultimately lead to the successful landings in France on June 6th, 1944.

With the results of the Dieppe operation having been carefully analysed, in January 1943 a new day fighter syllabus was issued which took into account that experience. Courses remained of nine weeks duration, with each intake increased to forty-four in summer. The main feature of the revision was the introduction of a new system of planned flying and maintenance enabling the intensive flying programme to be completed regularly to schedule. The new syllabus taught formation flying, with a particular emphasis on tactical formations as used in fighter squadrons, aerial gunnery and attacks, R/T procedure and homing bearings, dog fighting, aerobatics, low and dusk flying. The *"Pupil's OTU Guide"* advises *"Get your aircraft buttoned up. Learn to fly it as it deserves to be flown. Find out how to get the best out of it in climb, speed, fuel consumption, rates of manoeuvre and accuracy in station keeping. Learn from the instructors the basic principles of fighter tactics. They are in constant touch with the Operational Squadrons and will ensure that your instruction in this respect is up to the minute. Above all learn to shoot."* On marksmanship, this remarkable booklet points out:-

"Getting down to rock bottom, the main object of the RAF is 'Destroy the Enemy'. The most highly skilled flying in the world is of little use in a scrap if good marksmanship is lacking. A fighter is really a gun platform, a fighting machine which must be pointed in the right direction and hit what it is aimed at.

"Get 'deflection minded'. Keep an imaginary reflector sight in front of your eyes, not only in the air, but on the ground. Constant shooting practice is the only way to obtain complete confidence in your ability to kill.

"And close range is paramount. So get close and make sure of your bird."

On flying training, the book says:-

"Every term at OTU most of the avoidable accidents are directly attributable to bad discipline on the part of pupils. These acts range from disobedience of the Flying Instructors' injunctions as to the minimum interval between aircraft to which pupils may close when practising attacks upon each other, to such less serious acts as taxying across grass temporarily prohibited as unserviceable on account of the risk of upturning aircraft. The consequence of such indiscipline is a recurring and wholly avoidable loss of life and equipment that can ill be spared."

On the morning of Tuesday, 26th January, 1943, young Payne from Church Farm, Redwick, Gwent, was walking a herd of cows along the sea wall. As the incoming tide lapped at the shore, the tranquil pastoral scene was rudely disturbed by the snarl of Merlins overhead, as Spitfires from 52 OTU attacked a drogue being towed over the Severn estuary. At 1030 hrs the Flight Commander gave Purple Section orders to attack the target. Sergeant H. Clarke, in Spitfire Mk IIb P8207, swung round over the estuary from the English side and closed on the target. As he did so, Sergeant Eldon Howard Caldwell, in P8208, also made for the drogue, from the Welsh coast, roaring over the sea wall at about 500'. Over the water the wings of the two Spitfires collided. Sergeant Clarke managed to retain control of his machine, and fifty years later Mr Payne recalled the damaged Spitfire flying away up-river, belching out black smoke, to make a safe forced landing on the shore at Magor. Sergeant Caldwell was not so lucky. P8208 spun in half a mile out to sea and disappeared under the waves. For the twenty-two year old from Cardiston, Alberta, Canada, the estuary's cold and treacherous waters became his only grave.

The subsequent inquiry indicated that Sergeant Caldwell had arrived over Redwick early and received instructions to orbit and await his turn. Instead he attacked with the preceding section. Called again by the range control officer and once more told to await his turn, he again attacked which is when the collision occurred. Radio failure was not ruled out, and as Sergeant Caldwell had ignored such explicit instructions twice, I think that explanation quite possible.

Group Captain FG Argyle-Robinson, the Station Commander at Aston Down, later wrote to Sergeant Caldwell's parents:-

"It is with deep regret that I have to write you of the accident in which your son, Sergeant Pilot Eldon Caldwell, was involved whilst serving at this unit.

"The aircraft in which Sgt Caldwell was flying on January 26th, 1943, was seen to dive into the river Severn after it had collided in mid-air with another Spitfire. Although every effort was immediately made to recover the pilot, this could not be done and so your son has been officially posted as missing. But I am afraid there is no doubt that he has in fact been killed, and I wish to express to you the very sincere sympathy felt by myself and the officers and airmen serving on this station with you and your family in this grievous loss.

"The accident has been thoroughly investigated but no satisfactory reason for the mid-air collision has been found. The accident was witnessed both from the air and from the shore, and no attempt to bale out was observed. The Severn is a tidal river and attempts to recover the machine have so far proved unsuccessful, though it has been located. Following Air Ministry procedure, Sergeant Caldwell has been posted as missing. There will be some delay in presuming death unless the body is recovered.

"Sergeant Caldwell was first posted to this unit for target towing duties, but, at his own request, was transferred to operational training. He was a most likeable boy, very popular with his instructors and with other pupils on this station and there is no doubt that he would have made an admirable fighter pilot. By his untimely death both the Royal Air Force and the Royal Canadian Air Force have been deprived of the services of one of the finer type of lads who are the backbone of the force."

Eldon Howard Caldwell was born on November 12th, 1920, at Brocket, Alberta, Canada, and volunteered for aircrew training at Calgary, Alberta, on August 28th, 1941. Thereafter he completed his elementary flying training in Canada before arriving in the UK during 1942 to fly more advanced types of service aircraft. On December 8th, 1942, Sergeant Caldwell commenced his training at 52 OTU with No 26 Course. I have in front of me the log book of Sergeant Pilot Gordon Ingamells, of the same course, which lists numerous training sorties, including many gun firing exercises, with a total Spitfire flying time of forty-six hours and fifty minutes. In fact on January 23rd, Sergeant Ingamells also flew P8208, on *"Exercise 13A. Air combat above 5,000'."*

The twenty-one survivors of No 26 Course passed out of Aston Down on February 9th, 1943, three being posted overseas and the remainder to Spitfire squadrons in England. On August 19th, 1943, however, the Air Ministry officially notified Sergeant Caldwell's parents that their son was now *"presumed killed"* on active service.

There the story of Sergeant Caldwell and Spitfire P8208 may well have ended, if not for an increasing fascination, as from the 1960s, with investigating wartime crashes and recovering wreckage remaining at such sites. The interest became known as *"aviation archaeology"* and during the 1970s and 80s numerous amateur groups sprang up across the nation. A mad scramble for each organisation to investigate as many sites as possible thereafter commenced, with obvious results; sometimes both research and recovery work were undertaken in a slapdash manner. A huge amount of wreckage was recovered, often for display in scrap metal yard like arrangements relating precious little information regarding either the airmen concerned or their demise. It is not entirely a negative picture, however, as several capable author-historians fortunately emerged from their interest in aviation archaeology.

During the war, with aircraft falling out of the sky with an ever increasing rapidity, sometimes burying themselves deep in remote countryside, contemporary recoveries were not always possible. In such instances the airman involved was posted *"missing"*. The Ministry of Defence's view on such matters is that, so long after the event, a policy of *"letting sleeping dogs lie"* is appropriate so as not to cause further, undue, distress to families. Of course one could argue that all relatives would want their loved ones to be given a Christian burial, but there is evidence that on some occasions when the remains of *"missing"* airmen have been discovered by archaeologists, families have in fact been more distressed to have old coals raked over and painful memories evoked than for the status quo of *"missing"* to have been maintained. In 1986 the Government passed new legislation, the Protection of Military Remains Act, which, amongst other things, restricted the practices of the aviation archaeological movement. A licensing system was introduced whereby permission for recoveries was only given to bona fide individuals and groups with an historical interest, and only when there was no reasonable chance of human remains or live ordnance being encountered. Any application, therefore, to excavate the crash site of an aircraft whose pilot was not recovered for burial at the time, will, quite rightly, be automatically refused. On occasions, however, the RAF Aircraft Salvage Team have excavated such sites and have indeed recovered pilots for burial.

Such operations are obviously conducted totally professionally and with sensitivity in respect of dealing with the bereaved families involved.

During the early 1980s, a friend of mine formed an aviation archaeological group which was very active for several years. Many sites were dug, and much wreckage recovered, but unfortunately my friend was the only member undertaking any worthwhile research work. His positive efforts to record this information for posterity were sadly negated by the practices of other members whose motive was merely the collection of souvenirs, the great historical value of many of the relics involved not even being appreciated. Tragically the majority of these items have since been lost forever as members eventually dispersed and lost contact since the group folded and became inactive in the late 1980s. Unfortunately this situation is now all too common. Clearly for serious historians who have chosen to operate in a professional manner, and who make every effort to conduct research in the utmost of detail, such practices are deplorable.

In August 1984 this particular society discovered Sergeant Caldwell's Spitfire in the Severn estuary. The Merlin engine was still there, with propeller assembly attached, and all other major components besides. The engine and propeller, and a number of other significant items including many cockpit

Spitfire P8208 as first discovered by enthusiasts in August 1984.

Allan White.

components and the complete tail-wheel assembly, were subsequently recovered. My friend worked hard to have these items restored to some extent and displayed in a museum at an RAF station. Again others in the group were hardly as responsible; the engine was sledgehammered to facilitate access to the stainless parts within (valves etc apparently make nice trophies), and numerous other components have since gone *"missing"*. Fortunately my friend, whose interests have since diversified, recovered the P8208 items displayed at the station museum concerned when it closed, and has since kindly donated them to the Malvern Spitfire Team.

As is widely known following publication of my second book, *"The Invisible Thread: A Spitfire's Tale"*, which tells the story of a Spitfire which we recovered in 1987, the Team is also involved in the investigation of wartime crash sites, but believes the background research and human element to be of paramount importance. The physical bits and pieces are therefore merely the *"icing on the cake"*, as opposed to the team being motivated exclusively by their collection as are so many other organisations. The Team also has a serious Aeronautical Engineering Unit, headed by Dr Dennis Williams, himself a Ministry of Defence employed scientist. Dennis's research into the nuts and bolts of the Spitfire in particular is of the highest order. The wonders that he works with lumps of corroded metal, employing a *"secret"* chemical cleaning process, really have to be seen to be believed, each component being completely stripped and often restored to working order. The P8208 remains that the team inherited, therefore, have since been subject to his attentions and remarkable results have been achieved. The propeller is a De Havilland unit with duralumin blades, the angle of which the pilot could alter in flight, this having a similar effect to changing gear in a car. Incredibly those blades now once again turn into *"coarse"* and *"fine"* pitch, the entire unit having been dissected, restored and re-built.

When displayed, the lovingly restored items will be exhibited by honorary team-member Brian Owen, Keeper of Collections at Worcester City Museum, in a professional and intelligently presented setting indicating the relevant position in the aircraft of each component. Such interests amongst members therefore ideally complement the *"human"* research work conducted by Team secretary Andrew Long and myself, and superb artwork by Mark Postlethwaite G. Av.A., all of which equally contribute to fascinating presentations attracting many thousands of visitors. This unique blend of specialist skills, brought together under the umbrella of one responsible organisation with a very limited membership, is what has made the Malvern Spitfire Team so successful. Until recently the Team has been pleased to mount temporary exhibitions, particularly at Tudor House Museum, Worcester, but we now have so much material that only a permanent display is appropriate. We are currently seeking suitable premises and hope to achieve this objective within the not too distant future.

Dennis Williams and I collected the P8208 wreckage during 1992, and we also received Allan White's research files into the air war over south-west England, particularly as it affected RAF Aston Down. This material, the standard of which is impeccable, will now be put to good use, as indeed some of it has in this particular chapter. I had also long been aware of the P8208 story and during the late 1980s had been pleased to fill in some gaps for Allan in relation to that particular Spitfire's history. My research indicated that Spitfire P8208 had been built at the Castle Bromwich Aircraft Factory and was one of a relatively small number of cannon armed Mk IIs built. Delivered to 12 MU on March 26th, 1941, the Spitfire first served at RAF Northolt with 303 *"Kosciuszko"* Squadron and No1 Polish Fighter Wing between May 5th, and June 14th, 1941. That period was the time of early offensive fighter operations, and P8208 was flown on a number of training flights and bomber escorts over France by Group Captain Pawilkowski, Pilot Officers Paderewski, Wroblewski, Zak, Lapinski, and Sergeants Szlagowski and Giermer. All flights occurred without note, except on June 14th, 1941, when P8208, flown by Pilot Officer Wroblewski, was part of an escort formation to bombers on Circus 12. During the return trip the Poles were attacked by four Me 109s. One of the Poles fired back but without result.

The crash site re-located by the Malvern Spitfire Team in February 1993, and photographed by Dennis Williams from Peter Earp's Robinson helicopter. The item is part of the Spitfire's mainspar with an undercarriage leg attached. Note the chrome still gleaming in the area not barnacle-encrusted.

Dennis Williams.

A rudder pedal, with a part of the fabric foot-strap still attached, discovered at the site on the Malvern Spitfire Team's first visit.

Andrew Long.

Peter Earp's helicopter, used for reconnaissance work, "parked" on the crash site and adjacent to some wreckage. In the distance can be seen the sea wall, about half a mile away, along which Mr Payne was walking when he actually saw P8208 crash on January 26th, 1943.

Andrew Long.

As Dennis worked his miracles on the P8208 parts, information was received that since the war many people had visited the crash site, which was accessible on foot during periods of extreme low tides, and many other souvenirs had been taken away. What gave cause for serious concern, however, was that during the early 1980s human remains had possibly been discovered at the site and the appropriate authorities not informed. The Team was immediately disturbed to learn of this possibility and found obscene the prospect that Sergeant Caldwell's bones were still with the remaining parts of his machine and open to interference by sightseers. By coincidence an old fishing friend of mine and former police officer, Chris Carne, had since become a bailiff with the National Rivers Authority and was based at Chepstow in Gwent. As Redwick lay in his geographical area of responsibility, Chris was consulted regarding the spring tide dates, which would give the safest access to the site, and his professional experience enlisted to help plan a reconnaissance. I then contacted Martin Hill at the Ministry of Defence (S10) and explained the situation, putting across the case that as Sergeant Caldwell's remains were possibly still present, and therefore vulnerable, the P8208 site did not fall within the spirit of the Protection of Military Remains Act, especially as it lay just 500 yards offshore and accessible on foot. I suggested that a joint RAF/MoD/Malvern Spitfire Team operation should be mounted during the forthcoming spring tide dates and every effort made to both find the missing airman and clear the site. I indicated to Martin that although we had located Sergeant Caldwell's relatives in Canada, we intended to make no contact with them at this time, as in the event of nothing ultimately being found their hopes may only have been raised for nought, or in the event of the pilot's remains actually being discovered we were anxious for the news to be broken to the family by official sources. To all this the Ministry of Defence agreed, and a visit was arranged with Flight Lieutenant "Tex" Dallas and his RAF Aircraft Salvage Team, based at St Athan, for Monday, February 8th, 1993. The help of honorary team-member Peter Earp was also enlisted to fly down in his Robinson helicopter with Dennis Williams and locate the wreckage from the air, thereafter directing the walking party accordingly.

On the day in question, the Team and the RAF met at lunchtime in Redwick's village inn. We quickly set about convincing Flight Lieutenant Dallas of the seriousness of our interest, and quality of work to date, in addition to impressing upon him that in respect of this particular project, the safety aspect had been accorded especial priority, Chris Carne's professional and enthusiastic help in this sphere of course being invaluable. By 1.30 pm on what was a dull and miserable February day, the party was gathered on the seawall, awaiting Chris's instructions to head out after the rapidly receding tide. Eventually we clambered down the wall and slithered our way across one hundred yards of thick mud. Then came the difficult part; some two hundred and fifty yards of quicksand which had the texture of jelly. It was a frightening experience, but, breathless, we reached the hard shale some five hundred yards out on which the Spitfire was believed to lie. A large section of spar was found, but then all eyes were turned skyward as the Robinson appeared, Peter landing on the shale. Quickly airborne following a brief appraisal of the situation so far, minutes later Dennis, acting as observer in the aircraft, spotted a mainspar and undercarriage leg pointing skywards, just having been uncovered by the tide. The site, therefore, lay several hundred yards away from where the first spar was found. We all quickly made our way to the helicopter, which was hovering just inches above the water. Soon the site was completely dry, and there it was; all that remained of Spitfire P8208. All fuselage skinning and framework had long disappeared, and components were strewn across a large area of the seabed. Tony Bramhall's metal detector gave a continuous note over a wide area due to the large volume of metal present. The radiator was found, and the main spar broken in half, each with an undercarriage leg still attached, the chrome gleaming through in areas not barnacle-encrusted. The fuel tank and seat armour were found lying on top of the shale, but many other items were actually fossilising into the crust, and these had to be dug out. A rudder pedal soon came to the surface, and the bracket fitted adjacent to the reflector gunsight to accommodate spare bulbs for same. In this area *"Tex"* and his men started digging furiously, assisted by Team-members, hoping that it would be the position where the cockpit had settled into the bed. Soon two bones were discovered. Meanwhile the vast amount of wreckage was placed in one great pile. The problem was that it was dangerous enough to cross the quicksand carrying but a spade, so it was going to be impossible to return to the shore carrying the wreckage, some of which was extremely heavy. Peter managed to fly a small quantity back, but of course his small helicopter was not powerful enough to lift any substantial items. With the emphasis firmly on safety, Chris soon gave the order for us to start making the trek back to the sea wall, although I have to admit that on that occasion I cheated and returned in the helicopter!

The next day we all met in the village and made another visit to the site, the intention being for the Team to help the RAF dig deeper in the hope of discovering Sergeant Caldwell. We were all disappointed, however, to learn from Flight Lieutenant Dallas that the RAF St Athan Medical Officer had identified the bones collected the previous day as being of animal origin. Another bone was found on the second search, but this too was later similarly identified. On the previous day the weather had been quite mild, although overcast and dull, but on this second trip across the sand a bitter wind chilled deep, even through a Barbour jacket.

The wreckage was found still in a pile at the site, as we had left it, and St Athan's Sergeant *"Tiny"* Baelz estimated it to weigh well over 1,000lbs. The RAF's official interest in the project, however, only extended to recovering Sergeant Caldwell, and not the mangled remains of his aircraft, so a gratis helicopter lift was not going to be forthcoming from that source. The original idea had been to take a boat out on the morning tide, anchor up over the wreck, and load up the wreckage when the vessel became marooned by the receding tide, later being floated off when the water rushed back in. Unfortunately it was now feared that the rough nature of the shale might damage the boat's bottom, so therefore the only option was to somehow secure an airlift. Subsequently an approach was made to Bristow Helicopters Ltd, of Redhill Aerodrome in Surrey, and the Managing Director and Chief Executive, Mr Brian Collins, very generously agreed to sponsor the project with the use of a Sikorski S-76 helicopter and crew on the next spring tide date.

On Tuesday, 9th March, 1993, a fine, warm and clear day, apparently not unlike that on which P8208 had come to grief, Sergeant Baelz waved in the magnificent red, white and blue Bristow's machine to land in the field behind the sea wall. Captain Martin Forde, Bristow's Chief Pilot, kindly agreed to fly a shuttle service to land our party and equipment out at the site. Everyone was naturally delighted at not having to negotiate the quicksand, and soon the first party was away. Landing in the S-76 out on the shale, which had the consistency of rough tarmac, we discovered the pile of wreckage relatively intact, but covered in sand. Once everyone had been flown out to the site, the party split, some digging away at the cockpit area, others to free the pile, and the remainder loading items into the helicopter. The Robinson again appeared on the horizon and aviation artist and Team-member Mark Postlethwaite flew with Peter to take aerial photographs of the site and work in progress. Another bone was discovered, but we were all doubtful that it was human, and indeed this was also later officially identified as being of animal origin. With the site having been completely cleared, Chris called *"time"*, and Martin began shuttling everyone back to shore. Leaving the site we were all elated at the success of the recovery side of the operation, and particularly at the project's value as a public relations exercise, the Malvern Spitfire and RAF Aircraft Salvage Teams having worked together as one, but there was a prevailing element of sadness as we had not found Sergeant Caldwell which was our original objective and reason for defying the estuary and elements.

Captain Martin Forde eases down his S-76 at the site during the Team's second visit in March 1993. A pile of wreckage gathered during the previous visit can be seen already partially covered in silt.

Andrew Long.

"Operation Estuary" completed, participants pose for a team photograph. From left to right: David Malpas, Tony Bramhall, Anthony Whitehead, Captain Martin Forde, Sergeant "Tiny" Baelz (flanked by two Bristow ground crew members), Phil Jones, Dilip Sarkar, Mark Postlethwaite, Corporal Evans, Chris Carne (kneeling), Andrew Long, and two more helpers from Bristow Helicopters Ltd. Peter Earp hovers above in G-BSIT.

Dennis Williams.

Dennis Williams is currently hard at work on the P8208 remains which we plan to display in a forthcoming major exhibition dedicated to the memory of the unfortunate pilot. A preliminary post-recovery examination of the wreckage has revealed many valuable items, including the maker's plate, bearing the constructor's number CBAF 640, and detailing every modification that P8208 underwent, the reflector gunsight, with its glass lens intact, and a host of other fascinating relics besides. Dennis has kindly prepared the following authorative notes for the technically minded:-

"The first remains of P8208 to come into the custody of the Malvern Spitfire Team were items both large and small, which had been subjected to the attention of less well intentioned individuals in 1984. Included were the impressive De Havilland constant speed propeller, unfortunately minus the distinctive hub cylinder which had been smashed as a means of separating the rest of the assembly from the reduction gearing at the front of the engine. Six valves were all that remained of the once powerful Merlin engine, although fortunately the brass plate bearing both the Rolls-Royce and Air Ministry serials had survived. Cockpit items included the blind flying panel with part of the artificial horizon attached, pieces of the plastic instrument panel, the clock, the carbon dioxide cylinder for emergency undercarriage actuation, the windscreen de-icer pump and the oxygen stop-cock. The tailwheel, with its leg and shock absorber strut, was also present, as was one of the two under-wing oil coolers. Finally, the two Hispano 20mm cannon were retrieved virtually intact, together with one of the empty case ejector chutes. My first impression upon assessing this wreckage for preservation was of the relatively minor damage to many of the components. For example, although the propeller blades had each deformed rearwards, on eventual dismantling the only other crash damage to the propeller was found to be cracking of the steel thrust races at the blade roots. The conclusion is that the aircraft impacted at relatively low airspeed, perhaps in a belly-landing or ditching, or possibly in a spin, (ie in a stalled, rotating condition, rather than in a spiral dive in which the airspeed would have been high), this being consistent with eye-witness reports of the accident. However, corrosion damage as a result of several decades immersion in sea water had taken its toll, and for some thin-gauge ferrous components recovered in 1993, the decay was complete; only rusty impressions in concretions revealed their fossilised shapes. However, stainless steel and brass items had survived with only superficial damage, but most remarkable were the chrome plated oleo rams on the main undercarriage legs, also recovered in 1993, which had suffered practically no attack from the sea water. Most of the alloy skinning had already been lost when the site was located by the Team, but large sections of the concentric, multi-tube mainspar booms characteristic of the Spitfire wing were mainly intact and still attached to the undercarriage legs. Much of the wreckage was covered in calcified deposits, ranging from easily removed barnacles

to thick layers of scale. As cleaning of the P8208 parts has proceeded, chemical means have been used in preference to abrasion, with a variety of specialised methods being used for treatment of various alloys. Conservation versus restoration, and originality versus presentability are always carefully considered, with the general aim being to preserve and display the items in a corrosion-free, 'as crashed' state. However, in view of the excellent condition of some of the P8208 items, it has been possible to return them to working order, and this in itself is a tribute to the engineering standards applied to the Spitfire over fifty years ago."

Dr Dennis Williams hard at work restoring P8208's De Havilland airscrew which was initially recovered in 1984 but donated to the Malvern Spitfire Team by Allan White in 1992.

Dennis Williams.

Upon conclusion of the recovery, I received a letter from Martin Hill at the Ministry of Defence, part of which I quote:-

"I am sorry that the search for Sergeant Caldwell ended in disappointment, but in a way at least the uncertainty of whether he still lay with his aircraft has now been removed. I feel that this whole episode vindicates the MoD's policy, because to have raised false hopes of discovering Sergeant Caldwell might have brought a devastating blow to his relatives when nothing was found. It is a shame that not all aviation archaeological groups take the Malvern Spitfire Team's responsible attitude."

So Sergeant Eldon Howard Caldwell remains "missing, presumed killed", with no known grave. He is commemorated on Panel 186 of the Runnymede

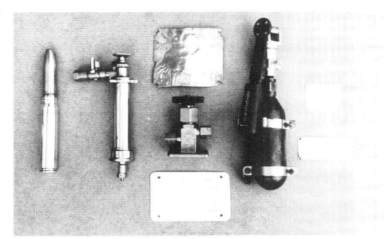

A small selection of P8208 items restored by Dennis Williams; left to right: 20mm Hispano Suiza ball round, windscreen de-icer pump, (top) Rolls-Royce Merlin maker's plate, oxygen supply cock, (bottom) manufacturer's plate including the serial number "P8208", the CO_2 bottle for emergency operation of the undercarriage system, (top) the SU carburettor plate and (bottom) a magazine instruction plate.

Dennis Williams.

Having cut a template to size, Dennis Williams is now in the process of re-building P8208's instrument panel using parts recovered from the crash site. Unfortunately when recovered in 1984, the Blind Flying Panel was complete, but all instrumentation had since gone "missing" prior to the item coming into the care of the Malvern Spitfire Team.

Dennis Williams.

Memorial dedicated to all Commonwealth airmen with no known resting place. At least, however, the participants of *"Operation Estuary"* can be sure that nothing now remains at the site to be interfered with, and that no more could have been done, fifty years after the crash, to find this young Canadian. The Team is currently considering the erection of a suitable plaque on the sea wall dedicated to Sergeant Caldwell, and in my mind's eye I picture the evocative sight and sound of a lone Spitfire roaring up-river in tribute.

To conclude, however, I would offer a word of caution. The Severn estuary is a dangerous place in which I would not have considered operating if not for on site professional advice. The Redwick site has also been totally cleared, so there is no longer anything to be seen. Please do not risk your life for nothing.

Chapter Nine

A RADIANT MEMORY OF YOUTH

Sergeant George Courtney Lock.
Mrs Joan Walter.

George Courtney Lock was born on September 14th, 1921, in the village of Fleur-de-Lys in Monmouthshire, the son of Courtney and Sarah Lock. Mr Lock had fought for his country in the Great War with the Devonshire Regiment and had received both the Distinguished Conduct and Military Medals for his bravery. During the war he had been wounded in Flanders when his face was hit with shrapnel. After the war Mr Lock took a position in charge of stores at the South Wales Health Sanitorium which treated tuberculosis sufferers (now Bronllys Hospital). Mr and Mrs Lock lived at Rose Villa in the tiny village of Bronllys with their two children, Joan and her younger brother George. The Welsh hamlet lies about eight miles to the north-east of Brecon, at the foot of the Black Mountains, and is overlooked by those imposing heights. Today Bronllys remains little changed since the days of the Lock family.

George was great friends with two local boys, twins Derek and Francis Owens. When pupils at the local school, their headmaster nicknamed the Owens *"Pudding"* and *"Pie"* respectively. Although *"Pudding"* never stuck as a nickname for Derek, twin Francis was known to all as *"Pie"* and he later attended Brecon Grammar School with George upon completion of their primary education at the village school.

In 1988 Derek Owens told me a little of those boyhood days:-

"My recollections of George are all very happy ones. Of course he was the best friend of both my brother and I. Being neighbours in such a small village and boys of the same age we were as close as brothers. We spent many hours in each other's company. When indoors we would play games but out of doors we would go for long walks across the Welsh hills, go on push bike rides or do a spot of mountain climbing. Of course there was no television so we had to find our own amusement. I suppose we did all the things that village boys got up to in those days."

George completed his Central Welsh Board Certificate of Education at Brecon Grammar School and left in 1938. At the age of seventeen he went to work as a clerk for a soup manufacturer in London. Soon afterwards he moved on to work in the offices of the United Kingdom Tea Company Ltd at the Empire Warehouse in London's dockland. George remained with the company until he joined the Royal Air Force Volunteer Reserve (RAFVR) in October 1940. Elder sister Joan also left Bronllys for London and worked as a clerk in the Ministry of Supply throughout the war, living in the capital throughout the blitz.

George Lock lived north-west of the Thames in Kentish Town throughout the around the clock attacks on London during the Battle of Britain. Along with the rest of the capital's population the young clerk took shelter, and in the morning, amidst the rubble and still smouldering fires of the night's destruction, went back to work as normal. Doubtless he watched with fascination the intricate patterns of white vapour trails being woven in September skies high above the capital as young men fought to decide their nations' destinies. On Saturday, 19th October, 1940, George went to his local RAF recruiting centre and volunteered for aircrew training in the RAF Volunteer Reserve. The recruiting Sergeant gave nineteen year old George his *"Notice Paper"*, being *"A Notice to be given to a Man at the time of his offering to join the Royal Air Force Volunteer Reserve."* George also signed the *"Oath to be taken by recruit on attestation"* which was worded as follows:-

"I, George Courtney Lock, swear by Almighty God that I will be faithful and bear true allegiance to His Majesty King George Sixth, His Heirs and Successors, and that I will, as duty bound, honestly and faithfully defend His Majesty, His Heirs and Successors, in Person, Crown and Dignity against all enemies, and will observe and obey all orders of His Majesty, His Heirs and Successors and of the Air Officers and

Officers over me. So help me God."

Joan was not surprised when her younger brother volunteered for aircrew training. Now Mrs Joan Walter, she recalls that:-

"George was always interested in flying but was adamant that he would only fly fighters and not bombers. If he was alive today I am sure he would be an aviation enthusiast."

George lived at 20 Bartholomew Road in Kentish Town, and on Wednesday, October 23rd, received his instructions from the Officer Commanding, RAF Recruiting Centre, Edgware Road, London, to report at that centre on Wednesday, October 30th, to *"be considered for the vacancy of untrained aircrew."* The letter went on to say that *"As the stay will be two to three days you should bring with you your ration book, shaving kit, sufficient clothing and a waterproof."*

Having successfully passed all of the tests at Edgware Road, George enlisted in the RAFVR *"For the duration of the present emergency"* on October 30th, 1940, just one day before the official close of the Battle of Britain. His service record shows that on that day he was mustered as an *"Aircrafthand/pilot."*

George now waited for the real test, his flying training which, under the provisions of the Empire Air Training Scheme, was to be conducted overseas in America and Canada, far away from the dangers of marauding German fighters. Having joined 1 Recruitment Centre, Uxbridge, as an Aircraftman 2nd Class on his day of enlistment, he was posted to Farnborough on December 6th. He joined 9 Recruitment Wing on April 5th, 1941, prior to arriving at the Initial Training Wing two weeks later and embarking for Canada, the *"square bashing"* over, shortly afterwards.

In late June 1941, Leading Aircraftman George Lock reached Canada and disembarked from a troopship after a trans-Atlantic Ocean voyage. In July, George and his fellow would-be aviators arrived for their first taste of flying at the Southern Aviation School, Camden, South Carolina, USA, as only the second British class to do so. At Camden the British pupils flew Stearman biplane training aircraft under the capable supervision of American civilian flying instructors.

One of a series of photographs reproduced from George Lock's photograph album and taken whilst training in America. George, at right, is wearing an American Army Air Corps hat, doubtless the property of an instructor!
Author's collection.

In October, the British students moved on from Camden to the Air Corps Basic Flying School at Cochran Field, Macon, Georgia, as a Camden newspaper reported *"to receive ten weeks of basic training in heavier type planes. In this phase of training they will receive instruction in aircraft, radio, cross country and night flying."* George found himself in 'B' Squadron flying the American Vultee BT-13a, a low winged radial engined monoplane trainer known affectionately by students as the *"Vultee Vibrator"*.

What a marvellous opportunity it must have been for youngsters like George Lock to travel to the United States of America, learn to fly and get paid for the privilege ! For a lad of not yet twenty from a tiny Welsh village community it must have been quite an experience. Throughout his training, George, a keen amateur photographer, made a photographic record of this period of his life. From the pages of his album stare back the fresh faces of boys embarking upon a great adventure, standing next to rows of smartly painted aeroplanes in their flying kit and posing with their instructors whom they clearly idolised. Perhaps it is the odd snap such as George sitting on a beach looking out to sea captioned *"Home's over there somewhere"* and *"Too far to swim Kelly"* as a friend does likewise, that reveal the inner feelings of these young men who were a long way from home. No doubt for many of the students it was the first time that they had ever been away from home, let alone travelled abroad. However, judging from the album, which is a tremendous historical record of the Empire Air Training Scheme and a credit to the nineteen year old who compiled it, George had no problems settling down to enjoy his new way of life and appears to have been popular amongst his colleagues. Recreation for the young fliers seems to have been mainly table tennis, volleyball, swimming, baseball, cinema and trips into the local towns sight-seeing.

"Home is over there somewhere".   *Author's collection.*

186

On November 2nd, 1941, *"Aviation Cadet Lock G"* wrote to his friend Derek Owens in Bronllys who was now a member of the local Home Guard unit:-

"Dear Derek,

"About a week ago I received a letter from you dated September 21st and I am always very glad to hear from you, all about the 'goings on' and happenings in Bronllys, although I realise that they are not exactly sufficient to write a book on! I was especially interested in your HQ activities and hope you continue with plenty of tactical and field training so that you can write and tell me about it. I expect that as now is the beginning of November the weather at home is being a bit on the chilly side. We had a bit of bad weather last week, cloudy skies and showers but this week-end the sun is shining again, still very warm, but when it goes down it gets pretty cool. The rain we had last week was the cause of our having quite a bit of flying cancelled. One day although the clouds were very low they decided we could fly and I went with my instructor to another landing field about twenty miles away where he was directing the solo students who were also over there practising landings. All we had to do was sit in the 'plane and give instructions over the radio to the other chaps. Eventually there were seven chaps over there when the weather closed in and ceiling was practically zero. It was impossible to fly in it. This was at half past nine in the morning and we waited there until nearly one 'o' clock. We could hear several ships who were still trying to make radio contact and get back to the field but two of them, both solo students, had to make forced landings. The weather showed no signs of clearing so they brought over a guard for our ships and transport to take us back by road. First of all we went to where the one ship had landed and watched a Lieutenant take off and fly instruments back to the airport. He only just managed to get out of the field, missing some trees at the end by inches. It was tea-time before we got back here and we had to pass a boring afternoon at ground school.

"Our upper class have left us now and in a day or two there'll be a new class arriving. We never find anything interesting to do and spend our weekends at the pictures and as upper classmen we also have the doubtful privilege of being allowed to the camp cinema on two nights of the week. We find life a lot better here than when we first arrived but it still gets pretty boring at times, especially when we don't fly. However we are already half way through and time is passing quickly. I'm looking forward to coming home again.

"Well, I'll say so long again Derek, remember me to the folks, I hope they are all well.

"All the best, your pal, George."

That letter tells us a great deal about the initial stages of aircrew training overseas. The enthusiasm for the job in hand and a love of flying rises above the boredom of everyday camp life.

In January 1942, George moved on for more advanced instruction at the Air Corps Advanced Flying School at Napier Field, Dothan, Alabama. During their time at the Advanced Flying School the cadets also received instruction at Eglin Field, Valpariso, Florida, where the pupils practised the basic skills of aerial gunnery. At this time George commenced a diary of each day's events and below are some extracts from this period:-

Wednesday 7th January 1942: "*Bad accident - Barlow and Bell crashed into a lake. Barlow killed, Bell injured.*"

Thursday 8th: "*Went by truck to Eglin Field, Florida. Very cold.*"

Saturday 10th: "*Dual gunnery. Gun jammed - didn't get a round out.*"

Friday 16th: "*Left Eglin by convoy at 1.30pm. Arrived at Dothan 6 o' clock. Opened post until 10.30pm then went to the pictures.*"

Monday 19th: "*Night cross country flight to Birmingham, back at 4am. Hopkins crashed and was killed.*"

Sunday 1st February 1942: "*Approx. 200 hrs flying.*"

"Come a shootin' bud!".

Author's collection.

Even from those few short entries we can see that training accidents were common and all too often fatal. For those who survived and passed the course was the ultimate prize - the coveted pilot's brevet or "*wings.*"

George Lock passed out from the Air Corps Advanced Flying School on

Friday, February 6th, 1942. As part of Graduation Class 4273, Sergeant Lock received his diploma from the Post Commander Lt.Col. Daniel, and his "*wings*" from the Director of Training, Lt.Col. Williams. As George had trained in the USA he was not only awarded the RAF flying brevet, but also the solid silver wings of the United States Army Air Corps. After the ceremony, photographs were taken of George and his friend Kelly, the fledgling pilots proudly sporting both flying badges on their tunics.

George's final grade sheet from Dothan shows that he completed 60.02 flying hours in his initial training, 70.25 flying hours in basic and 74.30 flying hours in advanced flying. Gaining his wings had taken a grand total of 204.57 hours in the air.

George Lock and his friend, Kelly, proudly sporting both the RAF flying brevet and USAAC pilot's badge after their "Wings" parade.

Author's collection.

George's final average was 92 per cent and his flying grade "*satisfactory.*" The grade sheet defines three grades: "*Satisfactory - satisfactory and acceptable, Unsatisfactory - Unsatisfactory and below the minimum standards and Failure - Inferior and dangerous; unable to meet minimum standards. Exhibits traits which are a source of danger to his life as well as the lives of others. This grade will require action by supervisory personnel.*"

He recorded in his diary: "*Graduation. Received wings and diplomas. Party tonight, Holden passed out !*"

The newly graduated pilots then began the long journey home, by road and rail to 31 Personnel Dispersal Centre at Moncton and across the ocean by troopship to the United Kingdom. These diary extracts relate those times:-

George Lock ready to go.

Author's collection.

Tuesday 10th: "*Got up at 3.30am, trucks at 6.00am for Montgomery, train at 10.30am.*"

Thursday 12th: *"Stopped at Toronto and took some pictures."*

Monday 16th: *"Life during these weeks at Moncton is so much the same, day after day, that daily entries would be tedious to read and write. We eat, sleep and sometimes visit town in the evenings. Having now been promoted to the illustrious rank of Sergeant we are allowed out all night but as yet I have not taken advantage of the privilege. The snow persists, as does the cold, but our quarters are very well heated and everyone is comfortable."*

Monday 23rd: *"We should have been posted days ago but we are still here. A draft of observers, air gunners and eighty three of our chaps have already left. Some Canadian trained Pilot Officers have also come and gone but we remain here, in the majority of cases flat broke. The weather has become milder. The snow thaws and continues to clear during the day then freezes up at night. Each day brings fresh rumours and duff gen and there is a general feeling of despair of us never leaving Moncton. An item of interest, something out of the ordinary, an eclipse of the moon."*

Wednesday 10th March 1942: *"Preparing to leave. Got out of camp by climbing wire fence !"*

Thursday 11th: *"Left camp at nine. Train left at ten to Halifax, Nova Scotia. On board the 'Orbita' at five, a fifteen hundred ton ship, hundreds of soldiers and airmen aboard. Lucky to have a cabin below."*

Saturday 14th: *"Left Halifax about 8.30am and land rapidly going out of sight by 10 'o' clock."*

Wednesday 18th: *"Everyone sticking voyage remarkably well, know of no one sick. Weather cold but not very."*

Saturday 21st: *"Excitement mounts as land nears - won £2 on roulette."*

Sunday 22nd: *"Reached Scotland this morning. In Clyde by 10 am."*

Monday 23rd: *"Parade at 8.30am, got ashore and train by 1 pm. Travelling all day via Carlisle, Crewe and Gloucester. Arrived Bournemouth 5am. Billeted in flats, lovely day, Bournemouth a great place."*

At Bournemouth the pilots joined 3 Personnel Recruitment Centre from where those arriving in the UK after training overseas were kept until they received notification of posting to further training units in the UK. From Bournemouth George embarked upon his first period of home leave since returning from Canada and the USA:-

Tuesday 7th April 1942: *"Caught 12.00 train from Paddington. Home via Newport at 6pm."*

Monday 13th: *"Back to London by 11.13, home for tea. Stayed most of the evening at Daisy's."*

Saturday 18th: *"Boring parades in preparation for posting."*

George was then posted to No.7 Personnel Recruitment Centre at Harrogate, Yorkshire, arriving by train at 8 am on Tuesday, March 21st, 1942. From his quarters at the Majestic Hotel, Kings Road, Harrogate, George wrote to Derek Owens:-

"Dear Derek,

"It only seems a few days since I left Bronllys but I'll tell you something of what has happened here since then. I rang 'Pie' up at his digs but as he wasn't at home I left a message for him to come over to Kentish Town but unfortunately he didn't get it so I was unable to see him Monday night. I haven't even got his address to write to so please let me have it as soon as possible.

"I made the most of my last couple of days leave and had a really good time but in no time at all it seemed we were back in Bournemouth. We didn't stay very long though and last night at 8 o'clock we started our journey northwards. Travelling all night in just an ordinary railway compartment wasn't any too comfortable and I wasn't sorry when we reached Harrogate at 7.30 this morning. We've been billeted in the Majestic Hotel - a huge place and of course we have a room about six storeys up. They are nice rooms and I think we'll be comfortable enough. As yet I haven't any idea what we'll be doing here but I imagine it will be a sort of refresher ground school course until we are posted for flying. The town itself isn't any too good for troops.

"Well, I think I'll say cheerio for this time, Derek. Remember me to all the folks, so long, Your Pal, George."

George continued his diary at Harrogate:-

Tuesday May 5th, 1942: *"Celebrated Kelly's twenty first birthday. Had a good night."*

Tuesday 12th: *"Yorkshire Moor to watch army manoeuvres. Didn't get back until late, terrible weather."*

On Saturday, May 16th, 1942, Sergeant Pilot Lock was posted to 14 Advanced Flying Unit (AFU) at Ossington in Nottinghamshire. His diary tells us what it was like being a pilot under training at the AFU:-

Sunday, May 17th, 1942: *"Dispersed camp. Poor huts, good mess. Long walk from one to another."*

Monday 18th: *"Flying twin engined Airspeed Oxfords."*

Tuesday 19th: *"Reported to flight but only got cockpit drill."*

Thursday 21st: *"Flew dual. Don't particularly like the Oxford."*

Friday 22nd: *"Am settling down to the daily routine at Ossington quite well. Flying is scarce but ground school is fairly interesting. Evenings are spent in the Sgts mess usually playing billiards and table tennis.*

Every day is a normal working day but we have one day off a week. The weather is most unsettled and is holding flying up quite a bit."

Tuesday June 9th, 1942: *"Got stuck on the perimeter track behind a crashed Oxford."*

Friday 12th: *"Transferred to Night Flying (NF) flight."*

Thursday 18th: *"Low ceiling stopped flying all day but flew a couple of hours tonight."*

Friday 19th: *"Getting ready to leave for Beam Approach Training (BAT) Course."*

Saturday 20th: *"Arrived at Holme approximately 3pm."*

Sunday 21st: *"Good billet, good mess. Issued with push bike to run around on."*

Monday 22nd: *"Got cracking on the beam, also Link trainer. Camp flicks, saw 'Virginia."*

Saturday 27th: *"Day off. Left at 12, caught 2.20 from York, Kings Cross at 6.20. Dais and 'Pie' came over after tea."*

Wednesday 1st July 1942: *"Flying all day, got six hours in. Talked to Dad on 'phone tonight."*

Tuesday 6th: *"Flying from X flew again this afternoon, did No.2 cross country landing at Watton."*

Monday 13th: *"News through that I'm posted on 21st July. Kelly posted to GR course at Harrogate. Went to Sutton but had to leave early for NF but did not fly."*

Sunday 19th: *"Posting postponed for seven days."*

Sunday 26th: *"Flying tonight, beautifully moonlit."*

Tuesday 28th: *"Spent most of the day getting a leave pass signed etc for five days leave."*

Wednesday 29th: *"Caught 11.50 from Paddington, home at 6 o' clock. Went out for a walk with Mum and Dad."*

Thursday 30th: *"Three of us went to Brecon, back on the 5 o' clock train. Played football with the kids."*

Returning to Ossington, George received news of his posting on Saturday, August 8th, 1942. On Tuesday 11th, he left Nottinghamshire at mid-day and travelled to RAF Cranfield in Bedfordshire, the home of 51 Operational Training Unit, the night fighter OTU, training young pilots and observers in the cat and mouse art of seeking and destroying nocturnal German intruders. 51 OTU opened at Cranfield on August 25th, 1941, providing fledgling night fighter crews with courses flying the Blenheim I & V. On April 9th, 1942, the nearby airfield of Twinwood Farm opened and served 51 OTU as a satellite. 51 OTU supplied intensive training experience to numerous night fighter crews until closing on June 14th, 1945, having served its purpose. RAF Cranfield is now the Cranfield Institute of Technology but remains largely unchanged since the 1940s.

As the *"Few"* had retained control of the air over Britain in daylight hours during the summer of 1940, Hitler had been forced to abandon his plans for invasion. The Luftwaffe switched its attacks to the night bombing of a number of British ports and cities. On the night of November 15th, 1940, over four hundred tons of high explosive was dropped on Coventry, destroying the city centre. The *"Night Blitz"* continued until the spring of 1941 when improved radar and new night fighters used by the RAF began to take their toll of the German raiders. No large scale bombing raids were mounted on the British Isles by the Luftwaffe until April 1942, when the *"Baedecker"* raids began in retribution for the attack by Bomber Command which decimated the historic town of Lübeck. These raids were mainly against lightly defended targets. Exeter, Bath, Hull, Grimsby, Southampton, Birmingham, Norwich, Canterbury and Bristol were all attacked by the German Kampfgeschwardern. On the night of January 17th, 1943, a raid of one hundred and eighteen aircraft was mounted against London. However by this time the defenders had made great progress in improving night fighting techniques and equipment. Losses sustained by the German bomber force over England's night skies in 1943 were severe. Times had changed and German night bomber crews were no longer free to roam virtually unchallenged over Britain as they had in 1940. In January 1944, Goering launched Operation *"Steinbock"*, a series of retaliatory raids on Britain. By May more than half of the bomber force had been lost to Britain's night defences. After the Allied invasion of Normandy on June 6th, 1944, the Luftwaffe's forward bomber bases slowly came under Allied control meaning the virtual cessation of German activities in British airspace.

The new art of night fighting was very different from day fighter combat. Night fighter crews required great patience and perseverance to stalk the German bombers and relied greatly on the speed, firepower and endurance of their aircraft, not to mention the reliability of their early radar sets. Like all air fighting, the night produced its aces, men like *"Catseyes"* Cunningham and Bob Braham. Having been awarded a bar to his Distinguished Flying Cross in December 1941, Braham had been posted to 51 OTU as an instructor. Whilst with the unit he destroyed a Do 217 on June 6th, 1942, before returning to his squadron the following month. By the end of the war, Braham had destroyed twenty-nine enemy aircraft. Cunningham enjoyed the distinction of shooting down a raider one night in May1942, when King George VI was an observer in the controlling ground station. Group Captain Cunningham's final score was twenty of the enemy destroyed. After the war he became a test pilot for De Havilland (later Hawker Siddeley) and continued an already distinguished career in aviation.

Sergeant Lock continued his diary whilst at the night fighter OTU:-

Wednesday, 12th August, 1942: "*Had a look round, quite a good station. Did a spot of Link and posted to satellite at Twinwood.*"

Sunday 16th: "*Flew dual in Blenheim V and solo in Blenheim I.*"

Thursday, September 3rd, 1942: "*Watched dinghy drill at Bedford Baths. Saw 'They Flew Alone' at flicks.*"

Sunday 6th: "*Did a cross country beyond Worcester. Lovely visibility.*"

Tuesday 8th: "*No flying, got cleared for leaving Twinwood.*"

Wednesday 9th: "*Exams. Caught 5.27 to St. Pancras, went for a walk to Primrose Hill.*"

Thursday 10th: "*Met Joan at lunchtime, saw 'Gone with the Wind' and played skittles down Bowman's.*"

The following day was George's twenty-first birthday:-

Monday, September 14th, 1942: "*Crewed up with Radio Observer 'Chuck' Dales. No flying. ENSA show, couple of drinks in Sgts mess.*"

Wednesday 23rd: "*Solo Airborne Interception (AI) flight. Turned about too much and made Chuck sick.*"

Thursday 24th: "*Another solo AI, all OK. Got some gen at the armoury. Have caught nine mice in billet in last three days.*"

On 27th September George wrote to Derek:-

"*Dear Derek,*

"*I'm not really sure whose turn it is to write so as your last letter is dated Aug. 24th I think it must be me. I expect you are back at work after your week's rest, which I hope you enjoyed. I'm looking forward to my next week off which isn't really so far away - only a couple of months and time passes quickly here.*

"*We are still having quite a good time here although everybody is glad we've just about finished ground school now. The weather of course rather tends to dampen one's spirit but we took advantage of those few hot days to do a bit of swimming in the river. I go to London for the day each time we get one off. I've been there three times since I've been here, the last time was yesterday. I get down there by about 7.30 in the evening so I spend quite a long time there considering it is just twenty four hours we get off. I managed to get a new fountain pen in London yesterday and Joan bought it me as a birthday present. They take a bit of getting hold of these days. Last night of course it poured with rain so we couldn't go out anywhere although the night before was fine and we had a nice walk over the heath.*

"*There doesn't seem to be much news these days. A couple of days ago I flew my* highest yet - reached 23,000' and it looks a long way to fall from up there. Well, I'll say cheerio again, Derek. Hope you and the family are all well, remember me to all. All the best, Your Pal, George."

On September 29th, George wrote further to Derek:-

"Dear Derek,

"Glad to hear from you with the local news - haven't been hearing anything about Bronllys since my mother's been in Aberystwyth. Thanks very much for the greetings telegram. I had a very nice time although nothing exceptionally hectic as one might expect of a twenty-first birthday. I still manage to make a trip to London every week or ten days and if I go this week I'll ring up 'Pie' and see if he can come over. We had a good long talk over the 'phone a week or two ago. Its about time I wrote to Fred Beavan again too - I try to write every few weeks regardless of whether I hear from him as I know that letters are worth their weight in gold to men overseas. Unfortunately I am not sure of his present address. I wonder if you could let me have it when you next write which will be soon I hope.

"I've just managed to get two films to fit my camera but I've left both camera and films with the folks in London. It is not worth the trouble of getting a permit to keep it with me.

"I was pleased to hear of your success at shooting and I hope you will forgive my reference to a spot of decent shooting I did today. It was on a miniature target over thirty yards with a .303 rifle. I fired 25 rounds as follows: 5 grouping, 10 application, 5 rapid fire, 5 snap shooting. Possible score 125 - I got 118, lost most of the points on rapid and snap of course. I got a possible on grouping and dropped one point on application but as you mentioned of your effort I'm also thinking it was more by luck than judgement ! I also fired 4 rounds with a .45 revolver but never having handled one before I had one bull, one out and two off the target. I wish we could get on the range more often as I enjoy a bit of shooting.

"I still haven't done a great deal of flying - my observer and I have only been on a few trips. I did a short trip yesterday afternoon testing the kite I had to fly the same night and took up three chaps who were there to see if they could get a flip. They were all stationed here and waiting to be trained as aircrew so naturally they were very keen and seemed to enjoy the ride. I flew nearly three hours solo at a stretch last night - not even my observer to chat to - but I quite enjoyed it.

"My bike is still going well but is suffering quite a bit from wear and tear. I really need a couple of new tyres on it and I can't buy a pedal to replace my bent one. My cyclometer is now registering about 120 on the second time around and still going strong. I've set up a dynamo now as well. Did I ever tell you that we discovered mice in our room ? Well I got a mouse trap and using bits of apple and chocolate as bait we caught fourteen mice since last Tuesday ! Our best effort was five in one day but now *they've either got used to us or there are none left.*

"I think I'll pack up now, Derek, and I hope I'll be hearing from you soon. So long, all the best, your pal, George."

The Fred Beavan to whom George refers was another air minded Bronllys lad who had joined the wartime RAF as an engineer. Mr Beavan served in the Middle East and later worked as an engineer at Bronllys Hospital. A keen radio enthusiast he is now retired and still lives in the village.

George's diary continues:-

Friday, October 9th, 1942: *"New at 4 Sqn, Beaufighters."*

Monday 12th: *"Bags of Link. Went to a show at the camp, 'Fol de Rols'."*

Friday 16th: *"First solo on a Beaufighter, 1 hour 50 minutes. Sgts mess dance."*

The Bristol Beaufighter was a sturdy aeroplane powered by two Hercules radial engines and heavily armed with four 20mm cannons in the nose and six .303 machine guns mounted in the wings. The *"Beau"* carried a pilot and an observer, the latter who sat on a swivelling seat beneath a transparent cupola in the rear half of the fuselage. The observer was able to monitor the displays and controls of the Airborne Interception (AI) radar fitted to the aircraft and which guided the nocturnal hunters to their prey. The Beaufighter saw service in many theatres of war; in the Far East the Japanese so feared the aircraft they called it the *"Whispering Death"*, and German sailors anxiously scanned Atlantic skies for marauding rocket-armed Beaufighters which mercilessly attacked enemy shipping.

Beaufighters remained the standard type with 51 OTU at Cranfield until February, 1944, when replaced by De Havilland Mosquito IIs.

In November 1942, Sergeant Pilot Lock completed his training and took leave of 51 OTU:-

Tuesday, November 17th, 1942: *"Said goodbye to the squadron, 2.30 transport to train, arrived London 6 o' clock and went to Daisy's until 9.30pm."*

George went home to Bronllys during his leave, his last before an operational posting:-

Wednesday, November 18th, 1942: *"Caught 12 train, home via Newport at about 6 o' clock."*

Thursday 19th: *"Didn't go out today, helped Dad sort spuds."*

Monday 23rd: *"Spent the afternoon up at school. Stayed in tonight playing ludo."*

His leave ended the following day:-

Tuesday, November 24th, 1942: *"Caught 11 am train from Talgarth, nearly missed the 1pm train at Hereford. Left Dais at Worcester, arrived at RAF Station Defford about 7.30pm."*

RAF Station Defford, about seven miles to the south-east of Worcester, was the home of the Telecommunications Flying Unit (TFU). Sergeant Lock joined the station strength of 67 officers and 1593 other ranks. Eight miles to the north-east of Defford airfield was RAF Pershore, the home of 23 OTU, and it was as a satellite to that station that Defford was first used when opened in September 1941. At first facilities were basic, and with just a mobile watch office only daytime flying was possible.

On August 1st, 1941, the RAF TFU was formed at RAF Station Hurn. It comprised the original A & AEE Special Duties (D) Flight which was formed in 1936 from the former Fighter Experimental Establishment at RAF Middle Wallop and the RAF's Blind Landing Detachment at the Royal Aircraft Establishment at Farnborough, to exclusively serve the airborne requirements of the emerging science of radar. At its conception, RAF TFU was under the administration of 10 Group, Fighter Command, but its functional activities were the responsibility of the Ministry of Aircraft Production through the Telecommunications Research Establishment (TRE) for whose service it was formed.

During the latter half of May 1942, TRE was relocated at Malvern and its attendant RAF TFU moved to the part completed aerodrome at Defford.

The TFU became the centre for developing and proving flying of all British airborne radars, its work being highly classified. At the Malvern based TRE, radars were developed which had a direct effect on ultimate victory. Airborne Interception (AI) radar was developed at TRE and Defford's TFU provided the experimental and *"guinea pig"* aircraft for its trials. *"Village Inn"* was devised here, the codename for trials with a radar operated tail turret. Experiments were conducted with ground controllers directing searchlight batteries as a fighter controller would direct a night fighter to its prey. Neither of these experiments were actually successful, but the *"H2S"* radar bombing aid was a tremendous achievement. This produced a map of the ground below on a cathode ray tube which was invaluable as a bombing aid for the RAF's night bombers. Other developments included *"Boozer"*, which warned bomber crews when they were *"painting"* on a night fighter's radar screen, and *"Serrate"* which enabled Mosquito intruders to home in on the radar transmissions of enemy night fighters. *"Window"* consisted of metal strips which when dropped in a predetermined pattern simulated an invasion force approaching enemy occupied France on the German radar screens and which had the effect of plunging the enemy defence system into chaos.

During 1943/44, the TFU employed around 2,000 personnel, consisting of men and women not only of the RAF but also the Fleet Air Arm along with resident TRE scientists and engineers.

The service aircrews at TFU were personnel of high competence selected for flying trials of the highest importance. No doubt Sergeant Pilot Lock and his observer, Sergeant Dales, had been selected to join the TFU as both were trained in night fighting and the operation of aircraft fitted with AI radar, an area of particular interest to the TRE scientists. By this time, as has been explained, the blitz as such was all but over, there being no urgent demand by operational squadrons for replacement crews. By such a quirk of fate then, Sergeants Lock and Dales were given a non-operational posting to Defford.

During the period of peak wartime activity, the TFU held up to 130 resident aircraft at any one time and handled 44 different types. By 1945, TFU had been involved with over 500 aircraft associated with R & D activities. Between August 1938 and the cessation of the Second World War on August 14th, 1945, twenty-nine RAF and eight civilian scientific personnel were killed flying in the development of radars. The incident with the largest single loss of life occurred on June 7th, 1942, when Handley Page Halifax V9977 crashed at Welsh Bicknor during H2S trials, killing the eleven on board. That number included both service aircrew and civilian scientists.

Post war, on October 12th, 1955, the unit's title of TFU was superseded by that of the Radar Research Flying Unit (RRFU) following the change of role and title of the parent establishment at Malvern in 1953, the TRE's new name being the Radar Research Establishment (RRE). The unit remained in service until the RRE's aerodrome at Pershore was closed on December 31st, 1976, and the RAF's RRFU was disbanded. The flying from Pershore post war until its closure was also quite intense, and as a child living in nearby Worcester I well recall the jet Canberras from the RRFU which were a familiar sight in local airspace for many years.

George's diary tells the story of his first few days with the wartime TFU:-

Thursday, November 26th, 1942: *"Wandered round in the mud. Wrote bags of letters."*

Friday 27th: *"Reported to 'A' flight Defensive Section. No hope of flying, bad weather. Wrote letters in the mess again this morning."*

Sunday 29th: *"1 hrs stooging round in an Oxford. Passenger tonight in a Wimpey (Wellington bomber)."*

Monday 30th: *"Flew over home in a Beau."*

Thursday, December 3rd, 1942: *"All set for a flip in a Spit but weather u/s ('u/s' being RAF slang for unserviceable). WAAF dance tonight not too bad."*

Friday 4th: *"Moved over to 'A' flight's dispersal. Got a flip in a Beau."*

Sunday 6th: *"Did a 15,000' stooge in a Beau, stayed in mess all night."*
Monday 7th: *"Beau target this morning. First flip in a Hurricane. Back to billet early, swept chimney and lit the fire."*
Tuesday 8th: *"Flew some boffins round in a Beau. First flip in a Spitfire. Back to billet early again."*

Most of the flying trials apparently took place to the west of Defford. This was for two extremely important reasons. Firstly the terrain between the Malvern hills and the Brecon Beacons provided an excellent backdrop for experimental purposes with the nearby industrial areas of South Wales, prominent coastal profile of the Bristol Channel and the offshore sea *"targets"* of the islands in the channel. Secondly the western airspace was relatively free from both enemy interference and the air traffic congestion found in the east. In a forty mile radius of Defford there were some fifty other aerodromes, the majority training establishments, and forty-two of these airfields lay to the east. It therefore made sense to use the western area for research and development purposes which became known as the Flight or Western Trials Air Space. Within its boundaries lay Bronllys, hence the reason why George Lock had found himself over his home village in a Beaufighter.

Exactly in which Spitfire Sergeant Lock had his first *"flip"* is not known. Of well over seven hundred aircraft handled by the Radar Squadron in forty years, embracing over forty types, only twenty-two single-engined fighters can be identified in the Defford era. This number of single-engined aircraft represents a mere three per cent of the total number of aircraft associated with the unit. Single-engined fighters were of little value as radar laboratory aircraft. Other than aircraft in use with the appended Naval squadron R & D laboratory, aircraft were invariably of twin or multi-engined types such as the Mosquito or Halifax which were able to carry crewmen as equipment operators and observers.

However single engined aircraft did provide air-to-air *"targets"* for the development of AI radars, as George's diary entry tells us regarding his *"flip"* in a Hurricane acting as a *"target"*. The fighters were also used in limited cases as carriers of Radio/Radar Counter Measures (RCM). Such RCM installations would have included *"Mandrel"* and *"Moonshine"* jammers against enemy *"Freya"* and other surveillance radars. The *"Monica"* device which gave early warning of rear attack might also have been tested on Spitfires and Hurricanes at Defford. Certainly both types would have been used in the continuing development of the Identification Friend or Foe (IFF) system and also *"Rebecca"*, airborne range, homing and approach system.

A secondary role of the fighters at Defford would have been as a defensive facility against daylight German intruders, although there is no record of them ever having been so used.

By this time the Spitfire Mk Ia was obsolete indeed in terms of front line operational efficiency and was therefore relegated to training or service with units such as the TFU.

One of only two Spitfires at Defford in February 1943 was Mk Ia X4918, which had arrived a few days after Sergeant Lock's first Spitfire flight. X4918 was built at the Supermarine Aviation Works at Woolston near Southampton at the end of 1940 under Contract No. 19713/39. I have been unable to ascertain exactly when or by whom X4918 was test flown from Eastleigh airfield. Chief Supermarine test pilot Jeffrey Quill, a patron of the Malvern Spitfire Team, checked his log book and discovered that he flew X4915 on a production test flight on New Years Day 1941, and X4917 three days later. Another aircraft in the same batch was X4922 which Jeffrey flew a great deal on performance and cooling tests. Fitted with a Rolls-Royce Merlin 45 engine, that particular Spitfire became the prototype Mk V. Although X4918 does not appear in the pages of Jeffrey Quill's log book, it was certainly tested around the same time as X4915 and X4917, possibly by his colleague George Pickering.

X4918's Air Ministry Form 78, or service history card, does not provide us with the exact number of the Spitfire's Rolls-Royce Merlin engine other than identfying the unit fitted as being a Merlin III. The Merlin III developed 880 h.p. at take-off, the power increasing to 1,030 h.p. at 16,250', being super-charged with a single-speed, single-stage supercharger.

Spitfire X4918 was initially taken on charge by 12 Maintenance Unit (MU) at Kirkbride in Cumbria on January 4th, 1941, prior to allocation to 72 Squadron at Acklington in Northumberland on March 2nd. Ten days later Sergeant Gregson made X4918's first recorded flight with the squadron when he patrolled Blyth at cloud base between 1230 and 1325 hrs. Later that afternoon he flew the Spitfire on a patrol of Ouston. On March 15th, Sergeant Mallet took to the air in X4918 to patrol base. Gregson then flew a number of uneventful patrols in the Spitfire between March 21st and April 10th, when a Pilot Officer Douthwaite was "scrambled" to "patrol base." At 1900 hrs the same day, Gregson scrambled in X4918 with Sergeant Lack in a second Spitfire. Ten miles north-east of Longhoughton the pair intercepted and probably destroyed a Junkers 88. The enemy aircraft was last seen with its port engine blazing, which had practically disintegrated, diving vertically for the sea at 1500'. The squadron diary records the victory as "a moral certainty". On April 24th, Sergeant Casey flew X4918 on a routine patrol as did Sergeant Harrison on the 28th. On May 5th and 7th, Sergeant Gregson took over again and made the remainder of the Spitfire's flights with the squadron.

On May 15th, 1941, X4918 was next taken on charge by 123 Squadron, which, although in the process of forming at Turnhouse in Scotland, spent only a few months in the UK before re-equipping with Hurricane Mk IIs and being posted to the Middle East. On May 25th, the squadron commenced training and made its first operational flight on June 6th. No aircraft serial numbers are recorded in the squadron's diary but it is known that on June 10th, Sergeant Pollock was flying X4918 when he overshot the runway and struck a pile of tyres on the perimeter track. X4918 was damaged and following repair was re-allocated by 43 Group Pool to 123 Squadron. On September 4th, the Spitfire was damaged again when Sergeant Harvey had the misfortune to suffer a burst tyre on the runway at Drem. This time the aircraft was repaired at Supermarines and afterwards was allocated from 12 MU to the RAF TFU at Defford on December 17th, 1941.

Aircraft at the TFU wore no unit identification markings, so secret was their work. In fact the only markings ever worn by the squadron was a squadron crest of two feet in diameter from 1967 onwards. It is believed that X4918 appeared at Defford in her original colour scheme of green and brown upper and "sky" undersurfaces.

Living and working amongst a multitude of aircraft from Spitfires to Lancasters, George Lock continued with his daily diary entries throughout his time with the TFU. He tells his own story of nearly three months at Defford with the following entries which although numerous I feel will be of great interest to the reader:-

Wednesday, December 9th, 1942: *"Boffins in a Beau."*

Sunday 13th: *"Weather fine, high wind. Topped 400 hours."*

Monday 14th: *"10 & 20,000' stooge in a Beau for two hours. In afternoon two more stooges - pretty cold up there !"*

Tuesday 15th: *"Heard of Bob Hooper's death in Wimpey crash."*

Monday 21st: *"Day off. Caught mid-day train to Worcester and went to the flicks."*

Tuesday 22nd: *"Flew morning, afternoon and night. Lovely moon, right night for flying."*

Wednesday 23rd: *"Short trip this morning. Going out on a night flying test pranged a wing tip. Night flying cancelled."*

Friday 25th: *"Got up the mess about 11.30am. Party starts and xmas dinner until about 5 o' clock. Slept off dinner for a couple of hours and went to the WAAF dance with Babs. Back 1am."*

Saturday 26th: *"Reported to flight but weather u/s for flying."*

Sunday 27th: *"News last week of Sqn Ldr Mould being shot down by Czech Spitfire pilots whilst flying a Beaufighter."*

At 1545 hrs on Wednesday, December 23rd, 1942, a TFU Beaufighter Mk VI, V8387, was shot down into the sea three miles off Kings Lynn, Norfolk. The Defford diary records that V8387 had been destroyed by *"friendly fighters"*. Both occupants of the aircraft were *"missing presumed killed"*. Squadron Leader HHB Mould and Dr AE Downing of the TRE joined the list of those who had given their lives flying in the development of radar. A Czech Spitfire squadron, 313, were responsible, but, as we have seen more recently in the Gulf conflict *"Friendly Fire"* incident when American jets destroyed a British personnel carrier, in war such tragic mistakes do happen.

Saturday, January 2nd, 1943: *"Took the Vega Gull to Hendon to pick up the Group Captain who flew it back stopping en route because of snow storms. Had a night in the mess and have an air gunner room mate."*

Tuesday 5th: *"About 4" of snow today. Sawed wood and played snowballs. Went home on the 5.20 from Defford, arrived Talgarth 10.15."*

Wednesday 6th: *"Derek came over as it was his half day. Started back 6.20, arrived Defford 11.50."*

Friday 8th: *"Flew Blenheim down to Farnborough and brought back Flt Lt Kay. Went by taxi to the hospital dance in Worcester. Had a lovely time and a nice partner, a Welsh girl called Anne."*

Monday 11th: *"Flew Beaufighter II on AI test intending to go to Colerne but the trip was cancelled. Local night flying until 11.30 pm when the weather closed in."*

Wednesday 13th: *"Took off at 2.30 for air test in a Beau II. Landed at Colerne at 4 o' clock, had tea and returned."*

Thursday 14th: *"Fetched the Beau II this pm. About tea time landed then took off again for Colerne. After some delay got airborne at 9 pm and had a very good trip with Wimpey and searchlight co-op. Landed at 12 had supper and slept at Colerne (an airfield in Wiltshire particularly used by night fighters)."*

Friday 15th: *"Late breakfast. About 14 Halifax bombers had landed. We couldn't get re-fuelled to return to Defford."*

Sunday 16th: *"Swung compass. In pm Malvern stooge one hour. Saw 'Charlie's American Aunt' at camp flicks."*

Monday 18th: *"Did two trips in the Spitfire in very bad weather. Visibility less than 2,000 yards. Went to a dance in Pershore tonight and danced mostly with Mary."*

Wednesday 20th: *"Two short trips in a Spit - VHF u/s each time. Rained all day without stop. Tried to get home but missed train at Worcester."*

Thursday 21st: *"Trip in a Spit."*

Friday 22nd: *"Pay day. Flew Beau, Lt Walker felt sick again circling at 15,000'."*

Saturday 23rd: *"Flew Blenheim this afternoon then went to a dance in Eckington on my own and navigated rather well."*

Sunday 24th: *"Rode passenger in a Mosquito. Heard of Chuck getting hit by a car in Worcester and is now in hospital."*

Friday 29th: *"Night flying with Sqn Ldr Brooke in Mossie. Pershore Wimpey crashed today."*

The *"Pershore Wimpey"* was Wellington bomber BK503 of 23 OTU, and which crashed at 1117 hrs near Earls Croome in Worcestershire. Two of the crew, both Canadians, Pilot Officer GG Weston and Sergeant JA Auclair were killed.

Sergeant Lock's diary continued in what was to be the last month of his life:-

Wednesday, February 3rd, 1943: *"Cycled down Pershore Road to see if the floods had abated. All OK. Biked to Pershore caught 12.28 train arrived Paddington 4 o' clock. Went down for Dais then up to Joan's."*

Friday 12th: *"Plenty of flying - tricks in the Spit. Did an orbit over Malvern for over an hour."*

Saturday 13th: *"No flying today. Went to Worcester and played table tennis. Went to a dance at the Guildhall, back on 11 o'clock bus."*

Sunday 14th: *"Speed take off in Spit. Climbed to 5,000' in eight minutes."*

Monday 15th: *"Beau flying, also Spit."*

Tuesday 16th: *"Flew the Beaufighter this morning, afternoon and night when I took a passenger."*

Wednesday 17th: *"Not much flying - low cloud. Airborne for about fifteen minutes in Hurricane. Back to bunk about eight and lit fire."*

Thursday 18th: *"Flew Hurri."*

Friday 19th: *"Flew aerobatics in Hurricane. Managed rolls OK but couldn't do a good loop. Sgts mess dance tonight, Babs came up but it was very crowded and not as good as usual."*

Saturday 20th: *"Flew Spit this afternoon, did a couple of rolls. Back to hut early tonight and talked in front of the fire."*

Tuesday 23rd: *"5.20 train from Defford, missed my train at Worcester so hitched a lift about fourteen miles then caught a lorry all the way home. Arrived 8.45pm. 'Phoned Dad who was waiting at the New Inn."*

Wednesday 24th: *"Got up about 10.30 and had a bath before dinner. Derek came over in the afternoon and stayed for tea. Saw Doreen this evening until about 8.30 then went out to a dance and had a good time there."*

Thursday 25th: *"Spent all morning indoors. Mum and I went for a walk to Talgarth, back down to catch the train after tea. Mum and Dad saw me off. Amy got on at Three Cocks so had company to Hereford."*

The next day is blank. On Friday, February 26th, 1943, George Lock was killed in a most tragic mid-air collision.

Nine miles to the north of Defford airfield on the outskirts of the city of Worcester was the home of 2 Elementary Flying Training School (EFTS) at the grass airfield of Perdiswell. This small airfield was where many young men from Britain and the Commonwealth gained their first experience of flying in the little wood and fabric De Havilland Tiger Moth biplane. The airfield itself was primitive, Nissen huts and tents serving as offices, but at least the trainee pilots were billeted in private houses in the city. The Tiger Moths from Perdiswell became a very familiar sight over Worcestershire as 2 EFTS adhered to a busy training schedule.

On the morning of Friday, February 26th, 1943, Sergeant 413013 John Francis Cameron McPherson of the Royal Australian Air Force took off from Perdiswell in Tiger Moth N9384 on a solo training flight. In 1943 there was no airfield surveillance by ground radar and McPherson was without radio communication facilities in his aircraft. It is reasonable to assume that as he soon arrived over the village of Pirton, approximately one mile to the north-west of Defford airfield, the young Australian had flown south along the Bristol railway line, the most dominant landmark, and had correctly kept the land reference to his left.

Every airfield has what is known as a circuit area which extends 6,000 yards (3.4 miles) from the centre of the airfield and 3,000 feet in height over that area. Whilst flying in a circuit area Circuit Rules for Service Aerodromes stipulate that *"the captain of an aircraft shall keep a sharp lookout for other aircraft in the vicinity, conform with or avoid the air traffic pattern, during circuit and approach make all turns left unless instructed otherwise, maintain a constant listening watch on the aerodrome radio communication frequencies and a sharp lookout for any visual signals and unless instructed otherwise land and take off as near into wind as possible."*

The rules also stipulate that aerobatics must not be performed if there is any chance that another aircraft would be put in danger. Air Force Standing Orders on flying activities are supplemented by a set of local flying orders which identify areas set aside for, amongst other things, aerobatics. Each order was directed at air safety and had to be signed as understood by all pilots.

When in an area set aside for aerobatics a pilot is required before commencing such manouevres to make a 360 degree turn and ensure that the airspace intended for aerobatics is well clear of other aircraft. Such areas were well away from airfield circuits.

The village of Pirton lies some distance within the Defford circuit. Over this area McPherson chose to commence aerobatic practice.It is not known whether he carried out a 360 degree turn.

At about 10.40 am the same morning, Sergeant Lock taxied onto the Defford runway in Spitfire X4918. Though unrecorded, it is quite possible that his intention was to link up with a laboratory aircraft and act as a *"target"* in an AI experiment, a theory supported by the role of single-engined types at Defford, and indeed George Lock's own diary entries regarding his previous sorties in Spitfires and Hurricanes.

When airborne, X4918 commenced a short climb, as Sergeant Lock made his left turn to leave the circuit area. If he had seen the Tiger Moth, the TFU pilot was entitled to accept that its pilot was on a training flight from 2 EFTS, that he was fully conversant with Air Force Circuit Rules and had knowledge of the nearby Defford airspace governed by those rules.

Written and reliable eye-witness evidence to indicate exactly what happened next is scant. However, Mr John Watkins saw the two aircraft collide:-

"Although it happened so long ago the memory is remarkably clear - not surprising perhaps for so dramatic an incident.

"I had just arrived at Clifton Court Farm, with tractor and cultivator, and chanced to look east. I noticed a Spitfire and a Tiger Moth, at the same height, closing on a collision course. As the planes passed the trainer made a violent banking manouevre but the Spitfire plunged earthwards, almost vertically. The impact seemed to have been relatively slight.

"The Tiger Moth, as I recall, maintained its northerly heading, though my strongest recollection is of focussing my attention on the stricken Spitfire. At a distance of 1 mile it was impossible to see clearly what had happened, but, as the Spitfire fell, it rotated slowly and appeared intact. The incident lasted only a matter of seconds, and the crash, near Pirton Pool, occurred out of my line of vision but sent up a pall of smoke some hundreds of feet high.

"The loss of the Spitfire pilot was such a sad loss when both man and machine were so desperately important to the war effort."

I also refer to the entry in the 2 EFTS diary, made in the absence of Sergeant Lock's evidence:-

"Aus.413013 Sgt McPherson JFC flying Tiger Moth N9384 when in the vicinity of Pirton, map ref: VP3368, came into violent collision with Spitfire X4918 flown by Sgt Pilot Lock of RAF Station Defford.

"Sgt McPherson had just completed a loop when the collision occurred at approximately 4,000'. The port wings and engine of the Tiger Moth were cut away but the pilot managed to abandon the aircraft and make a successful parachute descent. He only suffered a slight cut on the left leg and slight shock. The pilot of the Spitfire was trapped in his machine and was killed."

The TFU diary records only the briefest of details:-

"Spitfire I X4918 whilst flying in the vicinity of the aerodrome collided with a Tiger Moth from a nearby FTS. Pilot of Tiger Moth executed safe parachute landing. Sgt G Lock, pilot of Spitfire, killed in resultant crash. No damage to civilian property. Both aircraft unrepairable. Court of Inquiry to be held."

In view of the 2 EFTS diary evidence stating that the collision took place upon McPherson's completion of a loop, and no eye-witness evidence suggesting any evasive action by either machine, it is the author's personal opinion that neither pilot saw the other until either it was too late, or indeed not at all until the collision actually occurred. Had McPherson seen the Spitfire, however, and continued with his aerobatics in contravention of standing orders, in mitigation it should be remembered that at the time there was much aerial congestion; the Defford circuit area actually overlapped that of neighbouring airfields, and the sky was constantly full of a multitude of aircraft.

X4918 impacted in a field on the south side of Pirton Pool about three miles to the north-east of Defford airfield (approximately a quarter of a mile within the Defford circuit area) and two miles to the south-east of the village of Kempsey. Twenty-one year old George Lock was killed instantly.

Soon a crash party arrived from Defford which set about finding local eye-witnesses, and clearing up the crash site on Park Farm. Mr John Smith was a fifteen year old village lad from Kempsey at the time and remembers visiting the crash site shortly after the incident. There he saw a Queen Mary aircraft transporter in the field and airmen clearing up the smoking crater that was once Supermarine Spitfire Mk Ia, X4918.

Later that day, George Lock's parents received news of their son's death in a telegram:-

"Deeply regret to inform you that your son, Sgt George C Lock, lost his life today as the result of an aircraft accident stop Please accept my profound sympathy stop Letter follows stop OC RAF Defford".

Derek Owens remembers the sad news and paid tribute to his friend:-

"I remember the King's telegram arriving with the news that George had been killed.

A gloom descended over the village for days and I always recall George's father saying that the one person he felt sorry for was me, as I was so distressed.

"My recollections of George are all very happy ones, we were like brothers as neighbours in this village. We wrote to each other during his aircrew training and I always spent time with him when he came home on leave. Whilst stationed at Defford he flew over Bronllys on several occasions. George was a very kind and popular boy. When he came home from overseas he brought all of the pupils in the village school some chocolate. Of course chocolate was rationed then and the village very much appreciated his gesture.

"I still live in the same house opposite the village church and George is buried next to the churchyard gate. His memory is always with me."

"Chuck" Dales, George's navigator, came out of hospital in Worcester and received news of the accident. He wrote to Mr and Mrs Lock:-

"I am terribly sorry and grieved to learn of George's untimely death and hasten to send you my deepest sympathy.

"As you probably know I have been away for some weeks, the victim of a car accident, and only returned from leave last night.

"I understand that the funeral is to be private but as George's navigator and friend I would like to be present and feel that you will not mind.

"He was an extremely nice decent chap liked by all and the Sergeants here are very sorry to lose him.

"I do hope you are both as well as can be expected, try not to take it too hard - he died doing his duty."

On March 2nd, the news reached George Lock's former employers, the United Kingdom Tea Company Ltd and the managing director, Mr WGF Cristall, also sent a message of sympathy to Mrs Lock:-

"We very much regret to hear this morning that your son has been killed in a flying accident. You would probably like to know that he was well liked during the short time he was with us and we shall very much regret not having him back when the war is over."

Sergeant Pilot George Lock's funeral subsequently took place at Bronllys village church, St. Mary's, and he was buried in the churchyard.

Almost a month after the collision, Group Captain King, the Officer Commanding RAF Station Defford, wrote to Mr Lock:-

"I am writing to offer you on behalf of myself and all the officers and airmen at this station our heartfelt sympathy in your recent bereavement in the loss of your son, Sgt G Lock, who was killed in a flying accident near this station on 26th February 1943. I hope you will understand that I have not been able to write to you before this because I have had to wait until the proceedings of the Court of Inquiry had been completed so that I could tell you as much of the circumstances of the accident as possible. Unfortunately there is very little to say except that your son was flying a Spitfire aircraft on duty when, for reasons which it has been impossible to determine, he collided with an aircraft from a neighbouring unit with the result that both aeroplanes got out of control and crashed. From the evidence available the impact was so great that your son must have been killed instantly and could not have suffered.

"Although your son had not been serving long at this unit I had formed a high opinion of his abilities and devotion to duty. He was very popular with his fellows and his likeable personality had earned him many friends who mourn his loss keenly. It is some consolation to know that he died as he would have wished, doing his duty. He has given his life for his country just as gallantly as if he had been killed in active operations against the enemy."

Edwyn Owens, Derek Owens's cousin, remembered George Lock in 1993:-

"Although only a young boy at the time, my memory floods back to those war years and to George Lock who was our neighbour, close family friend and hero. Our small village community of just a few hundred people was closely knit, although many families, including ours, increased overnight taking evacuees from the London blitz. At that time, however, we young people felt safe and believed that George, in his Spitfire, would give our village special consideration and single-handedly would win the war for us. I vividly remember the times when we would rush into the school playground when the roar of his Spitfire was heard. George, visible in the cockpit, would fly low over the village and waggle his wings in salute as he returned to base. Then came that fateful day with the news of George's death that cast a dark cloud over the village. And I recall the sadness of his funeral in the village with our whole school attending. His memory will never be forgotten."

George Lock's neatly kept grave is marked with a Commonwealth War Graves Commission headstone with the inscription "Though sunshine passes and shadows fall, love and memory outliveth all". Mr Courtney Lock DCM MM passed away in 1958 and lies buried with his son.

Sergeant George Lock's grave in Bronllys churchyard. He is buried with his father, CW Lock DCM, MM.
Author's collection.

As a result of the aerial collision over Pirton, however, Sergeant McPherson became a member of the "Caterpillar Club",

208

founded by the Irvin Parachute Company for airmen who had saved their lives using a parachute. He later completed his course at 2 EFTS, Worcester, and eventually achieved his ambition to fly Spitfires. On May 31st, 1943, however, just three months after the collision in which Sergeant Lock was killed, 61 OTU at Rednal in north Shropshire suffered two flying accidents, one of which was fatal. The Operations Record Book recorded:-

"Only very limited flying today. Two accidents occurred today, one fatal. The first concerned Sgt Norris flying Spitfire P8319 who landed at RAF Montford Bridge with wheels up. The second, fatal, involves Sgt McPherson (Australian) who collided in mid-air with a Mosquito (HJ881) over Shrewsbury resulting in the deaths of both occupants of the Mosquito and Sgt McPherson. Investigation ordered. Sgt McPherson was flying Spitfire X4930."

The information for Sergeant McPherson's death certificate was provided by 61 OTU's Commanding Officer, Wing Commander Don Finlay DFC, a former Olympic hurdler and commander of 41 Squadron during the Battle of Britain. According to the certificate, McPherson's Spitfire crashed at Corporation Lane, Shrewsbury. Twenty-one year old Sergeant MacPherson now lies buried in the immaculate service plot of Oswestry town cemetery near Rednal airfield. His headstone inscription is a perhaps a fitting epitaph to all of the young men who lost their lives flying in the Second World War:-

"Now in God's Keeping He Remains a Radiant Memory of Youth."

Sergeant John F.C. "Jock" McPherson of the RAAF.
Mrs Margaret Horton.

Sergeant McPherson's grave in Oswestry cemetery, Shropshire.
Author's collection.

John McPherson's cousin, Mrs Joan Stephens, recalled that his death came as a great shock to the family; *"It was a real blow to us because he was so young and there were other members of our family who had gone off to the war but came back safely. He was a pretty nice sort of guy as I remember, a teaser. We all called him 'Jock' as his father was Scottish. Before he joined up, 'Jock' worked for the Nestles company in Sydney."*

Another of his cousins, Margaret Horton, added further detail:-

"His paternal family came from Manly, and the address on his Death Certificate, 192 Pacific Parade, Dee Why, was his grandparents' home. That house no longer exists as it has since been replaced by flats. 'Jock' was actually raised, however, in a country town in the southern highlands of New South Wales called Mittagong, and he attended Bowral High School. After matriculation he came to Sydney for further education. Whilst studying he lived with my grandparents at Hornsby as likewise did my own family. I therefore saw a lot of 'Jock' whilst I was growing up myself. I remember him being caring, intelligent, energetic, fun-loving, and, as Joan says, a bit of a tease. I never saw him in a bad temper, we all adored him.

"When I was eight years old I wrote a letter to Santa Claus, with quite a list of things that I wanted for Christmas, and but mere tokens for everyone else. My mother gave 'Jock' the letter to post. You can imagine my delight when I received a reply from Santa several days later (containing a mild rebuke for being greedy!). I was much older, of course, when I realised that 'Jock' was the writer of that letter. On reflection I realise how wonderful it was that he took the time, not many teenagers would have bothered.

"At night the whole family tried to be as quiet as possible to enable him to study. This was actually a wasted exercise as after half an hour 'Jock's' radio would be blaring out the latest pop tunes and he would be jigging around with text book in hand. I remember my grandfather slapping his hand on his knee and saying "Dash my rags, boy, I thought that you were supposed to be studying." Jock replied "Sorry, but it's too quiet and I can't concentrate." From then on that was how it was. One of his favourite songs at that time was "South of the Border", which he continually sang around the house.

"When war broke out 'Jock' was anxious to get into uniform. When he was of age, it was with mixed feelings that his parents gave permission for him to enlist, knowing that he would probably go ahead anyway. Whilst he was away, he always seemed to find time to write to us, and we all looked forward to receiving his letters.

"He and my mother had quite an affinity and would talk of many things. I remember her being most disturbed about a dream in which 'Jock' came to say "goodbye"; she feared for his safety and then a few days later the telegram arrived informing us of his death on active service."

In October 1986, over forty years after Sergeants Lock and McPherson collided, the Malvern Spitfire Team was formed to further historical aviation research. Although having a wide interest in the aeronautical events of yester-year, such local incidents as George Lock's accident came under the Team's microscope.

Knowing the significance of the wartime work carried out by the TFU and TRE, I felt that a memorial should be erected in Sergeant Lock's honour which would also be a tribute to all those killed flying in the development of radar from RAF Defford. Worcester City Council were supportive of the idea and suggested the Perdiswell Sports Centre in Worcester as a possible location for such a tribute. This was particularly appropriate as the sports centre stands on the site of the old airfield and home of 2 EFTS from where Sergeant McPherson had taken off that fateful day in 1943. George Lock's elder sister and only surviving relative, Mrs Joan Walter, was quickly traced to her home near Swansea and immediately offered her full support. Mrs Walter fully approved of the sports centre as the location for the memorial and added:-

"I feel that although the plaque will bear my brother's name it is indeed a tribute to all the young airmen who lost their lives. I hope that the young people who pass through the sports centre will give just a little thought to the young men of George's generation who gave their lives that we can enjoy our freedom today."

A letter was also received from George's boyhood best friend, Mr Derek Owens, who similarly offered help and support. Indeed Derek's help and encouragement has played a major part in this story being written. I am personally moved that despite George having been killed over fifty years ago, Derek's deep affection for his best friend has never faded.

Research work progressed and plans were made for a memorial service. It was decided that the tribute would take the form of, appropriately, a Welsh slate plaque with silver lettering. It was gratifying to receive donations towards the cost of the plaque from villagers of Bronllys who still remembered the young pilot's sacrifice. Following the first information regarding this project appearing in the Worcester *"Evening News"*, I was contacted by a former and very senior engineer from the radar squadron who wished to remain anonymous, but who kindly donated a TFU heraldic crest to accompany the plaque. Mrs Walter provided a wartime photograph of her brother which was framed to hang above the slate memorial.

The date for the service was set for 3 pm, Sunday, October 4th, 1987. Mrs Walter travelled to Malvern where she stayed for the weekend and met members of the team. The memorial had been fixed to the wall of the centre's foyer the previous week along with the photograph, crest and information regarding the TFU. On the big day, Derek Owens travelled to my home, from where both he and Mrs Walter, courtesy of team member Tony Bramhall's kindness, were conveyed to the sports centre in a Rolls-Royce.

At the sports centre over seventy invited guests had assembled and the cadets of 187 (Worcester) Squadron of the Air Training Corps provided a guard of honour. The pale blue limousine arrived on cue, and Mrs Walter and Mr Owens were met by representatives of the Malvern Spitfire Team, Worcester City Council and the officers of 187 Squadron. Inside the sports centre the local vicar, Wing Commander Canon Graham Lyle, commenced dedicating the plaque by reading John Pudney's moving poem *"For Johnny"* to the assembly:-

> *Do not despair*
> *For Johnny-head-in-air;*
> *He sleeps as sound as Johnny underground.*
>
> *Fetch out no shroud*
> *For Johnny-in-the-cloud;*
> *And keep your tears*
> *For him in after years.*
>
> *Better by far*
> *For Johnny-the-bright-star,*
> *To keep your head,*
> *And see his children fed.*

When Mrs Walter had unveiled the plaque a lone bugler played the *"Last Post"*, the haunting notes of which drifted across the playing fields, allotments and derelict buildings that now comprise the site of what was once a very busy wartime airfield.

After Mrs Walter had returned home, I received a package in my morning post containing an incredible gift. Concerned with being George Lock's only surviving relative and custodian of a number of rather unique relics, Mrs Walter had decided to pass on to me her brother's diaries, personal papers and the superb photograph album of his training overseas. Perhaps the most treasured item was his silver United States Army Air Corps (USAAC) wings which George can be seen wearing in a photograph taken after his

Mrs Joan Walter and Mr Derek Owens at the unveiling of the Malvern Spitfire Team's memorial to Sergeant George Lock at the Worcester Sports Centre, October 1987.

Andrew Long.

"*wings*" parade on February 6th, 1942. In recognition of team member Dennis Williams's early research work into her brother's accident, Mrs Walter sent him a USAAC officers cap badge which George had also brought back from overseas.

Sergeant Lock's USAAC "wings", given to Dilip Sarkar amongst a host of relics by Mrs Walter.

Dennis Williams.

A USAAC cap badge brought back from America by George Lock as a souvenir and given by Mrs Walter to Dennis Williams, in recognition of his input to this project.

Dennis Williams.

These precious relics will now be preserved in the care of the Malvern Spitfire Team. Access to the diaries and papers has proved a tremendously rich source of contemporary material and asset in the writing of this story. Copies of the papers and photographs also contributed greatly to the section telling the story of Sergeant Lock in the Malvern Spitfire Team's first major exhibition, "*SPITFIRE!*", at the Tudor House Museum, Worcester, which received 10075 visitors between June and October 1988.

As almost a sequel to the story, on a grey and damp day in November, 1992, my wife, Anita, and I met members of the Malvern Spitfire Team at Park Farm, Kempsey, the scene of Spitfire X4918's crash site. Our intention was to excavate the site and recover for restoration and display any items there remaining. Team stalwarts Andrew Long, Tony Bramhall, Dennis Williams and Mark Postlethwaite, were supported in our endeavour by Clive and Derek Davies, and Roy and Ashley Mayo (the latter aged three), with Bob and Kevin Jenkins providing and driving the JCB. An initial sweep with Tony's sophisticated metal detector proved disappointing, until an area some fifteen feet in diameter produced an extremely promising reading. The turf was carefully removed, and immediately wreckage came to light. Soon the JCB was at work, and Andrew Long and Mark Postlethwaite were in the hole, at one point standing ankle deep in aviation spirit and oil, directing operations and passing out many and varied lumps of Spitfire. Others carefully sorted through the buckets of earth displaced by the machine. Gradually, as items were placed on a sheet, a large pile developed until it became obvious that we were undertaking one of our most successful Spitfire recoveries. Dennis Williams, the team's technical research and restoration specialist, was on hand to identify many items on the spot following an initial scrub with a toothbrush and water. Amongst those items were the Spitfire's De Havilland Constant Speed unit, that governed the use of the propeller, a counter-balance weight from the metal airscrew, engine valves, piston and liners, con-rod sections, large chunks of engine casing, three kidney-shaped exhausts, numerous cockpit instruments, and many other relics besides. By the end of the day some four hundredweight of aircraft had been recovered from as deep as five feet down, more than enough to keep the technical section very busy throughout the winter months ahead. Despite our triumph, however, an air of sadness hung about us all throughout the day, not surprising perhaps considering our close association with the unfortunate pilot and his surviving sister. Our sadness was accentuated with the finding of a tunic button, a poignant reminder of the human tragedy amongst the wreckage of a war machine. It is intended that eventually a selection of restored X4918 remains will go on show permanently at the sports centre, alongside the memorial plaque, and other items will be shared with the public in our various exhibitions at Tudor House Museum. Ultimately we hope to obtain our own premises which will be a memorial in itself to those like Sergeant Lock whose tragic stories will be related. Dennis Williams has also prepared a report regarding X4918:-

"In contrast to Spitfire P8208, the subject of the last chapter and which was recovered from the River Severn estuary at Redwick, X4918 was known to have dived steeply into the ground. On locating the crash site and commencing digging, it was evident that the high speed impact had resulted in complete disintegration of the Spitfire. Components were identified from all parts of the aircraft, ranging from a propeller blade counterweight at the front to the tailwheel shock absorber strut at the rear. Practically no individual component had escaped serious damage, with even the heavily-built Merlin engine having broken up to the extent that normally resilient items such as the valves had been severely distorted. Recovery of the large number of small shattered items was made difficult as excavation revealed that below the topsoil the aircraft had been arrested by a layer of sticky, blue-grey clay, with wreckage extending to a depth of about five feet. After a long and difficult day's work, the Team were satisfied that all wreckage had been extricated, and after reinstatement of the ground the remains of X4918 were removed for preliminary cleaning and catalogued. The final weight of the wreckage was found to be nearly 400 lbs."

Members of the Malvern Spitfire Team following the successful recovery of Spitfire X4918 at Park Farm, Kempsey, in November 1992.

Mark Postlethwaite.

X4918's oil-filler access panel, recovered during the November 1992 excavation, and after subject to Dennis Williams's attention.

Dennis Williams.

Again, this moving story relates the life and death of a young Welshman who proudly stepped forward to serve his country in its darkest days. Let us not forget that all aircrew were volunteers and George Lock joined the RAFVR in most desperate times when Britain stood alone. Perhaps though we have now gone some little way towards repaying an immeasurable debt owed not only to Sergeant Lock, but also to his family and friends who had one they held most dear suddenly taken from them on that winter's day in 1943.

> *He shall not grow old, as we that are left grow old,*
> *Age shall not weary him, nor the years condemn,*
> *At the going down of the sun, and in the morning,*
> *We will remember him.*

Chapter Ten

THE DAREDEVIL

Sergeant Victor Jack Trafford Allen.
Author's collection.

ollowing the A49 Hereford Road south, about five miles from Leominster you will reach the village of Hope-under-Dinmore with its church of St Mary's. The small community is scattered around Dinmore Hill, a significant geological fault as a result of which the undulating landscape rises sharply from below 400' above sea level to over 600' in less than one mile. To the west of Dinmore Hill, looking towards Weobley and Dilwyn, the high ground descends steeply to the flat Wye valley flood plain. Hope-under-Dinmore is a sparsely populated area of predominantly black and white cottages and farmhouses. Largely untouched by the progress of man, it remains a haven of rolling green fields and woodland.

Turning right off the A49 opposite St Mary's church and following the narrow lane up its steep ascent, you will reach a rather quaint black and white cottage which stands alone on the northern slope of Dinmore Hill, commanding a superb view of the valley towards Leominster. During the war this cottage was the home of the Allen family and known as Buskwood Farm, surrounded by a pear orchard. I first visited this site in January 1987 with my good friend Jim Thomas from Hereford. Although we found the cottage empty and up for sale it was little changed since the Allens' day except for a small extension and the orchard being removed. Nothing remained as a grim reminder of the most terrible tragedy that befell the Allen family adjacent to their picturesque home on Thursday, 29th June, 1944.

Victor and May Allen had two children, an elder daughter called Pearl and a son christened Victor Jack Trafford who was born at Buskwood in 1925. Jack grew up to become a very popular character in the village and is remembered by his cousin Eleanor with quite some affection:-

"To me, a girl a couple of years younger, he was super, very witty with a great sense of humour."

Cousin Peggy recalls that:- *"Jack was quite a lad with a warm loving nature, the dare-devil with a great sense of fun."*

May Allen was devoted to her son. The Allen children apparently very much reflected the saying that *"He was his mother's son and she her father's daughter."*

Jack was a very intelligent young man who excelled at his studies. Family friend Mrs Apperley went to school with young Jack and recalls that his only wish from an early age was to join the RAF and become a pilot. For many years a wooden bus shelter stood near Dinmore Hill in which he had carved his name at the age of just thirteen: *"Jack Allen - Pilot"*.

Having attended the Larkhill Academy in Scotland and Lucton School in Herefordshire, Jack completed just one term at Trinity College, Cambridge, before joining the RAFVR on October 6th, 1941, *"For the duration of the present emergency"* and mustered as an Aircraftman 2nd Class. Like many other air-minded and educated young men of his day he seized the opportunity provided by the war to learn to fly at His Majesty's expense and serve his country in the process. At the age of just seventeen, Leading Aircraftman VJT Allen arrived in Canada to commence his pilot training under the Empire Air Training Scheme. This programme was to take him to the Elementary and Reserve Flying Training School at Caron, Saskatchewan, where he won his *"wings"* and later to fly the Hurricanes of 1 OTU at Bagotville near Quebec. In the autumn of 1943, Sergeant Allen returned to the UK for the final stage of his fighter pilot training at 53 OTU (40 Course) flying Spitfires at Kirton-in-Lindsey in Lincolnshire.

Throughout training Jack's companion was Frank Day, a young Hertford-shire lad of similar wit. However at the end of their course at 53 OTU the pair

Sergeant Allen seated in a Hurricane fighter during advanced flying training in Canada.
Author's collection.

Jack Allen, seventh from right, and Frank Day, fifth from left, whilst training in Canada.
Author's collection.

were separated by their postings and were never to meet again - Sergeant Day was posted to fly, much to his disgust, Hurricanes in the Scilly Isles and later, more to his liking, Mustangs in India. Sergeant Allen's dream came true when he and Flying Officer AGP Jennings were both posted on February 22nd, 1944, from 53 OTU to fly Spitfires with 616 Squadron at Exeter.

616 Squadron was originally an Auxiliary Air Force unit and in September 1939 was equipped with Gloster Gauntlet biplanes. Fortunately before the outbreak of war these obsolete fighters were replaced by the new, fast and sleek Supermarine Spitfire. The squadron saw action during the Battle of Britain but suffered particularly heavy losses. After a rest at Kirton-in-Lindsey between October 1940 and February 1941, 616 Squadron returned south and at Tangmere became part of the famous wing commanded by Wing Commander Douglas Bader. From 1941 - 1943 the squadron flew Spitfire IIs, Vs and IXs from various bases in the south of England but later re-equipped with high altitude Mk VI and VII Spitfires and was engaged on home defence duties in the west of England, commanded by Squadron Leader LW Watts DFC.

In June 1941 a review of Spitfire development had taken place prompted by the increased performance of the fighter's German adversary, the Messerschmitt 109, and the arrival on the Channel coast of Germany's most deadly fighter, the Fw 190. As we have seen, both of these enemy aircraft outclassed in many respects the Spitfire Mk Vs operated in the front line by the RAF, the Fw 190 particularly at high altitude, and so the Spitfire Mk VI was developed as a temporary expedient. The MK VI was basically a Mk V airframe fitted with a more powerful Rolls-Royce engine - the Merlin 61, a four bladed propeller and extended pointed wing tips to reduce the drag of wing tip vortices induced when flying at acute angles of attack at high altitude. The Mk VI was also fitted with a pressurized cockpit. On its first flight the Mk VI reached an altitude of 42,000' but although both 124 and 616 Squadrons received the new Spitfire to intercept high altitude raiders, the Merlin 61 proved to be not quite powerful enough to cope with the extra weight imposed by cannons and the pressurized cockpit. The quest for improved performance from a high altitude Spitfire resulted in the Mk VII. This new Spitfire not only retained the long wing span, 20 mm cannons, pressurized cabin and four bladed propeller of the Mk VI but also included new improvements such as a retractable tailwheel, a pointed broad-chord rudder and the most powerful Merlin engine yet produced - a Merlin 64 with a two stage blower. This new fighter provided the squadrons with the high altitude remedy that they so badly needed.

Only the 10 Group Culmhead Wing, which consisted of 124, 131 and 616 Squadrons, was equipped with the new Mk VII. 124 Squadron exchanged its

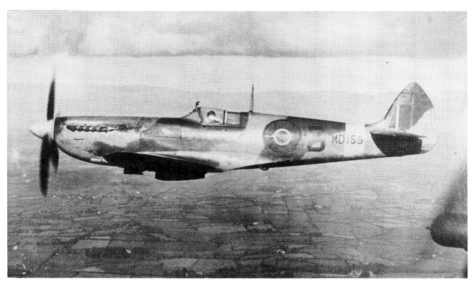

A Supermarine Spitfire Mk VII. Note the pointed, extended wing-tips, the pressurized cockpit and pointed rudder.

James Hellyer.

high altitude fighters for the Spitfire LFIX in 1944 when the squadron changed duties to a low altitude ground support role with the 2nd Tactical Air Force.

Sergeant Allen's first sortie with 616 Squadron was in Spitfire Mk VII "YQ-J" as Yellow 2 to Flying Officer JR Rich of the RCAF on a convoy patrol. After another convoy protection patrol the following day, he flew as Red 2 to Squadron Leader Watts on an escort mission on March 19th, 1944 when the squadron protected seven Mosquitos of 85 Squadron which were bombing targets in northern France. After a number of convoy and standing patrols throughout the month of March, Sergeant Allen flew as Red 2 in Spitfire "YQ-E" to Warrant Officer Des Kelly, an Australian, on a weather reconnaissance flight at 22,000' over the Amiens and Lille areas. April too continued with daily patrols of Dover, Dungeness and Portland. Towards the end of the month the squadron moved to Fairwood Common, again flying defensive standing patrols which continued into May. On the 23rd of that month Allen flew on Ramrod 131 when 616 Squadron's Spitfires escorted Mitchell bombers to bomb Dinard airfield. The squadron diary records that the Spitfire pilots witnessed some *"excellent bombing"*.

In June 1944, 616 Squadron was based at RAF Culmhead near Church Stanton, south of Taunton in Somerset. During this intensive build-up period to the Allied invasion of Normandy, the squadron found itself flying convoy protection patrols and sweeps over enemy occupied France. On June 1st, Sergeant Allen flew "YQ-F" Red 4 on a Rhubarb. The squadron diary tells the story:-

"Flt Lt Barry, Flt Lt Harrison, Flight Sergeant Woodacre and Sergeant Allen of 'A' Flight, Flt Lt Pennick, Sgt Cartmel, Pilot Officer McKay & Flying Officer Hobson of 'B' Flight took part in a 'Rhubarb' over north west France covering coastal railways. Added following score to squadron's 'bag': 2 locos, 6 wagons, many damaged, motor lorries and 1 gun post. Intense flak met over Landerneau. Flt Lt Barry returned safely to base after aircraft hit by 20 mm cannon. He now displays this souvenir found embedded in the rear of his cockpit."

The attacks on trains were actually part of a complicated overall plan approved by the War Cabinet and known as the *"Railway Plan"*. For *"Operation Overlord"*, the Allied invasion of France, to be successful, the enemy would have to be prevented from quickly moving his forces to the front. To achieve this aim, all eighty-five French railway centres were attacked. It was calculated that these attacks would cost the lives of some 10,000 French civilians. This deeply concerned the British Prime Minister, Winston Churchill, but it was argued that if successful Overlord would ultimately save the lives of millions. The Railway Plan comprised measures to attack road and rail facilities, and road and rail movement. In addition, neither reserve troops in billeting areas nor air transport were safe from attack. The War Cabinet felt that there was nothing to be gained from actually damaging roads before D-Day, but it was planned that on and afterwards attacks would be made on bridges over the Orne to create *"choke points"* through the towns of Lisieux, Caen, Bayeux, St Lô, Coutances and Valognes. The attacks on both railways and bridges by the Allied air forces were to be reinforced by sabotage by both the Special Air Service and Special Operations Executive.

On June 2nd, 1944, Sergeant Jack Allen flew on a cine-gun camera training flight, and the following day took off in "YQ-E" at 1500 hrs with Flying Officer Mullenders on *"low flying and cross country"*, landing at 1640 hrs.

The grey dawn of June 6th, 1944, saw the huge Allied invasion fleet anchored off the beaches of Normandy which were dubbed with the code names Sword, Juno, Omaha, Utah and Gold. Nearly 200,000 men were engaged in naval operations and 14,000 air sorties were flown. The liberation of occupied Europe began before first light that morning as Allied troops landed in France. By evening the beach-head was secure and over 156,000 men had been landed. The 616 Squadron diary has this to say of the long awaited invasion known as *"D-Day"*:-

"It has begun; the Allied armies have landed in France. Everybody is anxious for news and very excited. Convoy patrols made by seven aircraft off Portland and Start Point. Pilots returned with stories of the Channel swarming with ships of all sizes and the skies darkened with our aircraft. One section made air-sea rescue patrol for a Liberator bomber reported down near Start Point at 2030 hrs. Eight aircraft led by Sqn Ldr Watts DFC took off on a Rodeo sweeping Brest Peninsular. Squadron returned with bag of 2 locos and 4 military trucks. Some opposition from flak but no casualties or damage. The day ended with the news that the Allied forces had established themselves on the beaches between Cherbourg and Le Havre."

Sergeant Allen flew once on D-Day, as Grey 2 to his section leader Flying Officer M Mullenders. Although the sortie was a patrol with a *"nil report"*, what an incredible sight the invasion fleet, disgorging troops and armour ashore, must have looked, especially to an impressionable nineteen year old.

At 0930 hrs on D-Day there had been 6/10ths cloud at 2,000' over Northern France which was ideal for Allied fighter bombers. Unfortunately, however, the carefully laid plans for high altitude bombers to create choke points came to nought due to the low cloud. Although Bomber Command flew 1,000 sorties, results, due to the bad visibility, were poor.

Another young pilot who had also trained overseas with the Empire Air Training Scheme and in the UK with 53 OTU was Warrant Officer(later Flight Lieutenant) Bob George who had joined 616 Squadron at Ibsley in July 1943 whilst the unit flew the Spitfire MK VI. During his time at Culmhead, Bob's log book details numerous scrambles, standing and convoy protection patrols. On D-Day Warrant Officer George flew Spitfire VII MB825, coded *"YQ-P"*, on two sorties - firstly protecting destroyers dropping depth charges and secondly on a Rhubarb. In his log book Bob wrote: *"D-Day - It's come at last !"* and in relation to the Rhubarb - *"My first. Shared two trains and got a small military truck for myself."*

By D-Day the Railway Plan had been

Sergeant Bob George pictured shortly after his "wings" parade and wearing both RAF and USAAC flying badges.

Flight Lieutenant R. George.

successful, and the railway system of Northern France was completely unable to cope with the requirements of German divisions. Reinforcements were actually brought to the front at a lower level than that used by garrison troops before the invasion. The enemy was therefore forced to use the roads, which aggravated his motor transport and fuel situation in addition to presenting excellent targets to marauding fighter bombers. The small amount of railway traffic after D-Day was constantly harried by fighter bombers until by the end of June rail movement in Northern France ceased. The major factors in achieving this successful result were the destruction and exhaustion of locomotive power and repair facilities, the destruction of marshalling yards and regulating facilities, and the blocking of important routes. Air attacks on running trains, such as those carried out by 616 Squadron, actually had a more devastating effect than those conducted by Resistance groups, as the Allies later discovered when they experienced great difficulty in repairing the railway system.

Between June 7th and 12th, Warrant Officer George's log book details the sorties he flew with the squadron in further support of the Allied invasion:-

"June 7th - MB915 - Rhubarb - Pooped at a couple of trains, a truck and an RDF (Radio DirectionFinding) tower."

The squadron diary also records the Rhubarb of D-Day plus 1 in which Sergeant Allen again flew as Grey 2:-

"Busy day. At first light eight aircraft took off for a Rhubarb. 'A' Flight - Flying Officer Mullenders, Sgt Allen, Flt Lt Harrison and Warrant Officer Woodacre. 'B' Flight - Flying Officer MacKay, Flying Officer Hobson, Pilot Officer Clerc and Sgt Cartmel. Course flown as planned over St Brieuc, Morlaix and Landerneau. Two locos and one army truck damaged near Dinan. No enemy opposition from aircraft but flak near Guingamp and Landerneau. Flying Officer Hobson's aircraft was hit but made base safely. Warrant Officer Woodacre returned early with mechanical fault."

After the seemingly endless patrols and offensive sorties fatigue was bound to take effect. The squadron archivist records:-

"Pilots and ground crews feeling the strain after the past few days ops. However all are cheerful and ready for more. News flashes from the Allied beaches in Normandy give indications that all is well."

Bob George recorded in his log book on D-Day plus 3:-

"June 9th - MB885 - Beach Head Patrol - Bags of shipping but no huns."

The squadron diary elaborates:-

"Allied beach head patrol. Today the squadron was detailed for a beach head patrol. This was the thing every squadron pilot wanted to take part in. At 1820 hrs 12 aircraft took off on first patrol. Taking part were Sqn Ldr Watts DFC, Flt Lt Endersby,

Fg Off Cooper, W.O. Hart, Flt Lt Cleland, W.O. George, Fg Off MacKenzie, Flt Sgt Packer, Fg Off Rodger, Sgt Allen, Flt Lt Harrison and Flt Lt Jennings. It was a Culmhead Wing show led by Wg Cdr Brothers DFC & Bar. Patrol was made between Trouville and Barfleur approximately 2 miles off beach. No enemy opposition encountered. Pilots able to tell stories of seeing Allied warships shelling enemy positions and many fires on coast."

The Culmhead Wing Leader was Wing Commander Peter Malam Brothers who had joined the RAF before the war and flew Hurricanes over Dunkirk and during the Battle of Britain with 32 and 257 Squadrons. In January 1941 he formed and commanded 457 Squadron, the second Australian fighter squadron in the UK and led this unit until June 1942 when he was posted to command 602. The following autumn he was promoted to Wing Commander and led the Tangmere wing before leading the Milfield, Exeter and Culmhead Wings. By the end of the war his score of enemy aircraft destroyed stood at 15 and he had been awarded both the DSO and DFC. Peter Brothers retired from the RAF as an Air Commodore after a distinguished career in both war and peacetime. In 1988 Air Commodore Brothers emphasised that the invasion period was a *"very busy time operationally and one in which we were taking casualties."*

The following day, on June 10th, Sergeant Allen flew as Red 4 on a Rhubarb over the Rennes and Lamballe area. There was brisk action for the Spitfire pilots as the diary relates:-

"At 1000 hrs Sqn Ldr Watts led 8 aircraft on 10 Group Rhubarb 275. Operation made according to plan covering Rennes/Lamballe area. No opposition from flak or enemy aircraft. Sqn Ldr Watts hit loco near Loudeac and 1 lorry on Rennes/Lamballe road. Other claims were 1 truck at Lamballe by Flt Lt Graves DFC, 1 truck at Lamballe by Sqn Ldr Watts and Fg Off Rodger, Sgt Allen and Flt Sgt Wilson another truck at Quedillac and 1 loco by Fg Off Rodger near Plouguenast. A hutted camp was attacked by Sgt Allen near Plouguenast and lorries were attacked by Flt Lt Cleland and W.O. George together with the lock gates and high tension cables. On the way back Flt Lt Graves had engine trouble and was forced to ditch 40 miles south of Start Point. Seeing Flt Lt Graves in trouble Flt Lt Cleland jettisoned his hood and prepared to throw out his dinghy. Fortunately Flt Lt Graves managed to get into his own dinghy and was brought to air sea rescue base by Walrus aircraft. Taken to Royal Naval Hospital at Plymouth with head and leg injuries. All wish him well and hope he will be back to the squadron very soon."

Bob George recorded simply in his log book:-

"June 10th - MB808 - Rhubarb - Canal lock gates, armoured car, a truck and electric pylons. Mike Graves in the drink, ditched but OK."

During the following few days Jack Allen flew a number of patrols and Bob George continued flying on offensive operations over occupied territory:-

"*June 12th - MB822 - Rodeo -*   *Harrison bought it and Jack Cleland got two Fw190s but bailed out in the drink. Picked up OK. Me 109s shot down by Bob Hart and Flt Lt Harrison. FW190s by Mike Cooper, CO and Hobbie. Some damn fool went across my nose so I couldn't fire on two FW 190s !!*"

June 17th saw Sergeant Allen flying Red 4 "YQ-I" on an eight aircraft Rhubarb led by Flight Lieutenant Barry. Bad weather hampered visibility and all pilots returned safely without firing their guns but reported seeing a deserted Luftwaffe airfield near Planguenoval. The following day the squadron diary reports:-

"*Warrant Officer Kelly RAAF returned today to the squadron fully recovered from his eye injury. He is with us for non-operational flying duties for the time being. Keen as ever Warrant Officer Kelly hopes to be back on ops in the very near future*".

Bob George recalls the Australian Des Kelly as "*an excellent chap who lost an eye attacking an FW 190 which got through to Southampton around D-Day time - chased it all the way to Cherbourg airfield and shot it down whilst landing. It blew up and the debris hit his Spitfire*".

On June 24th, the Culmhead Wing flew to Tangmere and took part in three "shows". The first operation saw the Spitfires escorting Lancaster and Halifax bombers attacking flying bomb bases in the Pas-de-Calais. The sortie was successful and after a short rest the wing took off again on Rodeo 174 and apart from inaccurate flak experienced over Fontoise was otherwise uneventful. Sergeant Allen flew on all of the day's sorties.

Regarding the trip escorting the bombing of the flying bomb bases the squadron diary has this to say:-

"*Despite continuous bombing by the RAF flying bombs continue to penetrate south and south-east London although fighter squadrons of 11 Group report many destroyed.*"

The V1 was a new and sinister German weapon - a pilotless jet-powered aircraft bomb launched from bases in France towards London. Known by those who waited, watched and listened on the ground in fear as "*Flying Bombs*" and "*Doodlebugs*", the RAF's codename for the Fieseler 103 robot flying bomb was "*Diver*". The V1's dropping point was determined by a propeller-driven "*air-log*" which cut out the fuel supply at a pre-set distance. The fuel capacity therefore was generally sufficient to carry them to London, over which the bombs would plunge earthwards causing terrible destruction. Hitler had placed great faith in these secret weapons which considerably diminished the inspiration which D-Day had given the British people. The V1s destroyed 25,000 houses and killed 6184 people, virtually all in London. Eventually British defences took their measure of the flying bombs and by August the majority were being destroyed before they could do any damage. More devastating were the V2 rockets which commenced in September and which killed 2754 people. They gave no warning and there was no defence against them; plans were actually made to evacuate London but fortunately the Allies eventually overran the launching sites.

For 616 Squadron a great privilege lay ahead in being the first Allied unit to operate the revolutionary jet fighter - the Gloster Meteor, shortly after Germany entered her first jets into the fray. As from June 1944 the squadron's pilots began to attend conversion courses at Farnborough and by July most 616 Squadron pilots were familiar with their new mount. Warrant Officer George went to Farnborough on his jet conversion course on June 13th, and returned to operational flying at Culmhead on June 19th. Sergeant Allen, known by the squadron as "Johnny", no doubt impatiently awaited his chance to fly the Meteor; for him that opportunity would never arise. On June 29th, 1944, Bob George wrote a short note in his log book:-

"Johnny Allen killed".

One Spitfire on charge with 616 Squadron in June 1944 was MK VII (Supermarine Type 351) MB762. This fighter had been built at the Castle Bromwich Aircraft Factory by Vickers Armstrong against contract number 19713/39 and ordered on May 12th, 1942. MB762 was the 38th aircraft of only 140 built of that mark. Initially taken on charge by 39 Maintenance Unit (MU) at Colerne in Wiltshire on July 16th, 1943 the Spitfire was despatched to 405 ARF on September 1st and to 616 Squadron at Exeter on the 28th. When the squadron was at Fairwood Common, MB762 had received flying battle damage on January 21st, 1944, but unfortunately no details of this were recorded in the squadron diary. The damage was repaired on site and completed on February 26th, when MB762 returned to squadron strength. MB762 was to perish on Thursday, June 29th, 1944, with Sergeant Allen.

On the day of his death, Sergeant Jack Allen took off from Culmhead in Spitfire MB762 on "a gunnery and aileron test flight to be carried out in the vicinity of the aerodrome". In high spirits, no doubt flushed with the success of the Allied forces in Normandy and his own squadron's contribution to the invasion, the pilot set course for his parents' home on Dinmore Hill. Knowing full well that his actions were totally unauthorised and contrary to orders, Jack must have also calculated that as his Spitfire was capable of speeds of just over four hundred miles an hour, it would take but a few minutes to cover the ninety miles to Dinmore Hill and return, the gunnery and aileron test complete and no one in authority any the wiser. Brimming with optimism and confidence I doubt the thought that something could go wrong ever occurred to the young pilot. That *"dare devil sense of fun..."*

Reaching Dinmore Hill Jack banked his Spitfire to port and raced very low down the valley towards Buskwood Farm, south from Leominster. As MB762 hugged the contours of the valley villagers ran out of their cottages to see the green and grey fighter flash past lower than their houses perched on the slopes of Dinmore Hill. With the loud roar of the Merlin engine shattering the tranquil setting the Spitfire shot over Buskwood. Jack's sister Pearl came running out to watch and stood at the door with her baby daughter Beverley. His grandfather was working in a field a short distance from the farmhouse and he too stopped his work to watch the fighter circling Dinmore Hill rocking its wings. All eyes were trained skywards - schoolboys Bob Jaynes and Glen George excitedly watched the impromptu flying display, fascinated by the pilot's skill.

On his second pass Jack roared along the valley floor to pull up sharply in front of Dinmore Hill and again hurtle high over his parents' home. At the last second Jack Allen made a fatal error of judgement and his aircraft's propeller touched the ground in front of the pear orchard which rose up to Buskwood Cottage. The consequences were obvious; MB762 tore through the orchard

The crash site of Spitfire MB762. To the left is Buskwood Farm. The items discovered were found in front of the hedgerow to the right. At the time of the accident this field was an orchard.
Author's collection.

shedding panels and cowlings as it went. The Merlin engine broke free and hurtled up the hill, tearing through two hedges and coming to rest some 250 yards from the point of impact. As the Spitfire carved a crazy path through the trees it continued to break up and scattered wreckage in all directions. Eventually the screeching sound of tormented metal subsided and a shocked silence descended over the Herefordshire countryside.

Nineteen year old Jack Allen lay dead in the cockpit of his Spitfire, which was the only section of the aircraft to remain intact, his body hanging limply in his Sutton harness. Horrified villagers rushed to the scene from all directions to offer whatever assistance they could. First to the cockpit section was a local schoolboy, John Beaumont, who was soon ushered away from the terrible sight as adults arrived on the scene. High octane aviation spirit had gushed in all directions as the fuel tanks had ruptured - villagers virtually set upon Mr Beaumont senior as he lit his pipe but fortunately no harm was done. Bob Jaynes clearly recalls the wreckage being scattered over a large area and seeing the black and white identification stripes on what remained of the fuselage and wings.

Glen George recalls that Mr and Mrs Allen were spared the agony of witnessing the crash as both were working at the nearby Rotherwas munitions factory.

Soon PC230 Dick Tanner of the Herefordshire Constabulary arrived at the scene to give whatever assistance he could to the RAF party at the site. Dick remembered that the body was still in the cockpit when he arrived and that he helped carry it on a stretcher to awaiting RAF ambulance at the end of the adjacent lane. The late PC Tanner recalled that the young pilot had been killed by a piece of metal piercing his temple and brain, there being no other visible injuries.

The Operations Record Book of nearby RAF Shobdon, the home of 5 Glider Training School, states:-

"1535 hrs informed by flying control officer of aircraft crashed on Dinmore Hill, Herefordshire. Medical officer and ambulance proceeded and found Spitfire MB762 wrecked. The pilot, 1579427 Sgt J ALLEN of No.616 Sqn is dead having suffered partial ablation of the skull and a fractured right clavicle".

Sergeant Jack Allen was buried at St Mary's church at Hope-under-Dinmore the following Monday. The service was taken by the Revs. JA Hughes and E Charles. The latter had taught Jack at Lucton School and spoke with great admiration of the boy and said he had *"watched his career day by day until he had mounted to the height of his ambition. He was a brilliant scholar, intellectual and lovable."* Amongst the many mourners were two representatives from 616

Squadron; Flight Lieutenant Mike Graves DFC DFM, Jack's flight commander who was still on rest from operational flying duties after ditching in the Channel, and Pilot Officer Des Kelly DFC who was recovering from his eye injury.

616 Squadron's Commanding Officer, Squadron Leader Watts, found himself in trouble with the AOC 10 Group as a result of the accident. An RAF cover-up ensued and no mention is made in the squadron diary of Jack Allen even having taken off on the day of the accident, much less that he lost his life. His name merely ceases to appear in the records without mention as to why this should be so. Each aircraft has a service card called a *"Form 78"* on which are recorded all details of movement and the aircraft's disposal. The fact that MB762 was written off in a flying accident went unrecorded and the *"78"* states that

Sergeant Allen's grave at St Mary's Church, Hope-under-Dinmore, Herefordshire, prior to restoration by the Malvern Spitfire Team, in 1987.
Author's collection.

the Spitfire was *"presumed struck off charge on 21.6.47"*. Former PC Tanner remembered being told at the time that *"Sergeant Allen was on a training flight and as he was many miles off course that fact must not become common knowledge."*

Squadron Leader Watts DFC also lost his life in a flying accident, on April 29th, 1945, when his Meteor III collided with another jet fighter flown by Flight Sergeant Cartmel over Lübeck in Germany. Flight Lieutenant Graves died flying when testing a Gloster Javelin delta-wing jet fighter in 1955. The Australian Des Kelly is believed to have survived the war, and in fact later returned to Dinmore Hill to visit the Allen family, but nothing further is known of him. Bob George was later commissioned and after flying the Meteor jet he left the RAF as a Flying Officer in 1946. He is now a highly qualified biologist specialising in research into certain species of the flea insect. Bob lives in south-west England.

After the incident a copy of the crash signal from 10 Group HQ to 78 MU, which cleared the wreckage of MB762 from the Buskwood crash site, appeared in the RAF training manual called *"Tee-Em"*. The following note accompanied the signal as a warning to other headstrong pilots:-

"The sergeant pilot of a Spitfire was sent off to carry out a gun and aileron test but half an hour later was flying low over his father's house.

"Only six weeks previously he had carried out the same stunts at a low altitude in order to show his father how well he could fly. This time on his second run across the

village and up a valley on the far side he failed to allow sufficiently for the steepness of the hillside and crashed into it. On this occasion his father saw how badly he could fly for he killed himself instantly".

The 616 Squadron Operations Record Book indicates only one flight that Sergeant Allen could have previously flown over Buskwood: June 3rd, 1944, when he flew a low level cross country flight lasting one hour and forty minutes with Flying Officer Mullenders. Locals do recall that Jack had performed a low level beat up of Buskwood before the incident in which he was killed and it was probably on that sortie.

Mr and Mrs Allen remained at Buskwood Farm for many years after the accident but eventually moved to Mrs Allen's native Scotland. Both have now passed on. Mrs Allen never recovered from the shock of losing her son but always kept her grief close, which never eased in the pain of its tragic intensity. Pearl is believed to have married and emigrated to Canada but all efforts to trace her or daughter Beverley have failed.

No one could deny that Sergeant Allen lost his life and aircraft in the most foolhardy of circumstances. However I feel that one cannot wholly condemn him for his actions when put into context; Jack was only nineteen years old and flying the legendary Spitfire - more than enough to go to many youngsters' heads. He had also participated in dangerous operational flying and seen the start of the liberation of the occupied lands only three weeks before his death. He was certainly not alone in carrying out such unauthorised flying: Bob George's log book records that on 21.10.43 two other pilots *"pranged whilst shooting up girlfriend in Ringwood flying Tiger Moth. Both killed."*

Many highly trained pilots must have occasionally let their high spirits override their better judgement but a small number like Jack Allen paid the price. Indeed on April 9th, 1940, Pilot Officer Lancelot Steele-Dixon was killed in Harvard training aircraft P5846 when performing aerobatics over his parents' house at Winforton in Herefordshire. Pilot Officer Dixon's step-father was the author Rafael Sabatini who wrote the *"Captain Blood"* and *"Scaramouche"* books. The pilot's mother was a famous artist and sculptress who fashioned her son a bronze effigy of fallen Icarus which adorns his grave in Hay-on-Wye cemetery. Dixon would have undoubtedly joined the fabled Few had he not lost his life a mere three days after starting his basic day fighter course at 5 OTU, Aston Down.

I first heard of Sergeant Allen's crash from Jim Thomas of Hereford who had known the unfortunate pilot. Soon afterwards I was contacted by eye-witness Glen George and slowly the story began to piece together, albeit in very confusing fragments; local legend had fused the two separate incidents involving Sergeant Allen and Pilot Officer Steele-Dixon into one. The issue was further confused by there being no record of the accident in the 616 Squadron diary at the Public Record Office which meant that the serial number of the Spitfire involved could not be ascertained. This information was neither held by MoD's Air Historical Branch. Eventually Malvern Spitfire Team member Dennis Williams found the aircraft's number purely by chance in the RAF Shobdon station diary.

An appeal for other eye-witnesses to the accident provided an excellent response and brought a bonus through contact with several of Sergeant Allen's relatives and friends. As a result a number of photographs of the pilot were obtained. The grave in St Mary's churchyard was found in a terribly overgrown state and Leominster man Bill Sevier, himself a veteran of the Korean War, was so moved by the story that he offered to adopt and maintain the grave which by this time had been restored to its former state by members of the Malvern Spitfire Team. This action was very much appreciated by Sergeant Allen's relatives and also by the vicar of St Mary's, the Rev. Miller. Sadly Bill was to die prematurely himself, of cancer, in 1988.

An article appeared in the Hereford Times relating to the accident and my research in July 1987. Soon afterwards I was contacted by Frank Day, now

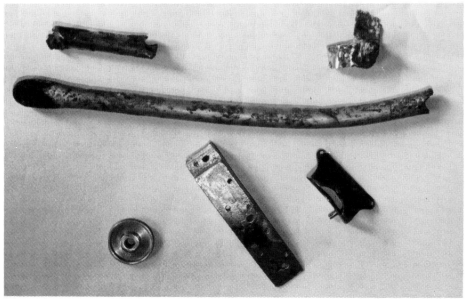

The pathetic remains of Spitfire MB762.

Andrew Long.

232

retired and living near Leominster, who had seen the article by chance. Until he had read the piece he had no idea that his friend of training days had been killed and had in fact made various efforts to contact him since moving to Herefordshire some ten years ago.

Following permission for a site investigation being obtained from the landowner and MoD, I paid a number of visits to the crash site in 1987 with various eye-witnesses and members of the Team. It was not expected to find any of MB762 remaining at the site so we were pleased when fragments of aluminium pipe and an electrical item were discovered buried just below the surface in the site of the old orchard and roughly in the area that the cockpit section came to rest. It is possible that other relics may have been lost when a large gas main was laid across Dinmore Hill, the course of which runs straight through the impact point.

Eye-witness Mr Bob Jaynes donated two small souvenirs removed by his father from the wrecked Spitfire's cockpit on that fateful summer's day in 1944. One item is a small wheel of about 1" in diameter numbered '30027/1981'. The '300' identifies the component as being from a Spitfire. Although 'Type 300' was actually the Mark I many parts used in its construction were also included in other variants of the fighter and would not be re-numbered with that particular mark's type number, ie those parts specifically produced for the Mk VII would be numbered '357' but those also common to Mark I construction would remain '300'. The second part of the number, '27' tells us that the item is from the main fuselage or hull - '1981' specifically identifies the individual component number but I am unable to positively confirm this from contemporary drawings. The second relic is a small spacing fillet of solid aluminium. On it the late Mr Jaynes senior has inscribed *"Spitfire. Crashed on Dinmore Hill 29.6.44."*

Now barely remembered across the span of almost half a century, the name of Sergeant Victor Jack Trafford Allen can at least be found in the Book of Remembrance in Edinburgh Castle.

Chapter Eleven

"ACHTUNG! JABO!"

Pilot Officer John Thould.
Author's collection.

John Thould was born at Upton-upon-Severn in Worcestershire, a small but picturesque riverside town in the shadow of the Malvern Hills, on August 16th, 1920, the eldest son of Frederick John, a self-employed plumber and electrician, and Edith Thould. The family lived at 36A Old Street, in the town centre. After attending the local primary school, John moved on to complete his education at the nearby Hanley Castle Grammar School. His younger brother, Jim, now a local magistrate who still lives in Upton, recalls that John certainly developed an interest in flying from about 1938 onwards. After war came, it was no surprise, therefore, when young John joined the RAF, volunteering for aircrew training, and reported for duty at No 1 Aircrew Reception Centre in London on July 7th, 1941. On July 26th, he joined No 7 Initial Training Wing at Newquay, to complete his *"square bashing"*. On October 1st, LAC Thould commenced his ab initio flying training at No 1

Elementary Flying Training School, Hatfield, making his first flight on October 3rd, in Tiger Moth R4751, gaining *"air experience"* with an instructor, Pilot Officer Bowden, at the controls. Thereafter followed some three flights a day, instruction in climbing, gliding, medium turns, taking off into wind, and spinning. On October 20th, John proudly recorded in his log book *"First solo"*, the flight being of ten minutes duration in Tiger Moth T5414. By the course's conclusion he had flown a total of 12.15 hours, 1.40 of them being solo. On October 30th, the Chief Flying Instructor endorsed the young pilot's log book as *"average proficiency as a pilot"*. Ab initio flying thus complete, Thould's next stop was at No 1 Aircrew Deportment Centre, Heaton Park, on November 5th. On November 21st, he was aboard HM Troopship and bound for foreign climes to complete the next instalment in his flying training.

On December 2nd, the ship reached America, and the following day Thould joined No 31 PD at Moncton. Stationed at Maxwell Field, Alabama, between December 18th, 1941, and January 10th, 1942, he commenced flying PT17 biplanes under instruction on January 12th, 1942, at Tuscaloosa Primary, thus beginning an intensive course that concluded on March 20th. At Gunter Field on March 29th, he progressed to flying BT13s, low-winged monoplane single-engined trainers. On June 2nd, he moved on again, to Turner Field, flying advanced AT6 and 17 trainers. The American phase of John Thould's training was completed on August 5th, 1942, and his log book was endorsed *"above average"*. Another young pilot on the course was Peter Taylor, later to fly Spitfires and Mustangs with 65 and 19 Squadrons, and from whom I was first to hear of John Thould nearly fifty years after the pair had parted company for their respective UK postings.

Arriving back in the UK on September 9th, 1942, Sergeant Thould subsequently spent one day at No 9 Advanced Flying Unit, Hullavington, before joining No 5 AFU at Ternhill in Shropshire on October 6th. There he flew the Miles Master on a variety of air exercises, but on December 2nd, 1942, his dream of being a fighter pilot came true when he flew a Spitfire, R6963, for the first time at 61 OTU, Rednal. Sorties on the basic day fighter course, which lasted from December 8th, 1942, to February 14th, 1943, included local map-reading, sector recognition, steep turns, aerobatics, formation flying and dogfight practice. A cross country exercise was conducted on January 15th, 1943, Sergeant Thould flying K9444, and the route from Rednal to Evesham in Worcestershire would probably have taken him over his hometown of Upton-upon-Severn. From Evesham the Spitfires flew to Aston Down, from there to Hereford and then home. Towards the end of the course, on January 29th, Sergeant Thould flew on a practice Rhubarb, in X4766, and the following day on a practice convoy patrol in P7674. On February 1st, Sergeant Thould moved from Rednal to its satellite at nearby Montford Bridge, to complete the last five days of flying. The following day, flying P7674, he practised air to ground firing, but on 3rd and 4th flew an Oxford with Sergeant Towstiejko on "*ack-ack cooperation*". Finally the course was completed on February 5th, the students flying a "*balbo*" fly past, Thould again in P7674. His log book was endorsed that he had flown a total of 58.20 hours on the Spitfire Mk I and II, 1.40 being at night. The Chief Flying Instructor rated his ability as "*Good Average*". However, it was not to a Spitfire squadron that John Thould was posted, but to 263 on February 27th, 1943, which was equipped with Hawker Hurricanes and Westland Whirlwinds at Harrowbeer, inland of Plymouth.

In 1940, 263 "*Fellowship of the Bellows*" Squadron had valiantly operated Gloster Gladiator biplanes against the Luftwaffe during the Norwegian campaign. Tragically, however, on June 8th, 1940, whilst being evacuated to the UK, all of the squadron's officers, and one Sergeant pilot, were killed when HMS Glorious was sunk by a Hipper class battleship. The squadron subsequently reformed at Drem in Scotland just two days later. On July 1st, 1940, Flying Officer Tom Pugh, brother of Pilot Officer Jack Pugh, both of whom we met in chapter one, was posted to 263 from No 1 RAF Depot. The squadron was equipped with Hurricanes at this time, but when Squadron Leader Eeles took command on July 6th, he brought a new fighter with him; the Westland Whirlwind.

A Westland Whirlwind fighter-bomber, P7110.

Author's collection.

237

The Whirlwind was the most radical of seven designs submitted to meet Air Ministry Specification F.37/35 for a heavily armed fighter carrying four 20mm cannons. The *"Crikey"* was powered by two engines, twin Rolls-Royce Peregrines of 885 hp. It had coolant radiators within the wing centre section which therefore offered minimal drag, the guns were grouped together in the nose, and the tailplane was mounted very high on the tail fin to keep it clear of the wake from the powerful Fowler-type flaps. Despite these flaps, however, the Whirlwind maintained a high landing speed which made it difficult to operate from grass runways. Furthermore, wing loading was high which made for poor manoeuvrability. It is perhaps a pity that a Merlin powered Whirlwind was not produced, for operation from the longer runways common from 1942 onwards; it may have proved a formidable fighter. As it was, the one hundred and fourteen, underpowered, machines produced were largely to see action in the ground attack role.

By September 1940, Tom Pugh had been promoted to Flight Lieutenant and had his 'B' Flight operational on Camm's Hurricane fighter. The squadron saw no action during the Battle of Britain, however, and in December moved to Exeter. The grass runway was soon found to be unsuitable for the Whirlwinds, which type the unit was converting to, and the squadron diary reports the airfield as being in a *"deplorable condition"*. The squadron flew continuous training flights with the Whirlwind, moving to St Eval in Cornwall in March 1941, although still very short of experienced pilots. The following month 263 moved again, to Filton, from where the Whirlwinds commenced flying numerous routine convoy patrols, protecting shipping in the Bristol Channel. These patrols continued throughout May and June, their frequency perhaps being best illustrated by statistics; during the latter month 67 such sorties were flown by the squadron's pilots.

On June 14th, 1941, came the occasion that the Whirlwind pilots had waited for; *"Warhead No 1"*, a proposed dawn attack by two pairs of Whirlwinds against the enemy airfields at Querqueville and Maupertus. It was believed that there was a larger concentration of Me 109s on the Cherbourg peninsular than was normal, I and II Gruppe JG2 and a part of III/JG26 at Maupertus, and III/JG2 at Querqueville. The plan was to attack at first light, exercising the element of surprise. The pilots selected to carry out the operation, Squadron Leader Donaldson and Pilot Officer Rudland, and Flight Lieutenant Pugh and Pilot Officer Mason, had flown to Ibsley in Hampshire the previous evening, staying there the night, and rising at 0315 hrs to find perfect conditions. At 0445 hrs the first pair, Donaldson and Rudland, took off, followed a minute later by Pugh and Mason. The former pair successfully attacked Maupertus's dispersal pens in a shallow dive descending from 1300' to 100'. Despite much return flak, the dispersals were hit, and the two Whirlwinds passed out safely under the protective screen of 234 Squadron's Spitfires. Flight Lieutenant Pugh had found his target covered in mist and so was unable to make an attack. Six Me 109s are reported as having been scrambled in pursuit of the fighter-bombers, but these were intercepted by the Spitfire escorts.

During July 1941 the Whirlwind saw no further action, but August, when Tom Pugh was promoted to command the unit, is recorded in the squadron Operations Record Book as being a *"menis memorabilis"*: *"The Whirlwind has at long last been completely vindicated and has just shown that it is an admirable machine. Many offensive sorties have been flown this month, mainly against enemy aerodromes at Querqueville, Maupertus and Lannion. Three Me 109s have been destroyed in combat, one damaged, and five Ju 88s, seven Ju 87s and some Me 109s also destroyed on the ground with others damaged. One 'E' Boat sunk and another damaged along with two tankers at sea. Gunposts, lorries, wireless stations and enemy troops also attacked and severe damage inflicted. No machine or pilot were lost during these operations."*

So it was that the Whirlwind found its niche as a fighter-bomber, as opposed to its originally intended role as a fighter aircraft, and the period heralded a new deployment in the ground attack role for many RAF fighter squadrons.

Sergeant John Thould, second from left, poses with other 263 Squadron pilots in front of a Whirlwind.

Author's collection.

By September 1941, 263 Squadron was also being used to provide Whirlwind experienced pilots for 137 Squadron which was newly equipping with the type and thus becoming the only other squadron to operate the Whirlwind. This was to have an adverse effect on 263, however, whose subsequent replacements were straight from OTU with no operational experience. October therefore saw no offensive operations flown by 263, but on the 8th, Squadron Leader Tom Pugh received a well earned DFC in recognition of his efforts to date. During November, attacks against the Cherbourg peninsular were resumed, enemy shipping becoming a favourite target, but no contact was made with the enemy in December.

Pilot Officer John Thould helping to "bomb-up" his Typhoon.

Author's collection.

In March 1942, 263 Squadron moved to Fairwood Common, and to Warmwell the following October, by which time Squadron Leader Pugh DFC had himself moved on to form 182 Squadron at Martlesham Heath, one of the first Hawker Typhoon equipped squadrons. It was at Harrowbeer, however, that Sergeant John Thould reported to 263 Squadron for flying duties on February 27th, 1943. His first flight was made on March 14th, in Miles Magister L8280, with Sergeant John Purkis at the controls, when the pair flew from Harrowbeer to Warmwell from where the squadron was to operate for some time thereafter. On March 23rd and 27th, Sergeant Thould flew Hurricane BD715 on local recognition flights of one hour, and twenty-five minutes respectively. On March 28th, he flew a Whirlwind for the first time, P7117, on a familiarisation flight of one hour's duration. During the next few weeks, he flew many training sorties in various Whirlwinds, such as cine-gun attacks, aerobatics, air-sea firing and formation flying. On May 7th, 1943, however, he *"put up a black"*; with a strong south-westerly wind blowing on a cloudy day, whilst coming in to land in P7057, Sergeant Thould held off for too long at 30', stalling, writing off the Whirlwind and nearly destroying the Watch Office in the process. The squadron commander, Squadron Leader GB Davies, had no sympathy. Attributing the accident to carelessness, the commanding officer immediately posted the unfortunate, and relatively inexperienced, young sergeant from his squadron in disgrace to the Aircraft Refresher Course at Brighton.

Sergeant Thould then spent several months *"out in the cold"*, flying Lysanders with 1498 Flight, an army cooperation unit, later flying Martinets on dull target towing duties at 11 Armament Practice Camp. Enthusiasm undaunted, however, he continued throughout this time to request a return to operational flying. Being a pilot of obvious potential, his persistence was eventually rewarded when on December 9th, 1943, he returned to 263 Squadron at Warmwell, still commanded by Squadron Leader Davies.

On December 12th, 1943, Sergeant Thould made his first flight having resumed association with his former squadron, circuits and bumps in Hurricane P7752. Only a few days previously, on December 2nd, however, the squadron had begun receiving the Hawker Typhoon Mk Ib, marking the end of 263's long association with the Whirlwind. The squadron diary records that *"All pilots who flew the Whirlwind on operations against the enemy had absolute confidence in and affection for their aircraft."* On December 13th, Sergeant Thould flew a Typhoon for the first time, JR129, gaining experience on the new type for forty-five minutes.

The Typhoon was another storm from Hawker to be unleashed against the enemy, being a direct descendant of the Hurricane and also designed by Sydney Camm. The Typhoon had first flown on February 24th, 1940, following which another experimental fighter, the Tornado, was abandoned. The Typhoon's Napier Sabre engine, a twenty-four cylinder powerplant, suffered serious problems, but the unit produced 2,180 hp and a maximum speed of 374 mph. The Typhoon's wing section was thick, causing high drag and limiting high speed performance. The high wing-loading and poor manoeuvrability produced a real performance far below that suggested by the designer. The cockpit of the Mk Ib had a *"car"* type door, which, in high speed dives tended to unlock and open due to suction on the external handle. Elevator flutter also caused rear fuselage failures, adding to casualties suffered as a result of engine failure and carbon monoxide poisoning. Not surprisingly perhaps, for the majority of 1942 the Typhoon programme was threatened with cancellation. Squadron Leader RP Beaumont, however, the Commanding Officer of the Typhoon-equipped 609 Squadron, became convinced that at low altitudes the Typhoon was actually as good as any other contemporary fighter, and indeed better than some. In anticipation of the fighter pilots' future role of supporting the Army when it eventually returned to Europe, Beaumont was particularly interested in the idea of the Typhoon as a ground-attack machine. First, though, he actually managed to prove the *"Tiffie's"* worth in intercepting the low-level *"tip'n run"* Fw 190s which no other Allied fighter could easily catch. The Typhoon's strong wings also made it capable of not only packing a powerful punch in the shape of four 20mm cannons, but also two 1,000 lb bombs, and eight 60lb rocket projectiles. The RAF eventually received over 3,000 Typhoons. During the course of production development, the original and unusual cockpit was replaced by a sliding tear-drop canopy, which offered an excellent all-round view, and the original three-bladed airscrew was replaced by a four-bladed propeller. Typhoons were soon roaming over enemy coastal waters hammering Hitler's shipping, or attacking anything that moved by either road or rail in France.

On December 22nd, 1943, Sergeant Thould reported to 1 Special Low-level Attack Instructors' School to learn the skills of ground attack which he would later put to good use on operations. On Christmas Eve, 1943, he made a *"sector recco"* in Hurricane KX188, followed by a low flying sortie at 50'. With Christmas Day off, the flying resumed on Boxing Day, Thould commencing the first of many 40mm cannon firing practice flights in Hurricane KZ711. On December 30th he undertook medium bombing in KW383, carrying eight ten pound *"eggs"*, and low-level bombing on New Year's Eve. The first day of 1944 saw no flying undertaken by No 1 SLAIS, but as of January 4th, 1944, Sergeant Thould commenced practising firing rocket projectiles with either four or eight 25lb missiles in Hurricanes KX538 and KX199. On January 11th the course concluded, and Thould returned to his squadron at Fairwood Common, no doubt eager to put his newly acquired knowledge to devastating effect against the enemy.

On January 23rd, 1944, 263 Squadron moved to Beaulieu, from where its training flights in Typhoons continued, without mishap, until January 28th when Flight Sergeant Thould's aircraft, MM965, suffered an engine failure. The pilot safely forced landed the machine at Dinton, and subsequently received high praise from Group Captain Legg, the Middle Wallop Sector Commanding Officer. Any reprimands in a pilot's flying log book are noted in red ink;

commendations in green. Legg recorded in Thould's log book, in green ink and under the heading *"Instances of Avoidance by Exceptional Flying Skill and Judgement of loss or damage to aircraft or personnel"*, that *"Flight Sergeant Thould was flying a Typhoon at approximately 1,000' when the engine cut and completely failed him. He made a successful forced landing, thereby avoiding injury to himself, and in so doing demonstrated his skilful airmanship in saving his aircraft and himself from complete destruction. He is accordingly to be commended."* No doubt John Thould reflected at this time on his Whirlwind mishap of May 1943, for which he had now more than made up.

On February 9th, 1944, Flight Sergeant Thould flew his first operational sortie, a scramble in Typhoon JR389, but his log book records that the result was *"no joy"*. Whilst Thould and other pilots continued their intensive flying training programme, the squadron's more experienced pilots were in action. On February 12th, Squadron Leader Gonay destroyed a Do 217, and an Me 109 the following day. On February 18th, Flight Lieutenant LWF *"Pinky"* Stark DFC reported from 609 Squadron and took over 'A' Flight. Stark was a very experienced exponent of the Typhoon, having previously flown with Beaumont himself, and an *"ace"*, having destroyed five and a half enemy aircraft.

From March 1944, Flight Sergeant Thould flew on virtually every operational sortie flown by 'A' Flight. On March 6th 263 Squadron moved to Warmwell and began a period of intensive operations against the enemy during the build up for the Allied invasion of Normandy. On March 12th, 1944, Flight Sergeant Thould was patrolling the Channel in JR382 and chased an *"unseen bandit to Alderney."* Four days later Squadron Leader Gonay led his squadron on a *"shipping recco"* of the Channel Islands area, looking for enemy vessels, but no targets were found. Three days later the squadron returned to Harrowbeer. On March 31st, a long standing member of 263 Squadron, Flight Lieutenant Racine, was reported missing from a Rodeo flown from Predannack, on which Flight Sergeant Thould was the *"spare"*. The following day he participated in the search for Racine over the sea north of Batz. Although the search was unsuccessful, Gerry Racine returned safely to London under his own steam, arriving there on April 17th, 1944.

On April 18th, 1944, Flight Lieutenant Stark DFC led his flight from Harrowbeer to Tangmere, from where himself, Flight Lieutenant Rutter, Flying Officer Purkis, Pilot Officer Green, and Flight Sergeants Handley and Thould undertook Rodeo 115, a fighter sweep over France. The sortie was to be extremely successful.

Flight Sergeant Thould flew MN476, *"HE-D"*, for the first time on Rodeo 115. This aircraft thereafter became his regular mount and he named it *"The*

Hawker Typhoon MN476, "HE-D", named "The Hawk" by John Thould and flown by him on numerous operational sorties. It was in this very aircraft that he eventually lost his life in action.

Author's collection.

Hawk". At 1517 hrs on April 18th, 1944, Stark led the Typhoons off from Tangmere, setting course to sweep anti-clockwise around Paris with the intention of *"destroying any Huns that they could find."* The aircraft flew in sections line abreast, from port to starboard the formation comprising Flight Sergeant Thould (Yellow 2), Flying Officer Purkis (Yellow 1), Flight Lieutenant Stark (Red 1), Pilot Officer Green (Red 2), Flight Lieutenant Rutter (Blue 1), and Flight Sergeant Handley (Blue 2). The Typhoons thundered across the Channel at zero feet, climbing to cross the French coast SW of Trouville at 8,000' above cloud. They then dived to zero feet, pinpointing on the railway line west of Bernay cathedral. Stark then led the flight SE before turning east between Chartres and Dreux. On a road between Ablis and Rambouillet a large camouflaged truck towing a trailer appeared, at which Stark fired a short burst. He saw cannon shell strikes on both vehicles. Following a bright flash in the truck's cabin it stopped as the Typhoons roared overhead in search of another victim. Flight Sergeant Handley was next to fire his guns when an airfield was encountered at Ecrosnes, between Chartres and Paris. Handley fired a short burst at an He 111 parked in the dispersal area and noted

244

strikes. The Typhoons then continued SE of Bretigny when an Me 410 was seen ahead, flying from starboard to port at 500'. Flying Officer Purkis fired a short burst without result from extreme range, but Flight Sergeant Thould chased the enemy aircraft, at a speed in excess of 360mph, closed to 250 yards and attacked, slightly to starboard and beneath from astern. The enemy's starboard engine was soon ablaze.The Me 410 made no evasive action, nor returned Thould's fire, but the pilot attempted to make a controlled forced landing in a ploughed field. However, Stark and Thould both saw the 410 explode upon impact.

After reforming, Stark led his Typhoons north of Villaroche airfield. Ten miles east of Villeve airfield he saw a Do 217 flying west at 200'. Flying Officer Purkis attacked first, noting strikes on the bomber's fuselage. Rutter, Green and Handley then attacked. The latter closed from 200 to 80 yards, firing continuously, and a piece of debris from his target lodged in his Typhoon's leading edge. Again the enemy aircraft failed to return fire, and this example suddenly went into a vertical dive, crashing in flames.

Reforming again, the Typhoons flew north, Flight Lieutenant Stark firing at a large grey staff car travelling NE between Paris and Soissons. The rear of the vehicle burst into flame and it careered out of control into a ditch. With both time and fuel now getting short, Stark flew NW. In the Cormeilles area, Flight Sergeant Handley fired at some twenty German soldiers but could not see the result of his attack. The formation then climbed to fly over Rouen at 11,000', and after crossing the coast west of Fécamp at 9,000' in a shallow dive at 400 mph, returned safely to Tangmere at 1715 hrs.

Flight Sergeant Thould's first Rodeo had certainly proved memorable. Hitler's Festung Europa may well have had a *"wall of fire and steel"*, but clearly it had no roof.

On April 25th, 1944, Thould flew MN476 on two *"armed shipping reccos"*, the Typhoon carrying two 250 lb general purpose bombs. The target was the wrecked destroyer Ebeling. Thould reported two near misses, but Stark went round again to score a pair of direct hits.The next day Squadron Leader Gonay led five of his pilots, including Thould in JR389, on a Roadstead to attack shipping in the Morlaix estuary. Both light and heavy flak was reported by the pilots. On landing back at base, the engine of JR389 apparently cut completely, but Flight Sergeant Thould made a safe landing without power.

During May 1944, 263 Squadron continued with its Roadsteads against enemy shipping, during the month flying sixteen offensive operations. This practice saw a great improvement in the standard of dive-bombing. On May 30th, Flight Lieutenant Stark led eight *"Bombphoons"* on Roadstead 116, an armed reconnaissance of the Brest approaches. Off the Goulet the pilots found a 3,500 ton merchant ship, towed by a tug, which they subsequently attacked and sunk. The squadron diary recalls that the attack saw the *"neatest results to date. Twelve of the bombs, which were 500 pounders, fell in the stern area of the ship, one causing a direct hit, and another producing debris."* John Thould's MN476 was hit by flak in the starboard bomb rack fairing. He recorded in his log book *"Good bombing! Three direct hits, about five very near misses. Lots of flak."* Later the same day Stark led Morgan, Thould, Heaton and Shelland on Roadstead 117. The brief was as per the previous sortie and a minesweeper and armed trawlers were located and attacked south of Ushant. Unfortunately, however, the high standard of bombing was not maintained, and no hits were recorded on the enemy ships.

The standard tactic employed by 263 Squadron on such sorties was to rendezvous with Spitfires at either Bolt Head or Predannack, before crossing the Channel at zero feet. From twenty miles off the French coast the formation would commence a rapid climb to 10,000', subsequently dive-bombing targets found from out of the sun, or from astern of ships. The aircraft would then orbit offshore at 3,000' to reform before returning to base.

The start of June 1944 found 263 Squadron undertaking a mixture of offensive and training flights. On June 1st, Flight Sergeant Thould practised bombing in MN487, and on the third firing rocket projectiles (RPs) in MN282. On June 6th, however, the squadron diary records:-

"After midnight a flap for twelve aircraft. Eight flew a Goulet recco in duff weather and returned to find it D-Day. Thus what has been demanded for three years, expected for two, and hourly awaited for three months arrived unheralded in 10 Group whilst the squadron was doing an armed ship recco, and continued whilst we did RP practice at Bolt Head and were bound in the dispersal. However, things are often better than they seem and the next hours and days were very much our busiest since Norway. That evening saw the squadron's first RP operation, a damaging attack upon a 500 ton motor vessel off Granville, and the start of 121 sorties in five days."

John Thould did not fly operationally until D-Day plus three, when he participated in a dive-bombing attack on the town of St Lô in Normandy. In his log book he wrote: *"Proctor, Cooper and I dive-bombed St Lô. Very little flak from Huns, but bags of all sorts of flak from the Allied Invasion Fleet as we came out over the beach-head."* The following day Flight Sergeant Thould flew on a Roadstead, in MN261 which was armed with eight sixty pound high explosive rockets, to attack a radar station on the island of Jersey. On that attack MN261 was hit by flak in both the port nose fuel tank and the starboard leading edge. Fortunately, however, Flight Sergeant Thould managed to return safely to base.

Later that day he flew MN300 on a Ramrod to attack the viaduct at St Brieuc, but the weather closed in as the *"Tiffies"* reached the French coast so the operation was aborted. On June 12th Thould was back flying MN476, dive-bombing a minesweeper in St Helier harbour. The German ship was fortunate not to be hit, but John's log book records that there was *"a lot of flak."* Later that day the St Brieuc viaduct was eventually damaged by 263 Squadron. On June 14th the squadron conducted an RP attack on armed trawlers south of St Helier, during the same sortie claiming its first U-Boat. However, Squadron Leader Gonay was subsequently reported missing. The squadron diary remarks that Gonay was *"the master of every situation. As a leader he was absolutely trusted, admired and loved as a friend."*

As of June 16th, 1944, 263 Squadron's specific task was to harry enemy shipping between Cherbourg and Brest. This, according to the squadron's Operations Record Book, was of *"great importance to the Normandy beach-head."* With the success of the Railway Plan and disruption of the enemy's communi-cation and transport means between the Contentin and North West France, the Germans were even to be denied the freedom of moving supplies by sea. On June 17th, Flight Sergeant Thould flew MN738 on a successful RP attack against a 1500 ton merchant ship in St Malo harbour. On June 20th, he flew MN282 on a Ramrod RP attack on the radar station at Ploumanach. Hits were scored on both the living quarters and northern target sites. The Operations Records Book recorded that the operation was *"a good evening prang of huts and buildings, but the burning of Cherbourg was an awful sight."* Two days later another Ramrod was flown against the same target, Thould in MN261, *"HE-N"*. The Freya and Würzburg radar installations were severely damaged. On June 27th, the squadron attacked the telephone exchange and repeater station at St Ivy College, Pontivy. Some of the Typhoons carried long-range auxiliary fuel tanks, and some RPs. This combination had been suggested by Flight Lieuten-ant Stark and meant that the squadron could either attack the same target in two waves, or simultaneously attack two different sites.

On July 3rd, 1944, Pilot Officer Thould, as he now was, flew MN476 on a Ramrod against the electricity transformer station at Mur-de-Bretagne. In his log book the pilot later wrote *"Many hits on transformer and control buildings. My wing-tip removed by bofors shell. Flight Lieutenant Stark baled out near Kerdert."* The next two Ramrods, on July 4th and 5th, both against a petrol dump at Guingamp, were both aborted due to 10/10ths cloud over the target. Two days later 263 Squadron flew another Roadstead, an RP attack on an 800 ton coaster near Trébeurden. There were no hits on the target, but light flak claimed Flying Officer Hodgson.

MN476 showing battle damage after its wing-tip was "removed by a Bofors shell" during a Ramrod on July 3rd, 1944.

Author's collection.

On July 10th, 1944, 263 Squadron moved to Hurn, near Bournemouth, and busied itself with further training flights, largely in respect of RP firing practice. Four days later, Flight Lieutenant Stark, shot down on July 3rd, was reported as having made his way safely back to England, his return in just eleven days being a squadron record. The month's also saw DFCs awarded to the squadron's Commanding Officer, Squadron Leader RD Rutter, Flight Lieutenant John Purkis, who had taken over as 'A' Flight Commander after Stark had baled out, and Flying Officer HM Proctor. With the move to Hurn, 263 Squadron correctly anticipated that it would soon be sent to France, flying with the 2nd Tactical Air Force from a new base in France. This assumption was correct, as on August 6th, 1944, the squadron flew from Eastchurch to landing strip B3 near Ste-Croix-sur-Mer in Normandy. Pilot Officer Thould wrote in his log book *"France at last."*

263 Squadron had been deployed to Normandy for the climax of the great battle. The Allied landings had successfully secured a foothold in France. Fierce fighting had taken place in the town of Caen, British and Canadian troops fighting against the determined young fanatics of the 12th SS Hitlerjugend Panzer Division. It took a month for Caen to fall into Allied hands. On D-Day plus ten the Allied advance was halted by the worst storm for forty years, which raged from June 19th-22nd, 1944. By July 1st, however, the Americans had cut off and captured Cherbourg. Von Rundstedt, once one of Hitler's most trusted commanders, made no secret of the fact that so far as he was concerned the war was already lost, and was immediately replaced in his command by Feldmarschall von Kluge. Feldmarschall Erwin Rommel, the *"Desert Fox"*, also disappeared from the scene in July. Germany proclaimed that the national hero had died of injuries sustained in an attack on his staff car by 602 Squadron's Spitfires on July 17th, 1944. On July 20th, the German Generals rebelled against Hitler but their plot to assassinate him failed. Retribution was swift and ruthless. Rommel was implicated in the plot so was given two choices; commit suicide and remain a hero with his death attributed to his wounds, or face a trial at the People's Court and subsequent public execution. The great soldier chose suicide. Meanwhile the Americans made slow progress on the Contentin peninsula.

On July 18th Montgomery began an offensive south of Caen, Operation Goodwood. On July 25th, the Americans broke out and at last advanced from St Lô. By August 1st their armour had reached Avranches. Kluge wished to fall back to the River Seine, appreciating that Germany had lost the Battle of Normandy, but Hitler refused. Instead he ordered Kluge to make a counter-offensive that would sever the American lines of communication at Avranches, isolate Patton by depriving him of essential supplies, before turning north to create chaos in the rear. Panzer Group Eberbach's subsequent attack reached Mortain. As usual, however, Hitler, detached from reality, made no allowances for Allied air superiority.

On August 7th, 1944, the day Hitler's Mortain counter-offensive commenced, 263 Squadron flew its first operational sortie from France. Pilot Officer Thould flew MN476, on an *"RP attack of gun and mortar positions west of Thury-Harcourt"*, the Operations Record Book noting that the target was *"well plastered with RP and cannon."* The following day, in MN738, he similarly attacked a wood north of Flers which was believed to be shielding panzers. The next day 263 Squadron attacked the village of Rouvres, again holding panzers, and on August 10th, Thould and MN476 participated in an RP attack on a *"Panzer HQ near Falaise. Lots of flak, chateau still burning from 'B' Flight's attack five hours previously."* On August 11th, 263 Squadron flew with the other units operating from B3, 266, 193 and 197 squadrons, as a Wing for the first time. The target was the Beauvais radar station. The next day it was back to Falaise, Thould destroying a troop-carrying lorry which Flying Officer Kemp saw burst into flames. On August 14th the squadron attacked tanks in a wood near Olendon, north of Falaise. On the 15th an *"armed recco"* of the area SW of Lisieux was conducted, several lorries and cars being destroyed by the Typhoons. Pilot Officer Thould attacked a large staff car, leaving it smoking in his wake.

By this time the carnage on the ground was staggering. On August 8th, the Canadians had launched Operation Totalize against Falaise, towards which Montgomery also moved. Patton swung round through France and turned north, the German army then being trapped between two pincers, but the gap remained open. From August 14th, Kluge's Mortain gamble having failed, the Germans had begun what was at first a slow withdrawal. That same day saw the launch of Operation Tractable, the second phase of the Canadian push to Falaise. By the 16th the German retreat was in full swing, the Germans streaming back into a small salient west of the Argentan-Falaise road. There France is a mass of tracks with thick plantations and sausage-shaped hills with very steep sides. The most incredible enemy targets presented themselves, the floor of the valley being alive with men cycling, marching and running, columns of horse-drawn transport, motor transport and armoured fighting vehicles. The Trun-Chambois road became a killing ground, known as either the *"Shambles"* or the *"Corridor of Death."* Aircraft of both the 2nd TAF and IXth American Air Force co-operated and strafed the columns of vehicles until it was too dark to see. The Canadians captured Falaise on August 17th. The following day, as the fighter-bombers hammered away at the *"shambles"*, complete panic was achieved amongst the enemy. The repeated RP and cannon attacks turned the withdrawal into a rout. By the end of the day, the RAF's 83 Group had claimed 1,074 motor transports destroyed along with 73 tanks, and 84 Group 230 and 37 respectively. The low flying tactics were costly, however, and those two groups lost a total of 25 pilots (Flight Lieutenant Ron Rayner DFC, who fought his way up Italy with 72 Squadron, often employed upon such strafing attacks himself, once remarked to me that he always feared being shot down and captured by troops that he had previously been attacking, an interesting point and one that I had certainly not previously considered). Meanwhile the Americans pushed on beyond Argentan to Chambois, thus drawing closer to the Canadians and so narrowing the neck of the Falaise gap. A partial link-up was achieved on the 19th, but the gap was not sealed, therefore not denying the retreat of any further German personnel to the Seine until August 21st.

The Allied air forces had undoubtedly played a crucial part in the Falaise victory, which sent the Germans rolling back to the frontiers of the Reich itself. In the battle area, however, the hour surely went to the British and American fighter-bombers, proving their worth in both armed reconnaissance and the close support of ground forces. During August the weather was fine which contributed to their success. At Mortain the Typhoons halted von Kluge's desperate attempt to reach the Atlantic and delay the Allies' advance to the Seine. A few days later, the German Army having cracked, its retreat was harrassed by the fighter-bombers and the roads east of Argentan became choked with wrecked transport. During the Battle of Mortain, the Typhoon squadrons flew a total of 294 sorties over eight hours. Subsequently 84 tanks were claimed as *"flamers"*, 35 as *"smokers"*, and 21 damaged, along with 54, 19 and 39 motor transports respectively. Ground fire had been less than had been anticipated, and only three Typhoons were lost. The fighter-bomber could be switched at short notice to any critical sector of the front and this flexibility, ease of control and weight of firepower that it could quickly bring to bear on any threatened point justified the confidence that Allied commanders placed in the weapon during the crisis. The deployment of the Typhoons was both timely and decisive, as, although fighting on the ground remained bitter for several days, large- scale attacks by panzer divisions were never renewed. Between August 13th and 16th, the 2nd TAF claimed to have destroyed 500 motor transports, and 40 panzers and other armoured fighting vehicles. The pilots repeatedly reported seeing Red Cross flags draped on German vehicles other than ambulances, but in the absence of photographic evidence permission was refused for such vehicles to be attacked. When the Germans did eventually cross the Seine one month later, Nazi domination of France was over. The Seine was actually reached two weeks in advance of Montgomery's target date. The enemy had suffered huge casualties in both men and equipment. Eleven panzer divisions were destroyed or so thoroughly disorganised that they were thereafter negligible as a fighting force. Twenty-three infantry divisions had been completely annihilated. The Luftwaffe, who had proved incapable of providing effective air cover for the withdrawal, also suffered a severe blow.

Research after the battle indicated that initial claims had actually been too high, particularly in respect of RP fire. It was discovered that only ten out of three hundred and one tanks had actually been destroyed by RPs, the remainder by cannon. The overall destruction, however, was nevertheless enormous. The Wehrmacht had lost 12,369 tanks, guns and vehicles in one of the greatest defeats ever suffered by the German army. It should be stated also that the role of the Allied air forces had not actually been to destroy the enemy, but to merely prevent an orderly withdrawal. No statistics, however, can indicate the effect of constant air attack upon the spirit of the German soldier, who was forced to shout "*Achtung! Jabo!*" (Attention! Fighter-bomber!) and take cover time and time again. The German Army also lost all faith in the Luftwaffe, a combination that had once proved so deadly.

Some indication of just how many Allied aircraft were operating during the Falaise battle is given in the log book of Peter Taylor,who had trained in America with John Thould and who at the time was flying Mustang IIIs with 65 Squadron as Flying Officer. The young Scot flew numerous dive-bombing and strafing sorties; on August 19th he wrote "*Forcing on with big strafe. Sifta Section dive-bombed, not so dusty, but too many Spitfires.*" Of another similar sortie later the same day: "*Same again, but area getting 'clapped'. Too many 'Tiffies' and too few trucks.*"

The roads were also strewn with the dead, both human and horses, and the area was so saturated with the stench of death that in the summer heat the smell even permeated the cockpits of aircraft flying 1,000' above the battlefield.

Hitler's forces were neither given respite at the Seine. On August 25th, 1944, 263 Squadron participated in operations along the river to prevent the German army crossing, successfully attacking barges. On that day, Flight Lieutenant

John Purkis DFC returned to the squadron, having been shot down over enemy lines on August 16th. Captured by the SS, he had been interrogated before being unceremoniously dumped in a civilian prison and forgotten when his jailers hurriedly left.

On August 26th, 1944, 263 Squadron was sweeping the Rouen area and there damaged more German transports. Pilot Officer Thould wrote: *"Mac and I got a poor bloke on a motor-bike."* The following day saw an uneventful *"Armed Shipping Recco NW of Le Havre"*. By August 31st, 1944, the enemy had retreated so far that the Typhoons were equipped with long range fuel tanks, although initially there were insufficient to go round. On that day, Thould flew MN476 on an *"Armed Recco: Dieppe-Forges-Poix-Eu. Carried long range tanks. First section destroyed two motor transports and damaged four. Our section destroyed four ammo lorries, one other truck and one car, all flamers. No hits with rockets, all cannon. My kite damaged by exploding ammo."* By this date Pilot Officer Thould had flown a total of 53.30 hours of operational flying, 15.30 of them that month. In total, he had flown 120.45 *"Typhoon hours"*.

During the first few days of September 1944, as the enemy eventually crossed the Seine, the strafing went on. By September 4th, however, the battle was well out of 263 Squadron's range. To be nearer to the front line, on the 6th, the squadron moved back to England and operated from Manston in Kent. As from three days later operational flying recommenced, largely on shipping strikes around the Dutch coast. On September 11th, the squadron returned to France, joining the Vendeville Wing near Lille at airfield B51. Operations continued to be conducted against targets around the Dutch coast. On September 16th, Pilot Officer Thould flew MN769 on a Ramrod to attack an observation post in a church at Zeebrugge. His log book records *"several hits on church, but none on spire."* Later that day another OP was attacked, in the lighthouse at Cap Gris Nez.

October 1944 heralded yet another busy period for 263 Squadron, on the 2nd of that month moving to airfield B70 at Antwerp where the pilots were billeted in houses, making a welcome change from tents. Targets were almost exclusively railway bridges over Dutch rivers at such places as Deventer, near Arnhem, Zwolle and Utrecht. On October 2nd, Thould had led an attack on a railway bridge near Utrecht, and recorded a direct hit on the line with a 500 lb bomb. As the German retreated through Holland back towards the Reich, he was similarly harrassed as he had been in France, roads around Oostburg also being amongst Pilot Officer Thould's targets. On October 7th, 263 Squadron made its first operational sortie into Germany itself, a Ramrod to attack the railway bridge north of Rees, Thould flying Typhoon PD518. The squadron's

Operations Record Book relates:-

"Today marked quite an event in the squadron's history as for the first time in this war an operation was carried out over German soil, the target being railway lines and train activity in the Ruhr area. Two direct hits were scored on the railway bridge and lines cut."

The next few days saw poor weather and no flying, but on October 11th it improved sufficiently to allow for a number of sorties against Oostburg, *"an innocent looking place on west side of the river Scheldt. Apparently enemy troops were firmly ensconced in the village and the army was having problems dislodging them. Naturally the 'Tiffies' were called in to dislodge the obstacle. A record day for sorties by the Wing, just under 200, with 41 by 263."*

On October 12th, the squadron flew its first operation using 1,000 lb bombs, Pilot Officer Thould in MN738 armed with two such weapons. The target on that occasion was *"Heavy flak gun positions west of Breskens."* Later the same day a low-level attack was made on the railway embankment across a lake near Kaldenkirchen on the Belgian border. The following day, HM the King, accompanied by Field Marshal Montgomery and Air Chief Marshal Coningham, visited the squadron and met pilots not flying on the morning's sorties, including Pilot Officer Thould. On that day, however, the squadron's Operations Record Book states that:-

"Two shows only carried out today, both close army support targets, some guns just south of Bergen-Op-Zoom and another batch of guns near a wood twenty miles NE of base. On the last operation the squadron lost one of its oldest and most stalwart members - Johnny Thould. Flying No 2 to Squadron Leader Rutter, the Commanding Officer, he was hit by flak whilst in the dive. The aircraft burst into flames and spiralled straight in. According to eye witnesses he had very little chance of baling out. A great loss to the squadron."

Pilot Officer Thould had only flown on the afternoon sortie, that entry being completed in another's hand in his log book, which on the same page is stamped *"Death Presumed."* During his operational career he had certainly amassed no mean amount of experience, but on that fateful day, luck just ran out for Johnny Thould and MN476, *"The Hawk"*, having previously escaped numerous brushes with flak. He now lies at rest in Merksplas cemetery, Belgium.

With the Battle for Germany underway, there was still six month's bitter fighting ahead until the war was won. The Luftwaffe was largely an ineffective fighting force by this time, ground down by the constant pressure of action across the globe, but occasionally showed that it still had teeth. As American four-engined bombers pounded the Reich by day, new shapes were seen in the air, namely the Me 262 and *"Komet"* jet-propelled fighters. These aircraft were revolutionary, but, as with the use of the terrifying "V" weapons, their introduction was just too late to have any long-term marked effect upon the war's outcome. On New Year's Day, 1945, the Luftwaffe made its last assault, a successful surprise attack on Allied airfields in Holland (see Postscript), coinciding with Hitler's last desperate, but ill-fated, gamble, the Ardennes Offensive or *"Battle of the Bulge"*. Montgomery crossed the Rhine, Germany's *"impassable natural defence"*, on March 17th, 1945, and on April 25th the Russians negotiated the River Elbe. The following day Soviet forces encircled Berlin itself. On April 30th, Hitler, still commanding phantom armies and ranting at his worn-out generals, committed suicide. At midnight on May 9th, 1945, troops on all fronts stopped fighting and laid down their arms. The long war in Europe had at last come to an end.

Those who died to win our freedom, like the men in this book, lie at rest in cemeteries across the battlefields, or in unknown spots. Two sayings come to mind, that *"a corner of a foreign field will remain forever England"*, and, another also encountered at military cemeteries around the world, *"When you go home, tell them of us and say, for your tomorrow, we gave our today."*

The survivors, men like Flight Lieutenant Peter Taylor, were retained by the service until the peril in the east had been neutralised, and the administrative machine, choked by the chaos that the end of the war created, could deal with their demobilisation and return to civilian life. On March 10th, 1946, Peter, at that time with 122 Squadron, flew Griffon-engined Spitfire Mk XXI LA282 from Dyce to his base at Dalcross. Upon conclusion of the twenty-five minute flight he wrote in his log book *"Last dice with Isaac Newton."* That line is deserved of the last in this study of RAF fighter pilots at war.

Pilot Officer John Thould's grave at Merksplas cemetery, Belgium, showing the original marker when photographed shortly after the war.

Postscript

Leutnant Hans Wulff pictured in 1944 whilst flying Fw190s with JG6.

Peter Wulff.

During the spring of 1992, the Malvern Spitfire Team staged a display in Herefordshire. Members were there approached by a retired gentleman who had shown interest in the stories exhibited, and who told them that he had also flown *"fighters during the war"*. Having immediately noted an accent, the Team, thinking he was Polish, asked whether the visitor flew Spitfires; *"No,"* he replied, *"Focke Wulf 190s!"*

Hans Wulff, who had changed his name to *"Peter"*, later attended the launch of *"The Invisible Thread: A Spitfire's Tale"* at the Abbey Hotel, Great Malvern, on September 5th, 1992, and was there welcomed by the numerous former RAF fighter pilots present. Peter was also kind enough to add his signature to those on the prints of the book's cover, produced to raise funds for the Surma Memorial Trust for Youth, which is named after the Polish pilot around whose story that book was based. The Trust, now a registered charity, exists *"to educate and assist young people in Malvern."* So far over £6,500 has been raised (prints of *"R6644: The Invisible Thread"*, from a painting by Mark Postlethwaite G.Av.A., are still available from this publisher).

As I watched these men at *"The Invisible Thread"* launch, mixing freely and swapping stories, I realised more than ever that fighter pilots of all nationalities are the same; these men were of similar age, social backgrounds, education and service training, and had even flown very similar aircraft. Peter Wulff had ultimately become a prisoner of war, as indeed had several of the former RAF Spitfire pilots present. Clearly Peter, although his fighter had been swastika emblazoned, had much in common with these men who were once his enemies.

Side by side in front of a Spitfire, former enemies meet as friends at the launch of "The Invisible Thread" *by Dilip Sarkar, September 5th, 1992. From left to right, Group Captain Gerry Edge, Wing Commander Bernard Jennings, Mr Fred Roberts (19 Squadron groundcrew, 1940), Leutnant Hans "Peter" Wulff, Squadron Leader Harry Welford, Flight Lieutenant William Walker, Flight Lieutenant Ken Wilkinson, Flying Officer John Lumsden (post-war), Squadron Leader "Buck" Casson, Flight Lieutenant Richard Jones, Warrant Officer Bob "Butch" Morton (standing in front), and Flight Lieutenants Peter Taylor, Peter Hairs, Hugh Chalmers, the late Tadek Turek, Kazik Budzik, and Tadek Dzidzic.*

Author's collection.

Peter had actually been born Hans Wulff on February 22nd, 1923, at Lübeck in Germany, the son of Hans and Elisabeth of Gartner-strasse 37. Hans was educated in Lübeck and developed a keen interest in flying from the age of ten when he experienced his first passenger flight, in a Fw Moeve, a twin-engined civil monoplane. After the Great War, the Versailles Peace Settlement of 1919, in an attempt to prevent Germany ever becoming a military power again, limited Germany's Army to 100,000 men with no General Staff, no conscription, no tanks, no heavy artillery, no poison-gas supplies, and no aircraft or Zeppelins. The German Navy was limited to vessels under 10,000 tons, and was forbidden either submarines or an air arm. On January 30th, 1933, however, Adolf Hitler became Chancellor of Germany. Later that day he appointed Herman Goering as Reichs Commissioner for Aviation. In fact Goering was Commander-in-Chief of the secret Luftwaffe. For many young Germans during the 1930s, their passion for flying was satisfied by flying gliders in ostensibly civilian clubs. In reality these organisations were providing ab initio air experience for future service pilots. Hans Wulff began gliding in 1937.

In December 1941, he was called up for full-time service with the Luftwaffe, and underwent infantry training at the Fl.A.R., Schleswig. In March 1942 he progressed to the Luftkriegschule (Air War Academy) at Breslau/Schöngarten, followed by a period at the 'C' School at Fürstenwalde. Having received his pilot's qualification badge, and completed his training successfully, Hans joined the Erganzungruppe (Training Wing) of Kampfgeschwader 53 *"Legion Kondor"*, flying He 111 bombers at Orleans. In July 1943 he joined III/KG53 at Augsberg for operational flying duties. Hans spent ten months with that unit, during which time he flew against the Russians, making a total of sixteen operational flights. On one of these his bomber was shot down. After making a successful forced landing, Wulff walked back to German lines.

In the west, however, the situation was becoming desperate for Germany with the American 8th Air Force bombing by day and the RAF's Bomber Command by night. The German defenders became hard-pressed, and Leutnant Hans Wulff volunteered to become a fighter pilot during the spring of 1944. He remembers that *"I had volunteered before, without success, but with the losses we were suffering by that time the Jagdwaffe just could not turn you down. I was given the choice of either flying single-engined fighters, or twins. To fly the former I had to return to training school, which I did not want to do, so I opted for twins, hoping for a night-fighter posting. However, I was posted instead to the Erganzungs Staffel of Zerstörergeschwader 26 at Sagan, later joining 4/ZG26 flying Me 410s at Köningsburg/Neumark near East Berlin. We were flying against the American B17s and B24s, which was okay if they did not have fighter escort. I was actually shot down on my first two operational flights, forced landing on both occasions. I did not even see what hit me either time, but it must have been fighters. Eventually the fighter escorts were able to penetrate as far as Berlin itself, and even to our bases, which started to make the situation hopeless."*

In September 1944, II/ZG26 became II/JG6, and Leutnant Wulff became a member of 8/JG6 which was equipped with the single-engined Fw190 at Quakenbrük. He remembers that the Geschwader Kommodore was an Austrian, Oberstleutnant Kogler.

Having made nine operational flights with 8/JG6, Leutnant Wulff then participated in Operation Bodenplatte on New Year's Day, 1945, the Luftwaffe's last-ditch, superbly executed, surprise attack against 2nd TAF airfields in Holland.

On that day, Leutnant Wulff taxied out across the airfield at Quakenbrük in Fw190 A-8, blue 4+, and took off with the 5th and 8th Staffeln of JG6 at about 0830 hrs to shoot up Volkel. The 6th and 7th Staffeln operated from Vechta and were to join the rest of the Gruppe over Quakenbrük. The Staffelkapitän of 8/JG6, Oberleutnant Paffrath, was grounded due to an injury, so a deputy had been appointed to lead the unit for this attack. However, whilst that pilot was taxying to the take-off point his aircraft became unserviceable, so at the last moment, Leutnant Wulff was detailed to take over as leader. This placed the twenty-one year old in an awkward position; the 8th Staffel was to take off immediately before the 5th, which was led by Hauptmann Katz. Leutnant Wulff had misgivings about preceding the more experienced Hauptmann. He duly took off, however, followed by his No 2, and the No 2 of the pilot who had stayed behind. After some manoeuvering during the assembly period, Leutnant Wulff's formation followed the 7th Staffel. A Ju 88 actually led the entire formation, followed by the Geschwader Kommodore, Oberleutnant Kolger, and his No 2, Hauptmann Naumann, leading II Gruppe, the remainder of Naumann's Schwarm, 6th, 7th, 8th, and 5th Staffeln, III Gruppe, and I Gruppe.

The Geschwader flew in this order between 50-150 meters and to the southern shore of the Zuider Zee, before turning south until reaching the Lek, at which point the Ju 88 turned away. The fighters had been briefed to switch off their navigation lights at this juncture. Leutnant Wulff did not do so, however, discovering that he had actually forgotten to switch them on during the confusing take-off!

Leutnant Wulff, in common with others in the formation, actually suspected that the Geschwader was off course, due to the southerly turn, which should have been made at Spakenburg, actually having been made considerably to the west of that location. Ground markers had been arranged to indicate the correct turning point, but these had not been seen.

Immediately after the Ju 88 turned away, Leutnant Wulff saw two Me 109s in the area shot down by anti-aircraft fire, in addition to noting five Spitfires and

Tempests, although battle was not joined at that stage. Shortly afterwards flying time indicated that the Geschwader should be over the target, so, in accordance with instructions, III Gruppe began pulling up to 1500 meters, at which height they were to provide top cover, whilst I Gruppe climed to 500 meters to provide medium cover for the other units attacking at low-level. Leutnant Wulff followed in the wake of the Kommodore, who was to lead II Gruppe past Volkel in order to approach the airfield from the south. He remained at a height of 50-100 meters in an effort to find the target.

When about 5 km south of where III Gruppe had climbed, the point where, according to calculations, Volkel should have been, Leutnant Wulff saw some convoys on the road ahead, and, as they were directly in his sights, he opened fire on them. Although instructions had not included orders to attack such transport, he thought that as the chances of finding Volkel were slim, a target of opportunity was better than nothing. As he turned away from attacking the convoy, he saw a dogfight taking place between several Fw109s and *"a superior number of Spitfires and Tempests."* He climbed into the fray, shot down a Spitfire, but whilst watching the result his own aircraft was hit, sometime between 0945-50 hrs, over Venraij, 40 km ENE of Eindhoven. Foty-eight years later, "Peter" Wulff remembers:-

"It is interesting that I always thought that I had been hit by anti-aircraft fire, but my interrogation notes state that I was shot down by a Tempest. I am surprised at this as I believe that a fighter would have finished me off. I was very low to bale out, but had read the book written by Hanna Reisch, Germany's famous female test pilot, in which she described practising the escape procedure even in bed; I had therefore done the same and it was this that saved my life. I blew off the hood, undid my straps, and whilst actually standing up in my seat pulled the ripcord. This was so as to maintain as much altitude as possible for my descent. The small 'chute deployed, pulling the large one out of its pack and plucked me out of the aircraft. I was afraid of hitting the tail as I came out, and did strike the elevator which broke three ribs and damaged several vertebrae. I cannot recall anything of my short parachute descent, but I landed in a farmyard. The Dutch occupants put me to bed as I was in a bad way. I asked them to hide me until dark, to which they agreed, but two hours later a jeep arrived. A pistol came round the door and I, in no position to resist, was captured. I was taken to the base of a Scottish artillery regiment stationed nearby and stayed in the Sergeants' Mess. The Sergeants were still celebrating Hogmanay, and I was given chocolate and Scotch. Later I was collected by an Airman who tried to steal my high quality Swiss flying-watch. That is war, if a victorious soldier does not have a watch he takes that of the defeated, but the Scots went wild! A furious argument ensued between them and the Airman, during which the latter appeared somewhat

frightened and as a result of which I kept my watch. There was also a negative side to this, however; such watches were highly prized trophies so very few aircrew in captivity still possessed them. As I had mine, other prisoners were later suspicious of me and suspected that I was an informer! I reached the Interrogation Centre at Eindhoven during the evening of New Year's Day. The RAF were very angry about Operation Bodenplatte as they could not understand how such a large attack had been kept so secret. The interrogation was therefore a bit rough, although I do not blame them, they were very angry. The questioning went on throughout most of the night until I collapsed at about 4am. I kept telling them that they would get nothing out of me, and that I was only behaving as their sons would be expected to behave should they be captured. It was strange, after being treated so roughly, that later the filing clerk was kind enough to share his supper with me. I was then transferred to an Allied officers' hospital. The other patients insisted that a screen be put up around my bed. When I could walk I went to another hospital in Ghent. There our clothes were taken away every night, to prevent us from escaping. One morning when my uniform was returned, it was minus belt and gloves. I was not bothered about the belt, which was a nice souvenir for someone, but I was annoyed about my gloves being stolen as it was a cold winter and I needed them, I complained, saying it was not the impression I had of the British, who were supposedly honourable and fair. A week later a despatch rider arrived, all the way from Brussels, with a package for me; my belt and gloves! We were treated otherwise perfectly whilst in hospital, but arrangements were soon made to fly us to England and captivity proper. I was with another fighter pilot called Tudeck, who had flown with 4/JG27 during the Battle of Britain, later becoming Staffelkapitän of 4/JG2 and eventually a GruppenKommandeur with JG27. Anyway, Tudeck, incredibly, still had his pistol hidden in a flying boot. He suggested that we should try to seize a Dakota and escape, and that I, being conversant with twin-engined types, should fly it. I agreed to this adventure, but we were separated before the flight. During my last night in Brussels before departure for England, Johnnie Johnson came to visit us. The next day we were flown to Northolt and taken to an interrogation centre. So far the RAF had been unable to place my unit as they had three Wulffs on file, but as I walked in Kogler was sat there, who said "Hello, Wulff", and gave the game away. They did give us a whisky, though! I was later sent to be a prisoner at Crewe Hall in Cheshire. After the war, but whilst still in captivity, I volunteered for agricultural work in Pembrokeshire. This was great as we had much more freedom, the Corporal in charge just requiring us to attend roll-call, the rest of the day being ours. We used to go to the beach a lot, and one day I was sat there when a pretty girl rode by on horseback. Her name was Phoebe and we later married. After my release in 1948, I did not return to Germany but stayed in Pembrokeshire, farming. I started gliding again during 1952, with the Midland Gliding Club, at Long Mynd in Shropshire. I gained my licence to fly powered single-engined aircraft in 1957. I met an industrialist in Pembroke, who was actually refitting a frigate bought from Britain by the new German Navy, who asked me whether I would fly an aircraft for him if he bought one. I agreed, received my twin-engined licence, and subsequently began the happiest six years of my life, flying first an Apache then a Do 28, the latter being a superb aircraft. I was farming three days a week and flying the rest."

When quizzed about his combat victories, however, Hans "Peter" Wulff is less forthcoming: "I did shoot down a Spitfire on New Year's Day, 1945, but it is not something that I either like to remember or talk about now." Perhaps that is an appropriate sentiment with which to conclude "Through Peril to the Stars".

Acknowledgements

Many people have helped with the twelve projects that this book represents, but before I mention those individuals who kindly assisted with specific chapters, I would like to thank the following organisations which have assisted throughout: the Ministry of Defence Air Historical Branch (Richard King), Department S10 (Martin Hill, Steve Bryant, Ted Watkins and Gina Taylor), the RAF Personnel Management Centre (Mrs S C Raftree), the Commonwealth War Graves Commission, and the Keeper of the Public Record Office. Especial thanks, as ever, are accorded to Wing Commander NPW Hancock OBE DFC RAF Rtd, Honorary Secretary of the Battle of Britain Fighter Association for his unfailing assistance in tracing surviving members of the Few.

I am particularly honoured that Group Captain Peter Townsend has kindly written the foreword to this book, one of the Few whom I have long admired not only as an airman but also as a man.

Sincere thanks must also go to my close associates Andrew Long, Dennis Williams (both of whom also went to great time and trouble proof-reading the manuscript), Tony Bramhall, Mark Postlethwaite, Bob Morris, Brian Owen, Allan White, and Chris Goss, the latter who unfailingly provided excellent photographs and information in respect of the Luftwaffe. In addition thanks are also accorded to my other historian friends, Dr Alfred Price, Andy Saunders, Chris Shores, John Foreman, Winfried Bock, Cambell Gunston, Don Caldwell, Edna Murray, Ken Wakefield and Ken Wynn. I am also grateful once again to Gilbert Davies of Victor Studios, Hay-on-Wye, Herefordshire, for his excellent photographic work.

I owe an additional debt to Mark Postlethwaite G. Av. A. for another superb cover painting. Anyone wishing to obtain information regarding Mark's work should contact him direct at 11 Sheridan Close, Enderby, Leics. LE9 5QW, England, Tel: 0533 751894.

My wife, Anita, knows she has my gratitude for suffering my obsession with the dramatic events of fifty years ago.

Pilot Officer J.C. Pugh:
Squadron Leader R.M. Pugh AFC RAF Rtd & family, Air Marshal Sir Denis Crowley-Milling KCB, CBE, DSO, DFC RAF Rtd, Jeffrey Quill OBE AFC FRAes, Mr Powell, Radio Wyvern, Farnborough Mail, Express & Star, Dilwyn

Parish Council, Herefordshire Aero Club, 151 (ATC) Squadron, West Mercia Constabulary, In Flight Promotions, Mrs K Stanfield, Mr Dennis Fletcher and the late Mr Lionel Weaver.

Pilot Officer A. Bird:
Mr Allan White for his research & Mrs Marjorie Whittaker.

Pilot Officer J.R. Hamar DFC:
Mr & Mrs Fred Hamar, the late Air Commodore E.M. Donaldson CB CBE DSO RAF Rtd.

Pilot Officer H.L. Whitbread:
The Shropshire Star, Ludlow Advertiser, Mrs Margaret Jones, Mrs Sally Stubbs, Mrs Muriel Harvey, Councillor David Lloyd, Mr Ken Brown, Mrs Pauline Morris, Air Commodore E.W. Mermagen CB CBE AFC RAF Rtd, Wing Commander T.A. Vigors DFC RAF Rtd, Group Captain Brian Kingcombe DSO DFC RAF Rtd, Group Captain J.H. Hill CBE RAF Rtd, the late Flight Lieutenant R.B. Johnson RAF Rtd, Flight Lieutenant D.G. Gibbins RAF Rtd, Group Captain A.R. Wright DFC RAF Rtd, Squadron Leader J.I. Hutchinson RAF Rtd, Air Commodore E.W. Wright CBE DFC DFM RAF Rtd, Group Captain E. Graham RAF Rtd, Air Vice-Marshal R. Deacon-Elliott CB OBE DFC AE RAF Rtd, Flight Lieutenant N.H.D. Ramsay DFC RAF Rtd, Squadron Leader G.H.A. Wellum DFC RAF Rtd, Wing Commander R.E. Havercroft AFC AE C.Eng RAF Rtd, Flight Lieutenant J.P.B. Greenwood RAF Rtd, Major Eduard Neumann, and Mr *"Joe"* Crawshaw.

Sergeant K.C. Pattison:
Mrs Joan King, Mrs Joan Dawson, Wing Commander Sir Kenneth Stoddart KCVO, AE, JP, DL, K St. J, Hon. LL.D., RAF Rtd, Flight Lieutenant K. Wilkinson AE RAF Rtd, Flight Lieutenant D.H. Nicholls AE RAF Rtd, Squadron Leader M.P. Brown AFC RAF Rtd, Wing Commander P. Olver DFC RAF Rtd, Squadron Leader D.A. Adams RAF Rtd, Air Vice-Marshal FDS Scott-Malden DSO DFC RAF Rtd, the late Wing Commander R.J.E. Boulding RAF Rtd, the late Mr Don Angus, Mr Alex Henshaw MBE.

Pilot Officer W.P.H. Rafter:
Mrs K.H.E. Barwell, Mr Graham Perkins, Mr Martin Hallam, Group Captain G.L. Denholm DFC RAF Rtd, Wing Commander P. Olver DFC RAF Rtd, and Squadron Leader J. Stokoe DFC RAF Rtd.

Squadron Leader T.H.D. Drinkwater DFC:

Mr Les Drinkwater, the late Wing Commander P.I. Howard-Williams DFC RAF Rtd, Squadron Leader E.D. Glaser DFC RAF Rtd, Squadron Leader W. Dilks RAF Rtd, the late Squadron Leader V.H. Ekins MBE DFC RAF Rtd, the late Squadron Leader R.L. Stillwell DFC DFM AE RAF Rtd, Flight Lieutenant P. Taylor RAF Rtd, and Flight Lieutenant Tony Minchin RAF Rtd.

Sergeant E.H. Caldwell:

Allan White once again for his research, Flight Lieutenant *"Tex"* Dallas RAF, Sergeant *"Tiny"* Baelz and the RAF Aircraft Salvage Team, Bristow Helicopters Ltd., Mr Mike Evans of Rolls-Royce plc, Mr Chris Carne, Mr Peter Earp, Mr Payne, Mr Mike Parry, and the Polish Institute.

Sergeant G.C. Lock:

Mrs Joan Walter, Mr Derek Owens, Mr Edwyn Owens, Mr Bill Sleigh, Mrs Joan Stephens, Mrs Margaret Horton, Tim Lake and the Manly Daily, Mr Charles Hodgetts, 187 (ATC) Squadron, Mr John Watkins, Mr John Smith, and Mr Bob Jenkins.

Sergeant V.J.T. Allen:

Mrs Eleanor Boyle, Mrs Mary Apperley, Mr Jim Thomas, Mr Glen George, Mrs Peggy Brown, Mr Frank Day, Air Vice-Marshal J.E. Johnson CBE DSO DFC RAF Rtd, Air Commodore P.M. Brothers CBE DSO DFC RAF Rtd, Flight Lieutenant R. George RAF Rtd, Mr Bob Jaynes, Mr John Beamont, the late Messrs Bill Sevier and Dick Tanner, and the Hereford Times.

Pilot Officer J. Thould:

Mr J. Thould JP, Flight Lieutenant Peter Taylor RAF Rtd, Flight Lieutenant Ron Rayner DFC RAF Rtd.

Leutnant Hans (Peter) Wulff:

Mr Peter Wulff & Flight Lieutenant Chris Goss RAF.

Bibliography

During the research for this book, I consulted over sixty documents at the Public Record Office. Although too numerous to list, these are available to anyone with a valid reader's ticket.

I have also had access to the personal papers of many of the pilots whose stories are told in the book, in addition to their diaries and in some cases their flying log books. I am also indebted to survivors Flight Lieutenants R. George and P. Taylor for allowing me access to their own log books which have proved similarly invaluable.

The following books, which are not listed in any order, were essential background reading, and in some cases more of an inspiration:-

The Battle of Britain Then & Now, Mk V Edition, Edited by WG Ramsey, After the Battle, 1989.

The Blitz Then & Now, Volumes I & II, Edited by WG Ramsey, After the Battle, 1989 & 1990 respectively.

Spitfire The History: Eric Morgan & Edward Shacklady, Key Publishing, 1987.

Aces High, Christopher Shores & Clive Williams, Neville Spearman Ltd., 1966.

Fighter Squadrons in the Battle of Britain, Anthony Robinson, Arms & Armour Press, 1987.

Men of the Battle of Britain, Kenneth G Wynn, Gliddon Books, 1989.

Spitfire Squadron, Dilip Sarkar & Sqn Ldr BJE Lane DFC, Air Research Publications, 1990.

The Invisible Thread: A Spitfire's Tale, Dilip Sarkar, Ramrod Publications, 1992.

Air Aces, Christopher Shores, Presidio Press USA, 1983.

Air Ministry Pilots' Notes, Spitfire Mk IIa & IIb Aeroplanes (Air Publication 1565B), July 1940.

The Last Enemy, Fg Off Richard Hillary, Macmillan & Co Ltd, 1942.

Fighter Pilot, Wg Cdr Paul Richey, Hutchinson & Co Ltd, 1941.

The First & The Last, Adolf Galland, Methuen & Co Ltd, 1955.

Harvest of Messerschmitts, Dennis Knight, Frederick Warne Ltd., 1981.

The Second World War, AJP Taylor, Hamish Hamilton, 1975.

German Fighters over England, Bryan Philpott, PSL, 1979.

Action Stations 3, David Smith, PSL, 1980.

Battle Over Britain, Francis K Mason, Aston Publications, 1990.

The Battle of Britain, Richard Hough & Denis Richards, Hodder & Stoughton, 1989.

Spitfire Command, Grp Capt RW Oxspring, Grafton Books, 1987.

Spitfire into Battle, Grp Capt D Smith, John Murray, 1981.

JG26: Top Guns of the Luftwaffe, Don Caldwell, Orion Books, 1990.

Messerschmitt Aces, Walter Musciano, Tab/Aero Books, 1989.

Wings of the Luftwaffe, Captain Eric Brown, Pilot Press Ltd., 1977.

The Luftwaffe War Diaries, Cajus Bekker, Macdonald & Co Ltd., 1966.

The One That Got Away, Kendal Burt & James Leasor, Companion Book Club, 1958.

Luftwaffe Fighter Units: Europe, 1939-41, Jerry Scutts, Osprey Publishing 1977.

RAF Squadrons, Wg Cdr CG Jefford, Airlife, 1988.

Battle of Britain: The Forgotten Months, John Foreman, Air Research Publications, 1988.

The Battle for Normandy, Eversley Belfield & H Essame, BT Batsford Ltd., 1967.

Panzers in Normandy Then & Now, Eric Lefevre, After the Battle, 1983.

Sigh for a Merlin, Alex Henshaw, John Murray, 1979.

Battle of Britain Day, Alfred Price, Sidgwick & Jackson Ltd., 1990.

British Fighters of World War 2, Bill Gunston, Hamlyn Aerospace, 1982.

Axis Aircraft of World War 2, David Mondey, Temple Press, 1984.

Dieppe: The Day of Decision, Jacques Mordal, Souvenir Press Ltd., 1964.

Duel of Eagles, Grp Capt Peter Townsend, Corgi, 1972.

The RAF Handbook, Chaz Bowyer, Ian Allan, 1984.